BY MARGARET PARTON

The Leaf and the Flame   (1959)

Laughter on the Hill (1945)

THE LEAF AND THE FLAME

THE LEAF AND THE FLAME

BY MARGARET PARTON

NEW YORK   ALFRED A KNOPF   1959

920.5
P274l

This is a BORZOI BOOK, *published by* ALFRED A. KNOPF, INC.

FIRST EDITION

To the memory of ❀ *Unni Nayar*

Preface

NOT so very long ago, as Indian time goes, I lived for five years in India, as a staff correspondent of the New York *Herald Tribune* and the wife of a British correspondent. This book is a distillation of those years, discarding the transient and retaining what seems to me to be of permanent emotional value and objective interest. It is not, I believe, out of date in the essentials. Most of India is timeless.

I am deeply indebted to the New York *Herald Tribune* for permission to use material which originally appeared in that newspaper.

THE LEAF AND THE FLAME

acharya	a teacher
ashram	a retreat, usually including a religious school
ayah	a personal maid for babies, children, and women
babu	a clerk
bheestie	a water-carrier, particularly in a garden
brahmacharya	the practice of chastity
burra peg	a long drink, usually whisky
chappaty	a kind of whole-wheat pancake
charpoy	a light cot, webbed or string-bottomed
chokra	a boy
dal	edible yellow split pea
dak	the mail, or post
darshan	an auspicious view of a holy person or place
darzee	a tailor
dhobi	a laundryman
dhoti	a length of cloth, usually white; tied around a waist and hitched up between the legs
harijan	an untouchable; literally, "Child of God"
Mela	a festival or fair
namasteh	a greeting, usually said with the palms joined before the face. It means "hello" or "good-by" and literally, "Reverence to you!"
panchayat	a village council; literally, a council of five
puja	a prayer, or prayer ceremony
punkah	a ceiling fan, manipulated by someone pulling a rope or (more usually) by electricity
punkah wallah	the man who pulls the rope
Ram	one of the names of God; also Rama, the seventh incarnation of Vishnu
sadhu	a Hindu ascetic or holy man

January

❀

Delhi | January 7

I T I S evening, the cow-dust hour. But here in Delhi
it is not cows returning to the villages which make the blue haze
through the trees, but the smoke of hundreds of supper fires. In
dark little chimneyless kitchens Indian wives are squatting now,
cooking chapatties and *dal* on low, mud-brick stoves.

Under the heavy trees, as I walk home to the hotel from the
hairdresser's, the mist is light and blue. The sky darkening, two
stars faint. The crows cawing and flying.

On the hotel lawns the dhobi's wife is folding the sheets which
have lain in the sun all day. Swathed in white cotton, she squats
before an immense pile of white sheets, folding, folding.

From behind the prickly hedges which separate the lawns from
the servants' quarters a few dark-eyed Indian children watch the
white children still playing among the flower borders—the last
delicious five or ten minutes before their ayahs take them in to
supper and bed. One little English boy is chasing a tiny girl round
and round the sundial in the marigold garden; they have the air
of children running perpetually, as in a dream, or on Keats's urn.

Two little girls and a small boy sit in a circle under a *peepul* tree, talking earnestly. Their tall ayah stands beside them, but they pay no attention to her. The four-year-old girl is lecturing the other two, but it is fairy talk I cannot understand. I wish I could sit on the ground with them and listen to what they are saying, but I am exiled forever in the world of grown-ups.

The quality of the air, the evening! And the children, what have they to do with this enchantment? Faintly, at the back of my mind, I look down long chestnut avenues of memory, and a tiny, an almost imperceptible light flickers for a moment. What is it, what is it? Playing hide-and-go-seek or tag in the dusk, and the voices crying "You're out! You're out!" And some book— what was it?—the girls in white frocks with roman-striped sashes and a party on the lawn with Chinese lanterns, and a little girl named Dolly . . . But that was far away and in another country, not here, not here at all. This moment is sheer Kipling, even now in the days of the Indian Republic. The crows and the wash on the lawn, the blue haze and the smell of cooking fires, the glimmering figures of the dark patient ayahs saying *"Salaam, Mem-sahib"* as I go by. And the children on the lawn who will grow up one day to say: "Yes, I was born in India. Yes, I lived there as a child." The children, the bright-haired, alien children, running, running around the sundial.

Delhi ❀ *January* 10

I am glad I live at the Cecil Hotel, in Old Delhi. Of course, I should be living in a mud hut with an Indian family, or at least that's what I thought when I first came to India three years ago as a foreign correspondent. "Live with the people," I told myself then. "Become one of them. Sink into the life of India."

Why didn't I? Well, for one reason it is not easy to "live with the people" or disappear into local life when the color of your skin makes you as conspicuous as a white skin does in India. In the jungle towns of southern India I have been surrounded by five hundred dark people staring so intently that the force of their silent gaze seemed to have an almost physical impact. That was understandable, for not many white people had visited those villages. But I cannot understand why here in the north, where the Indians have seen so many British and, more recently, Americans, the appearance of a Westerner is greeted so incredulously, as if one had never before been seen. Not on the main streets of New Delhi, of course. But always in the villages and often in the city's native bazaars I am followed down the street by a band of stragglers, not begging, but only curious to see what I will do, where I will go, what I am interested in.

Oh, for a dark skin! But even then I would be betrayed, for even by an effort of the will one cannot throw off for long the years of Western education, of Western culture, of Western philosophy. And now I know that after one has been saturated with the outer glamour of India, has been enraptured to the point of surfeit with the colorful and the strange, after one has settled down to living here, the old training returns. So it is that I cannot but pity the man dying on the sidewalk amid disinterested passers-by; yet an intellectual Indian told me not long ago that I am wrong. "It is his karma, his fate," said my friend, shrugging his shoulders. "Nothing to do with you or me." Yet I feel pity and concern, and cannot help myself any more than I can help liking clean sheets or preferring usually to eat with fork and knife rather than dipping my fingers up to the polite second knuckle in a bowl of rice and curry.

Why do we Americans feel so guilty about these prejudices? Sometimes I look at the British in wonder, for they seem never to question their own separation from the real life of the country in which they make their home. It would never occur to any of them (except the eccentric saint or explorer) that they ought to be living Indian-style in India. "For heaven's sake, why?" they would inquire mildly and a little disdainfully.

Someone warned me, before I ever came to India, that I would suffer from a feeling of guilt. I have, and I do. India is a country which makes you want to be good, yes, to be noble. You do not become calloused to the refugee children living in drain pipes, looking as if their little bodies had been pinched up from dust and at the next monsoon would blow away again. You do not become hardened to the patient misery of the untouchables, the blank, stricken eyes of the village mother who holds out her sore-infested baby for you to see. But there are so many of them, so very many. What can you do but flee, turning over in your mind some mad, symbolic gesture of renunciation? And then you feel guilty, because you are angry and a little frightened, and incapable of renunciation or sainthood.

Some American women have, of course, put on cotton saris and gone metaphorically barefoot into the villages, and after the Indians became convinced of their sincerity of purpose they stopped sneering. But could the correspondent of a daily New York newspaper, the wife of a "proper Britisher," do that? No, say I (justifying, or justly?). She can live for days at a time in a village, as I have done. She can travel often, as I do. She can keep her eyes and her heart open to the life of India, as I try to do. But there must be access to news and to a telegraph office. You cannot disappear into the life of "voiceless India" and still expect to be in touch with the political rumors of the capital.

But these are justifications; when I am dazzled with the exotic, bewildered by the noise and dust and confusion of India, I find refuge in the orderliness, the simple beauty of the Cecil Hotel.

Our three-room apartment opens onto a courtyard, in the midst of which is a rectangular pool where salmon-colored water lilies grow. Over the pool is a little bridge, and beyond are the arcades of another block of rooms, the arches dripping with magenta bougainvillea. From our front step, we can see the shimmering green swimming pool, the surrounding tubs of nasturtiums. Beyond the pool, lawns and rose gardens stretch to the high stone wall which circles the hotel grounds. At the front of the hotel is the wide verandah where we sit in the evening, drinking coffee and brandy. Across the little hotel road is a terrace under the big neem trees; these cool, crisp afternoons we sit there in the green wicker chairs, drinking tea and watching tennis on the two courts below. Beyond the tennis court are the fountain with the green bronze frog, the pansy and marigold beds, the lawns where the children love to play—and a little graveyard for the deceased dogs of hotel residents.

Most of our fellow guests are European diplomats waiting to be assigned a permanent bungalow by the Indian government. In the two years we have lived here I have rarely seen an Indian guest, for most Indians who apply for a room (unless of maharajah rank) are politely but firmly turned away by the proprietress, Miss Hotz. Miss Hotz, who comes of a Swiss family with strong British overtones from many decades of running hotels in pre-freedom India, has strong ideas on the subject.

"Westerners and Indians have quite different standards," she insists. "The most educated Indian is quite likely to slip out of his sandals as he sits at a dining-room table, curl his bare feet under him, and scratch his toes as he talks! Or to clean his fingernails with his fork!"

Yes, I know, I know. I saw the same thing over and over again when I lived for a year at the Imperial Hotel in New Delhi. But as I watch Miss Hotz bustle away on still another of her eagle-eyed inspection tours, I remember Christmas.

Christmas night is the one night of the year when the decorous residents of the Cecil Hotel (who normally never recognize each other unless they've been introduced) indulge in comparatively uninhibited gaiety—perhaps to forget that at Christmastime, more than any other time, the Christian becomes sharply aware of his heritage, forlorn and alien in this sea of oblivious Hinduism. Our servants, I discovered, had no idea why white people celebrated Christmas. I told them the story, illustrating it with the little crèche under our tree, and later found that they believed that I had been telling the story of the birth of the Lord Krishna! They were so delighted that we should be celebrating the birth of one of the Hindu gods that I hadn't the heart to disillusion them.

For the party, the starchy Cecil dining room is decorated with crepe paper poinsettias, holly, and red-cellophane lanterns. Eric Jones, the Goanese flower-arranger, longs to try something "modern," but Miss Hotz won't let him move one holly leaf away from the traditional. The tables are pushed back, a band is installed where the cold buffet usually stands, ladies put on their fanciest evening dresses, men their tails and tuxedos, everyone wears paper caps from the Christmas crackers, and the dance is on.

This last party, like all of them, was a fine one, for it is in the Cecil tradition that no one gets drunk, no one gets obstreperous, and the mood is one of old-fashioned gaiety and friendliness. And through the gaiety moved the majestic, heliotrope-clad figure of Miss Hotz. Miss Hotz dodging Christmas kisses from elderly admirers, Miss Hotz embarrassed and flushed with pleasure as the guests toasted her and sang "For She's a Jolly Good Fellow," Miss Hotz rushing off to order a waiter not to serve any more champagne to a table of over-loud Frenchmen. And the dancers swirling, and the music lilting, and the balloons drifting down at midnight . . .

But there were ghosts at the feast. Pressed against every wide window were the faces of Indians, most of them the families of hotel servants, their dark eyes staring, staring at what probably seemed a fantastic scene to them. Men dancing with women, the low-cut dresses, the wine and whiskey and champagne, the endless platters of food. We must have seemed like creatures of another world to them as they, that dark, expressionless audience, seemed to me. I was glad when they drifted away after midnight. In their eyes, their moist black-olive eyes, another future shone.

Such moments are rare. Ordinarily we live our days, our weeks, our months, and our years with an unconscious assumption that they will continue this way forever. The sweet peas will blossom in the late fall, the flame trees in the spring. Abdur Rahman is our table bearer, has always been so, will always be so. There will be a choice between curry and the regular English food on Wednesdays and Sundays. The hotel will provide champagne for any large parties we wish to give, and box lunches for our picnics. From time to time we will travel about India, and always we will return gratefully to comfort and order.

Most of our daily comfort depends on Bhag Singh, our personal servant, or bearer. Bhag Singh is a tall, thin, solemn young man who works as a servant in order to support his family farm up in the foothills of the Himalayas. Sometimes his wife and four children are here in Delhi; sometimes they are back in the hills. They seem to come and go rather mysteriously, but Bhag Singh is always here. He is devoted to Eric, for whom he worked before we were married, and, by extension, to me. Actually, I think I am still on probation.

Life without him or somebody like him would be unimaginable. He brings us morning tea, bananas, and the newspapers at seven o'clock. At eight he brings us breakfast in bed, and while we eat he supervises the cleaning of the living room and the bathroom. After we have dressed and gone off on our rounds, he makes the beds, dusts, and takes our laundry to the dhobi. We never have to think about clean clothes and polished shoes; Bhag Singh thinks about them instead. Also, he drives the car, mixes drinks, takes Jimmy the Dachshund for walks, and darns Eric's socks. When the hot weather comes, he puts away our woolens amid leaves from the neem tree, which seem to be just as effective as moth balls. When cold weather comes, he takes the woolens out of the big black trunks, shakes off the dried fragments of leaves, and sees that the clothes are aired and pressed before they are returned to our closets. When we tire of hotel food, he drives to Moti Mahal, the "Pearl Palace" in the bazaar, and brings back to us two hot, spiced, charcoal-roasted chickens wrapped in newspapers, and a huge wheaten pancake still warm from the grill. He spreads a small tablecloth on the Persian carpet in front of the fireplace, drops cushions around it, uncorks a bottle of red wine, and retires silently. No doubt he thinks us crazy, but he never says so. He says very little, in fact, and what he thinks about us and our ways I don't know.

The fact that Bhag Singh is happily willing to perform for us all the mechanical tasks of living which normally harass people in the servantless West, means that we are free *all* of the time to live the life for which our education, our experience, and our good fortune has fitted us: the life of a foreign correspondent. He does his job, he is extremely well paid, and he is, I know, contented. Therefore we are free of tiresome routine and may do our jobs and live our lives as well as we are able.

The life of a correspondent is, I think, the best life in the world. Not because of the comfort, although that is delicious. Not because of the glamour, for one grows used to tonga bells and silken saris. Not that at all.

It is the best life because it is cohesive, coherent. Our fundamental job, as I conceive it, is to understand India, and to a lesser degree the countries around it which we sometimes visit—Afghanistan, Pakistan, Ceylon, and Burma. But to understand, we have to extend our curiosity into many fields: psychology, sociology, politics, art, music, nature, architecture, economics, costume, folk lore, dance, cooking, sport. Always, every minute of the day, one can be thinking about and learning about one of these absorptions. Even at play, even in indolence. And if one wonders occasionally "Oh Lord, where can I find a good psychiatrist?" immediately one is taken up by the question of why aren't there any, and what do Indians do when they need one. Continually we are pulled out of ourselves and into the life of the country. And this is good, for this is an existence of total absorption in something greater than oneself.

Always there is more to learn, layer beneath layer to explore. What is a Sikh, for instance, besides being a man who wears a beard and a turban and doesn't smoke? What is a Moslem, besides being a man who believes in one God, recites the Koran, feels oppressed by Hindus, and doesn't eat pork? What is a Hindu, besides being a man who believes in thirty-three million gods, practices the caste system, runs India, and doesn't eat beef? Why is it all so important? These are questions asked by newcomers to India, and by now I know many answers. But some of my answers are wrong, and perpetually they are subject to revision and further exploration. So every year in January I try to re-examine some of the basic questions, to see what I need to learn in the year ahead about religion, economics, politics, people, and all the other impossible paradoxes. I always end up by telling myself: "Everything."

Tomorrow, though, I can stop thinking and start looking again. We're driving down to Jaipur, in the Rajasthan desert, to see elephants and ceremonies. Bhag Singh has already packed our bags, and all is ready.

Jaipur ✿ January 14

Last year, when my ever-eager mother and her friend Lucile visited us in India, they too stayed in Jaipur, but under somewhat different circumstances. For weeks they had sought and sometimes found spiritual values among our Indian friends, but they had seen little of the blazing color of India, the old feudal splendor which still exists. Eric and I decided that Jaipur would be just the place for them, and mentioned the matter to an official in the State's Ministry. Since there was no hotel in Jaipur, it would be necessary, we knew, for them to stay at the State Guest House, where a minor functionary and a few servants would probably be assigned to look after their comfort and entertainment.

In due time an invitation arrived from His Highness Lieutenant-General Saramd-i-Rajahai Hindustan Raj Rajendra Sri Maharajah Dhiraj Sir Sawai Man Singhji Bahadur, thirty-ninth Ruler of Jaipur, inviting the two ladies to come and stay not at the guest house, but at his palace! Knowing that there had been some misunderstanding about the importance (or possibly ages) of the two ladies, we packed them off by train and awaited their report with only mild trepidation.

"Well, it was very interesting, but not quite what we expected," Mother said when she returned to the Cecil. "We were met at the station by a palace official and a chauffeur who drove us to the palace. We had adjoining rooms about the size of a basketball court, with marble floors and chandeliers and huge four-poster beds. They told us that cocktails would be served on the terrace at eight o'clock and Please Dress. I'm certainly glad I took your advice and brought along that nice Macy evening dress, although it's years since I wore one. Well, we went down a great flight of marble steps to the terrace, and there was the Maharajah and a lot of elegant-looking young people in saris and tuxedos, and some very good martinis, too.

"Well, the Maharajah is an Indian, so naturally I began asking him about the Bhagavad-Gita, and telling him of my own deep spiritual interest in Hindu philosophy. He was very polite, but he looked a little bewildered, and after awhile he began talking about his polo ponies and some kind of automobile in which he seemed interested. I believe he called them sports cars. Dinner was at ten o'clock, and the champagne was lovely, but everyone talked about horses. It all seemed very odd, considering that we were in India, where everyone is supposed to be so spiritual.

"The next morning, just after I had finished dressing, I saw a mouse in my bedroom. Well, you know how terrified I am of mice, so I screamed and jumped on the bed. After awhile a servant came in, but he couldn't understand me, and just looked at me as if I were simply another silly foreigner doing morning exercises. I kept squeaking and imitating a mouse, and finally he grinned and went away. A long time passed, and then another servant came with a great big cage about the size of a bird cage, and put it on the floor.

"We went sight-seeing all day with one of the palace officials and didn't get back until evening. Sure enough, there was a mouse in the cage! Then I called a servant, but he only shook his head and went away. Then another one came and explained to me that the job of taking away mice belonged to one particular caste. Maybe it was the untouchables, but I can't remember. Anyway, it was Sunday, he said, and those men were all off duty. Nobody else would do it, so I would have to wait until the next day for the mouse to be removed from my room.

"That night we weren't invited downstairs. But cocktails and a delicious dinner were served on the balcony outside our rooms. It was very luxurious, and very peaceful.

"I knew, though, that I couldn't sleep with that mouse in the room, squeaking and running around in the cage. So I waited until long after midnight, when the palace was finally quiet. Then I pushed the cage with my toe over to the door. I opened the door and peered out along the corridor. There was nobody around, just moonlight and shadows. So I pushed the cage down the corridor to the top of the long flight of marble steps which lead down to the terrace where the Maharajah drinks his martinis. Then I gave the cage a big boot out into the moonlight. And that was the last I saw of it. I slept beautifully, and the next day we left. All in all, it was a very interesting time, as I said."

We, too, are having an interesting if not quite so exotic a time in Jaipur, which we are seeing for the first time. "A rose-red city, half as old as time" . . . No, that was Petra. Yet the line seems appropriate here, where houses and palaces are painted a lovely rosy pink, decorated with white scrolls and geometric designs and flowers. And where the feudal traditions of pageantry, opulence, fighting, luxurious mustaches, glorious turbans, and turned-up toes of golden slippers go back several thousand years. Now the Congress government has very properly taken over, and the writing is on the wall for all the princes of the Rajasthan desert. Yet the glamour lingers.

We saw the mingling of the old and the new on our first day here, when His Highness held a durbar (a formal reception) in his marble-pillared throne room. Around the great room, open on one side to a magnificent garden, stood tall guards in cream-colored uniforms, with blue-and-gold sashes and turbans with a cockade of silver plumes. The Maharajah, who presided from his crimson-and-gold throne, wore tight black trousers with a red stripe, a white jacket festooned with gold, and a glittering turban of red and gold, with a gold cockade. The old Rajput nobles appeared in flowing brocades and brilliant turbans of scarlet and orange, lime and pink. Each dignified, curly-mustached old gentleman carried a long curved sword symbolic of the ancient fighting traditions of Rajput nobility.

Then arrived the Indian Congressmen, representing the people of free India; the politicians and bureaucrats who actually govern Jaipur today. They straggled in late, a procession of fat, unshaven, graceless men in wrinkled and often dirty white shirts and flapping dhotis, bare feet in dusty sandals, and crumpled Gandhi caps.

That night His Highness gave a reception for two thousand guests in the gardens of his City Palace. On a bluff high above the city, the old, deserted Tiger Palace was festooned with lights and seemed to float in the darkness among the stars. Down in the gardens where we were, fountains played, many of them illuminated in yellow, red, and green. All the trees were hung with strings of blue and green Christmas lights. At the far end of the garden a little orchestra played soft Indian music, and at a distance peacocks mourned among clipped cypresses. Drinks flowed for several hours, and at eleven o'clock a buffet supper of English and Indian food was served from long tables. Then a carpet was spread at one end of the lawn, chairs were re-arranged, and for an hour we listened to nautch girls, sedate in silver saris, sing plaintive songs of ancient Rajput love. After the first ten minutes I thought them a deadly bore, for they danced only by waving a languid arm now and then, and to Western ears their songs all sounded the same. However, now I can say I've seen dancing girls at a prince's palace.

Perhaps because they disapprove of lavish hospitality in times of austerity, perhaps because alcohol was served, the Congressmen who had been invited did not appear. And I must admit that I was glad that for this one enchanted evening the good, colorless men of India's future had left the field to the possibly wicked but definitely colorful men of India's past. The Congressmen, one hopes, will give the peasants bread; the princes gave them only circuses. Inevitably, the princes and all their glory must vanish. But how the recalcitrant heart mourns for the disappearance of pageantry!

We have been staying for four days at the Maharajah's State Guest House, where white peacocks wander over the green lawns, and food and drinks are free. A lovely arrangement. And we have done so many things I'm dizzy. We watched His Highness play polo. We wandered through the city and talked to people. We looked at jewels in a famous shop patronized by princes; sat cross-legged on cushions on the floor and let streams of pearls and rubies trickle through our fingers. We didn't buy any, but we dreamed a little over the sixteenth-century enameled necklaces.

One morning we went up the steep hill to the old Palace of Amber, once the capital of Jaipur, but now uninhabited. It is still kept in a perfect state of preservation, and we wandered for hours under marble archways and among elegant, airy rooms where walls inlayed with tiny mirrors could reflect the light of a single candle a thousand million times. Before we left, we took off our shoes and socks, watches and belts—anything associated with leather—and visited the white marble temple of Shila Mata, the presiding deity of the House of Jaipur, where grave young priests in scarlet robes rang golden bells.

This afternoon we watched an elephant-keeper painting complicated floral designs on the trunk, head, and legs of one of his charges in preparation for the great religious procession which was

held this evening. And just at sunset we climbed a winding stair-
case to an assigned place high on the City Palace battlements,
and watched the procession.

Blazing with color and light, led by three of His Highness's
elephants in golden trappings, it wound through the city and
finally passed below the royal box on the palace walls.

Following the elephants came twenty camels, twenty white
horses, and finally one hundred men of the palace staff, all in
red tunics and pink turbans. Behind them they pulled a chariot
lighted by pink flares of phosphorescence. It bore the golden
image of Gangor, the goddess of plenty, in whose honor the procession is held. At the end came one hundred more men, each
carrying an enormous black shield and a gleaming silver sword.

Lights blazed, dust tinged by sunset and pink phosphorescence
swirled above the marching men, the watching crowd shouted,
the drums throbbed. With a final triumphant blast of conch
horns the goddess and her attendants disappeared beyond a gate
in the rosy palace walls.

There will be a few more processions in years to come, a few
more garden parties. But not forever, and always with diminishing
grandeur. The Maharajah, whose privy purse has been sharply cut,
will sell off his elephants, for at the moment he owns fifteen, and
each one costs a thousand dollars a month to maintain. The
polo ponies, the court musicians, the mace-bearers, the dancing
girls, and the sword-polishers will go.

With their disappearance will come democracy and a better way
of life for the notoriously oppressed peasants of Rajasthan. It is
all very good, very right. But also rather sad.

Delhi ❀ January 30

A few years ago Rajghat was a marshy stretch of empty
ground between the Jumna River and the walls of Old Delhi.
Today it is a spacious, ten-acre park with straight, red-sandstone

paths, rectangular pools, flower beds, lawns. At the center are a raised platform and, within an enclosure, a plain concrete block inscribed in Hindi with a sacred name of God: *Ram*. On this site the body of Mahatma Gandhi was cremated after his assassination by a Hindu fanatic in 1948, and it was from this place, say the devout, that his soul ascended in perfumed smoke to heaven.

On every other day of the year Rajghat is a quiet place, visited only by gardeners, an occasional devotee, or a delegation of foreigners wishing to pay their respects to the man who is now a legend. If a diplomat or a tourist wishes to be correct in Indian eyes, he will visit Rajghat before he does any sight-seeing in Delhi. And if he wishes to meditate in solitude, he will not go to Rajghat on January 30, the anniversary of the assassination.

But if by chance a visitor to India had had only one day in which to study this amazing country, he would have found it all in microcosm today (as on every anniversary) at Rajghat. For here on this day civilizations and centuries meet, the noble blends with the ignoble, the sacred with the profane, the learned with the ignorant, the beautiful with the ugly. And in all these the heart of India beats.

Walking toward the grounds early this morning, Eric and I thought we had strayed by mistake into a village fair. Just outside the entrance to the park a little Ferris wheel had been set up, and was already revolving merrily with a burden of shouting children. Nearby, swarms of vendors sold hot nuts, balloons, marigold garlands, and badly colored pictures of Gandhi and the other gods of the Hindu pantheon. Lepers and professional beggars mingled with the noisy crowd, the lepers silently pleading, the beggars whining and clutching. Here was the mass of India in all its various aspects of noise, gaiety, illiteracy, and poverty. Here was the India that bangs gongs in temples to summon the gods, the India of conjurers and tricksters, of brass pots and swinging silver earrings, of betel juice and dancing, of breeding and dying. Here was the India that has survived all invasions and achieved almost without realizing it a free republic, the India that fascinates and repels so many foreigners, the India that Gandhi loved.

Within the gates, the atmosphere was different. Along the sandstone paths little family groups strolled toward the central platform, bearing their garlands of reverent tribute. Other families relaxed on the grass around the platform, laughing and chatting and enjoying the pleasant midwinter sun. From time to time processions of schoolgirls appeared, their black pigtails straight down their backs, their expressions shifting from holiday to solemnity. Children tumbled everywhere, tossing their balloons high as they played.

We walked over to a far corner of the lawn, where Indian political leaders, Congress workers, and schoolboys sat cross-legged and barefoot under a yellow tent, performing "sacrificial spinning" on small wooden spinning wheels—an emphasis on Gandhi's favorite solution for the economic difficulties of India. Earlier this morning Prime Minister Nehru and President Rajendra Prasad had taken part in the spinning.

On a simple mat nearby knelt three young men and two girls, chanting Gandhi's favorite prayer, to which he himself added the last two lines:

> *Ragupati raghava raja ram*
> Redeemer of sinners, husband of Sita,
> Isvar and Allah, both are thy names,
> Give wisdom to all.

Today this prayer and other sacred songs would be chanted by these young people, and by others who would replace them, for twelve hours. In some cities the chanting is to go on for twenty-four hours, and in one or two places for forty-eight hours.

As we listened to the chanting, we studied the crowd in front of the yellow tent. Most of them were men, most were young, most were barefoot. Among them moved a thin young man with a gentle face, in snowy-white homespun dhoti and tunic. In a soft voice he was talking, to anyone who would listen, about the virtues of home spinning and the necessity of cottage industries for India. Most of the men in the crowd looked unconvinced, but interested.

"It takes a long time," the young man explained to us. "We send out spinning wheels and cotton to people, and we try to teach them how to do it, but they don't understand always, and there are never enough of us to explain."

His name was Moti Lal, he said, and he was a worker for the Indian National Congress Party, that curious blend of Gandhi's idealism and Tammany Hall which Gandhi directed for many years and which now controls India. Moti Lal never saw Gandhi, but he guides his life by Gandhi's teachings. There are hundreds of thousands of men like Moti Lal in India, and to millions of people beyond the gate of Rajghat they symbolize Congress and, therefore, government.

"I became a follower of Gandhiji in 1942, when I was a student at the University," he told us. "That was the time of the civil disobedience campaign led by the Mahatma. So I joined Congress, and since that time I have devoted my life to the party.

"Of course, there are three aspects to life: body, mind, and soul. And since Congress doesn't pay salaries for workers like me, I have to support my body by selling medicines and tonics from door to door. But my mind, soul, and all my spare time are given to Congress work."

Every evening Moti Lal goes to his local Congress headquarters and looks over all the important news developments which he thinks the people in his ward should know about. Then in the morning, before he starts selling his medicines, he gives little speeches in the neighborhood park, explaining land reform or new sanitation methods to any one who will listen.

"This is my real day's work," he said, "and I hope it is work Gandhiji would approve of, for the people know nothing except what I tell them. But my long-range objectives are more important, and they are based on the principles I learned from Gandhiji's teaching: that the distance between the haves and the have-nots in India must be lessened and that everyone in India must have what you in America call equality of opportunity. Because of Gandhiji, I and thousands of men and women like me will devote our lives to achieving this end."

On the nearby mat two singers changed places, but the chant continued in the same rhythm. A plump, cross-legged Congress member in the yellow tent looked uncomfortable, but continued to spin devotedly. Some of the men in the crowd began to imitate the spinning gestures experimentally, as if wondering whether they too could learn. Moti Lal said he would see us later, and darted off to encourage them.

And so at last we walked back to the center of it all, took off our shoes, bought garlands of marigolds, and stood in line with the other mourners. Up the steps of the platform and around the white palings of the central enclosure, long lines of Indians moved slowly—and here one began to approach the heart of Rajghat. For as shoes were discarded, so too were the noise and confusion which are so difficult for the Westerner to reconcile with the spirit of reverence.

And here inside the final enclosure was the heart itself, the profoundly reverent heart. Silently the line inched around the flower-draped concrete slab: A holy man in his saffron robes. A young mother teaching her baby to make the prayerful gesture with flattened palms which the Indians call *namasteh*. A coolie in rags who could afford to buy only four rose petals. A bright-eyed college student carrying a book on organic chemistry in one hand and a marigold in the other. An off-duty policeman still in uniform, an untouchable, a farmer, a richly dressed merchant, a well-known politician, a housewife, and a swami. One by one they dropped their garlands and their petals, bowed deeply, brushed the tears away, and moved out again into the sun, into the park, into the noisy fairground, into India.

As we walked toward the gate, Moti Lal came to say good-bye. Proudly he waved his hands at the crowd. "This is happening all over India today," he said. "Children are singing, people are making speeches and listening to speeches. Processions are marching, hospitals and schools are being dedicated—all because Mahatma Gandhi lived. Government may forget sometimes, but we workers, we people, do not forget."

Neither do I. And so, this shining blue afternoon, I have been thinking of all the things the name and the personality of Gandhi have meant to me.

He was a revered name in the Quaker household of my childhood. He was a banner of courage flying against the legions of oppression. He was the voice of humanity and love in a world gone mad. All this before I came to India, before I learned that nothing is black or white in India, even where a holy man is concerned.

And at last to me he was a quiet voice of moderation at the twilit prayer meetings in a Delhi untouchable colony. While the temple bells tinkled, he was a drone and a whisper, like the whisper of the cricket-conscience in *Pinocchio*. He was a man too great for an ordinary reporter to want to interview, and yet, when I did interview him, he was a tired old man who lay on his back while two beautiful girls gave him a mud bath, and was cold and rude. It was in the midst of the riots; he was weary and heart-sick —and no doubt I should not have troubled him with my own agonized questions about the cold war.

"I have no interest in the troubles of the Western World," he said. "I am only interested in India."

From Gandhi, it seemed a blow and a betrayal. I left him, and in the rain outside the door, stopped and wept.

When I remember the great drama of the end, certain scenes and persons are etched in emotional lightning. Bhag Singh, running to my door and shouting: "Come quick! Mahatmaji is dead!" I looked in amazement at his contorted face, and my ears heard "Masterji is dead!" I thought he meant Eric, and began running beside him down the hotel corridor, crying "What? What? How?" Until, in a great burst of relief, I saw Eric waiting by the car.

Then we were outside Birla House in the blue dusk, and a crowd was already assembling, although it had been only twenty minutes since Gandhi had died. We pushed through the crowd and stood on tiptoe to peer into a downstairs room. Gandhi was lying on his back in the middle of the room, his head resting on the knees of a girl, a granddaughter probably. There were other people in the room, all crying, praying, kneeling. There were lights flickering and confusion.

It was still unbelievable, completely unbelievable. In a daze we wandered around the garden where the assassin fired his fatal bullets, talking to anyone who saw, anyone who could tell us who and why. Why? We talked to police, to soldiers. We peered into a little tool shed and saw the assassin, with the police questioning him. But hardly any of this can I remember; mostly I remember the vast sense of relief that the assassin was a Hindu, not a Moslem. For if he had been a Moslem, I think most of India's forty million Mohammedans would have been dead within a day.

And then Nehru strode out of the house, his face tragic and set. He shoved his way through the silently milling people and climbed up on a picket fence to speak to them. We could not hear him, so we crawled on our bellies under a thorny tree until we were close enough. Nehru spoke brokenly, attempting to quiet the crowd, but finally crumpled in tears and went back into the house.

The crowd was pushed back into the street, but still it stood there; still more came; Hindus, Moslems, Sikhs, untouchables, aristocrats, scholars and villagers, men on bicycles, barefoot girls, donkey-drivers, cow-herders. Now there were several thousand standing silently in the darkness, or whispering softly *"Darshan, darshan."* Finally they were given *darshan*: the glimpse of holiness which gives a mystical blessing to anyone who sees it. The body of Gandhi, stretched on a simple string charpoy, was carried on to a flood-lighted balcony and tilted so that the crowd could see his face. Near the bed burned a lamp with five flames symbolizing the five elements of air, light, water, earth, and fire. The silence in the street below was absolute.

Then we were back at the hotel, and I was huddled on a couch, clutching a drink and listening to the voice of Nehru on the All-India Radio. "The light has gone out of our lives, and there is darkness everywhere," he said, his voice husky with sorrow. "The light has gone out. Yet this light which has illumined this country for many years will still shine, and will shine one thousand years from now."

And at last, late at night, I sat with my fingers poised over typewriter keys, my hands shaking because I knew that the story I must write was the most personally moving and probably the most important I would ever write. Today, looking at the clipping of the story, which I have no memory of writing, I am amazed that it is so factual, so clear-cut, so devoid of emotion. That was, perhaps, just as well for a news story. But it still seems to me inadequate.

Thirteen hazy days intervened, and then the pictures come clear again: we of the press were riding in an army truck immediately preceding the flower-decked carriage which bore the copper urn containing Gandhi's ashes. Nehru rode cross-legged at the front of the carriage, his face sad and withdrawn. The seven-mile line of march from the railway station to the confluence of the sacred Ganges and Jumna rivers at Allahabad (where the ashes were to be immersed) was guarded by soldiers; beyond them millions upon millions of Indians pressed forward for *darshan* of the urn.

The procession moved into the Mela, or fairgrounds, where two million devout Hindus had gathered to observe the annual festival of bathing in the two rivers. From the truck we could look over the heads of the soldiers and see holy men almost naked and smeared with white ash and mystical red marks, and could hear the ringing of their wild bells and the beating of their drums. Suddenly, one of them, savage, naked, smeared with cow-dung, broke through the ranks of soldiers and leaped into the space directly in front of the funeral carriage. From a side of the carriage he grabbed a huge wreath of laurel leaves and draped it over one shoulder and under his other arm, capering and grinning. A soldier stepped out and shoved him back into the crowd.

But not before I had looked at Nehru and seen his expression
as he watched the insane holy man. And on Nehru's face was a
look of tragedy and pain and hopelessness, and in his eyes there
were tears.

For years my attitude toward Gandhi had swung wildly between cynicism and reverence.

When Gandhi traveled by train, an entire third-class carriage
would have to be emptied for the convenience of the great man
and his party. Dozens of peasants would then have to wait many
hours for another train.

When Gandhi came to the untouchable colony in Delhi, he
took over the local schoolhouse, and the children had to move
out to a tent under the baking sun. Dozens of workers were detached from their jobs at the Birla Mills and sent to police the
colony.

The goats' milk Gandhi preferred had to be sent from out of
town, at considerable expense, and so did his honey and special
brand of grain. "If the world only knew what it cost us to keep
Gandhiji in the poverty to which he is accustomed!" that acid wit,
Sarojini Naidu, once remarked with loving exasperation.

There seems to me much truth in the assertion of many Indians that Gandhi did not wish to change the caste system, but
wanted only to make people good and clean and contented in
whatever way of life God had chosen for them. The fact that he
called untouchables *harijans* or "children of God," and main-
tained that they should be kindly treated, did little to eliminate
untouchability. Some people say that his constant discussion of
the *harijans* only emphasized their separation from the rest of
Hindu society.

The same attitude of "let's clean up the status quo and keep it"
seems evident in his economic solutions for India. He opposed industrialization. He wanted the peasants to remain in their mud

villages, but to practice compost-pitting, the use of latrines, spinning, chastity, and noble thoughts.

In a country which has for centuries amply demonstrated its capacity for hysterical violence, Gandhi was constantly telling Indians how peace-loving they were. In a country where the scramble for the fast rupee is as animated as anywhere else, he continually reminded them of their spiritual superiority. In a country where sex is the only recreation of the masses, he preached absolute chastity. In a country which has never been addicted to liquor—and which in fact manufactures none worth drinking—he was a fervent prohibitionist.

In the steaming May of 1947, when the vital political conferences with Mountbatten were being held at Government House, the air conditioner had to be turned off because Gandhi insisted on wearing only his little scraps of homespun rags. Everyone else sweltered.

And when he was once asked who he thought should be the first president of free India, he answered: "A pure young peasant girl."

Much of this seemed absurd, not only to Westerners, but also to some sophisticated Indians. "Gandhi is a hypnotist, a charlatan, and a minor archangel!" a brilliant politician once told me.

And yet I know now that none of the seeming absurdities was as absurd as it seemed.

India, particularly where the masses are concerned, is a land of symbols. Light is a symbol, so is water and the powdered dust of flowers. And when a man who could be wealthy adopts semi-nakedness, a starvation diet, a string bed, and a third-class railway carriage, these become symbols of renunciation for the sake of others, the greatest of virtues. A leader who wishes to attain the kind of leadership Gandhi had (and it was greater than Nehru's) must use all of these symbols. The Indian may not always be a good man himself, but he invariably responds to what he conceives to be goodness in others.

Gandhi almost always talked symbolically. The "pure young peasant girl" meant really that he hoped India would be governed in the interests of the Indian peasants, and by goodness and vitality. To ask people to renounce liquor and sex is, symbolically, to ask them for self-control in all areas of life. Spinning, I suppose, is a symbol of quietness and creativity, as well as of independence of British mills.

Gandhi, like most great religious teachers, used the trick of telling people that they are already the kind of people one hopes privately they will become. If materialism and greed are evident in people, you tell them they are spiritual. If violence possesses their hearts, you tell them they are peaceful. It's a little like talking to a naughty but beloved child: "You're a very *good* child, aren't you? You wouldn't *dream* of pulling up the flowers, would you? No indeed, you *love* flowers!" This is not as silly as it sounds, for when it came to Gandhi, the Indian people were his children. And what did they call him? *Bapu*—which means "Father."

And today as a person he remains as mysterious as any universal father must always remain. But of one thing I am certain: that it no longer matters what Gandhi really was, but only what the people of India believe him to have been. There comes a time when legend is more important than reality.

February

✿

Delhi   February 8

THE United Nations is having another of those flaming debates in which India and several Asian nations are involved. The papers have been full of it; radio news broadcasts carry hourly transcriptions of the debates; and no one talks of anything else in government or newspaper circles.

Today I thought it would be interesting to get some "man in the street" opinion on the subject—and besides, it was a lovely blue and windy day for a walk through the bazaars. I asked Nand Lal, our part-time secretary, to come along with me and interpret, and he came, although of course he thought I was crazy. Indian newspapers rarely interview "the masses," as the common man is not thought to have any opinions worth listening to.

We drove to Subzimundi, which means vegetable market, but which is now just a busy section of shops and tenements. We parked the car at a corner of the main street and began walking slowly along the pavement. Our first subject was a pan-seller squatting on the sidewalk in front of a brass tray covered with green leaves, betel nuts, spices, and pastes. Nand Lal explained that we just wanted to ask some questions about the current debate before the United Nations.

"What's the United Nations?" the pan-seller asked. And then he added, with possible irrelevance: "I'm very happy, you know!"

Behind him a fat Hindu merchant had a little shop stocked with pencils and chalk, a few burlap bags of rice and flour. He shook his head when we asked him whether he had ever heard of the United Nations, and said no. Next door an old man presided over an aluminum tea kettle, a charcoal stove, a few benches. We sat down and bought a cup of tea.

"The United Nations is another name for America," he told us positively.

From another bench a young porter just off duty from the textile mill around the corner looked at the tea-seller scornfully. "The United Nations is all the people of the world trying to help each other," he announced. "India should help too, but I do not yet know how." Some of his fellow employees, the ones who read newspapers, discussed these matters, he said, and that is how he had learned what he knew.

We walked on down the busy, self-engrossed street. We came to a group of about twenty men lounging on a bit of grass under a tree—villagers in town for a day's sight-seeing and shopping. None of them knew what the United Nations was. Nearby, a barber sat cross-legged on a cloth on the ground, clipping a young man's hair. "I don't know," said the barber. "I only know how to cut hair."

In the dim green vegetable-shop beyond, a middle-aged man gave the same answer: "I sell vegetables. That's all I know."

The Moslem meat-seller next door was better informed. "The United Nations is a body which makes decisions which nobody follows," he asserted. But when we asked what some of these decisions were, he couldn't tell us.

A gaunt schoolteacher wearing a spotless white dhoti and carrying a black umbrella was just closing the doors of his small private school. "The United Nations exists to help the oppressed," he

told us. Then he turned to the scattering of boys who were await-
ing him on the sidewalk. "Do you hear that, children? We must
always help the oppressed!" The boys, wide-eyed in the presence
of strangers, nodded solemnly.

We spoke to a bootblack at the corner. He shook his head. "I
am an illiterate," he explained.

Down near the corner, a short little man sold sugar cane at
a small stall. "I have no time to know these things," he said. "I
spend all my time earning a living from day to day. If I don't sell
sugar cane this afternoon, my family won't eat tonight."

A hawker of men's socks butted in. "I know all about it," he
declared. "But it's no good! How can you tell, when the U.N. has
stopped the fighting, that it won't start again?" That seemed to be
the end of his thoughts on the matter, and he went his way,
muttering.

We came to the door of "The Hindustan Band Instrument
Company," and walked into a small room full of battered drums
and trumpets and cymbals. A few men lounged around on the
floor, looking disconsolate.

"We don't know anything about what you ask, for we are all
illiterate," one of them explained. "All we know is that we play
music for wedding processions six months of the year, and the
rest of the year we go hungry. Right now is the hungry time of
year."

Outside again, we walked on, unconsciously keeping step with
the jangly movie music coming from a loudly tuned radio in one
of the shops. A Sikh carpenter in a small lumber yard said he had
heard of the U.N., but didn't really know what it did. A bicycle
repairman told us that he had been taught to read and write in
school, but had now forgotten how because he never reads a newspaper and there is nothing much else to read. A Sikh tailor
who had been in the Indian Navy for six years remarked dourly:
"The United Nations is concerned with literary people." The
driver of a horse cart, a homesick refugee from Pakistan, asked:
"What did you say that name was again?"

Leaving the bazaar, we asked our final question of the corner policeman, a nice young man in short khaki pants and jacket. He scratched his chin and looked puzzled.

"I couldn't quite tell you," he said at last. "But I could show you on the map, maybe."

Delhi ✤ February 24

One of my favorite days in India is *Basant Panchmi*, which to Indians, at least in the north of India, is the first day of spring. The great fields of mustard are yellow and tender green, and the peasants put on clothing to match the colors—yellow saris on the women, little yellow or green caps on the children, yellow shirts on the men, or green, the color of the fields. Last year at this time I was in Pakistan, and I remember how the schoolgirls, wandering hand in hand through the mustard fields, wore green pajamas, pale yellow tunics, and gauzy green scarves. The beauty of India is often a by-product of tradition or necessity.

This year I was driving through the flat plains of the United Provinces, or Uttar Pradesh, as the Indians now call it. Pat and Bob Lubar (of *Time* and *Life*) and I have just come back from a wonderful ten-day trip which was really, between sight-seeing and note-taking, a ten-day, non-stop discussion of Hinduism, India, national character, Russia, Christianity, and everything else in the world. We drove all the way to Benares and back, and found the roads surprisingly good, if you discount hazards like bullock carts, pigs, chickens, children, horses, carriages, monkeys, and peacocks. We took with us a large supply of beer, crackers, sardines, and cheese, bought oranges and guavas at villages, and picnicked every day by the side of the road, much to the polite amusement of passing villagers. At night we stayed in decaying British-style hotels, with ghosts of British district officers in the mosquito-netted beds, flyspecked pictures of Queen Victoria on the dining-room walls, and thunderboxes in the bathroom. Why, oh why, will such places insist on serving cold mutton and boiled potatoes to any Western guest? But they are so proud of being able to produce these delicacies that they'd be terribly hurt if you rejected them in favor of curry and rice. Personally, I'd take curry and rice every time.

We write (because we believe in it and want to) so much about the progress of modern India and the enlightenment of New Delhi that this trip was almost like a vacation. For we did not go to see the village projects or the new dams; we went to see the old India, the India of fakirs and swamis and religious excess.

We went first to Allahabad, to see the annual mela at the junction of the sacred Jumna and the even more sacred Ganges. The mela is an enormous gathering of Hindus who come each year by the hundreds of thousands to bathe at the confluence of the rivers during the month of *Marg,* and in particular to bathe on the night and morning of the dark of the moon.

The mela encampment on the packed sand peninsula between the rivers is really one of the tremendous sights of India: Naked sadhus smeared with white ashes, their hair twisted with ropes. Yellow-draped holy men carrying the sacred spear of Shiva. Fat, greasy priests sitting cross-legged in their huts, accepting the worship of their followers. Rows and rows of beggars, the lepers segregated but hideously unmistakable. Rows of men selling powders in the different shades of crimson and scarlet and saffron which are used in painting the Hindu caste mark on the forehead. Boats darting back and forth across the waters, children running, everyone shouting, flags and banners flying.

We wandered among the crowds, undisturbed and undisturbing. Then we were taken by an Indian friend to visit the mela temple. We bought marigolds from a booth outside, took off our shoes, and walked stocking-footed among a big crowd pushing at the entrance of the temporary tin shack which served as the temple. Being foreigners, we were moved ahead by the police (they always do this, and they mean well, but it is embarrassing), and we found ourselves going down a flight of stairs with dozens of

Indians, and into a small, rectangular room where a red-painted statue of Hanuman, the monkey-god, lay at the bottom of a watery pit, with a railing all around. The garish wooden statue was covered with petals and garlands of flowers, and a barelegged priest stood ankle-deep in the water and blossoms, fishing in the muck for "sacred" fruit which he sold to devout worshippers for a few annas.

The police pushed from behind; the crowd roared "*Hanuman ki jai!*" ("Long live Hanuman!") and tossed their flowers into the pit. We tossed ours in too, then paddled out through the mud, flower petals, and spit.

Outside, there were images of other gods, mostly Kali, wife of the god of destruction—a black goddess with several arms, each hand bearing the severed head of some human victim, hideous to me, but meaningful and symbolic to Hindus. There were sacred cows, too, each decorated with an embroidered blanket. For a few pennies, the cow's owner informed the devout, she would guarantee to carry the giver safely across the river of death when the time came.

The Brahmin "parish" priests too have cows by their tents, and are involved in a nice little racket with them. A lower-caste Hindu, it seems, gains tremendous advance along the reincarnation scale of life if he gives a cow to a Brahmin. So the priest keeps a cow by his tent, "sells" the cow to a devout parishioner for a few rupees, and the devout parishioner then "gives" it back to the priest. The priest grows rich on the rupees, and the poor peasant advances a few more transmigrations toward Nirvana!

Not very sadly, we left Allahabad and drove on to Benares, "holy citadel of Hinduism."

Benares is built atop a tall bluff overlooking the Ganges, and facing east. From the river's edge up to the top of the hill rise flights of steps and stone platforms, and here and there are the soaring pillars and bastions of various maharaja's palaces. Between, in nooks and crannies, are sandwiched the temples: temples to Shiva, the principle god of Benares; to Sitala, the goddess of smallpox; to Shiva's bull, to Shiva's lingam . . . to all the thirty-three million gods and goddesses of Hinduism. To worship at these temples, to bathe here in the Ganges, to make the "pilgrim's march" around the city, to die in sight of the sacred river, all bring blessing—perhaps even freedom from the eternal wheel of life. But if you die, by mischance, on the *other* side of the river, you will be reincarnated as an ass.

At dawn, as the sun rises over the river, the bathing platforms and the river shore are thronged with men, women, and children in various stages of taking the sacred morning bath. In the water old women bob up and down, shivering, bow to the sun, turn around three times, and scurry to shore. Ceremoniously the Brahmins move their sacred thread of caste from left shoulder to right. A gaunt young man stands unmoving, waist-deep in water, staring straight into the sun. A young girl, her dripping sari clinging to her figure, climbs the steps from the water and modestly drapes a clean dry sari around her before slipping out of the wet one. She is very graceful, very grave.

On the platforms priests sit on little raised daises, under great bamboo umbrellas, each priest presiding over his own flock. Some paint caste marks on the foreheads of their followers after the purifying bath is finished. Others sit in contemplation while those around them pray wordlessly. Another is reciting the names of the gods. Surrounded by a great throng, one priest is chanting the story of how the young god Krishna danced with the milkmaids.

Up and down the three-mile stretch of steps and platforms there is an incredible noise of voices chanting, drums beating, and bells ringing in the temples, of children shouting. The smell is of dust and jasmine, of river and sun and humanity. And of smoke.

Squeezed in casually between a temple and a bathing platform is the burning ghat—the place where bodies are burned, the ashes to be thrown into the river and thence float on down to the sea. From the little boat in which we are riding on the river, the place seems just a debris-strewn mud stretch, with cows and dogs wandering through it, with the untouchables who burn the corpses poking at the smoldering pyres. Nearby stands a group of mourners staring expressionlessly. On the steps lie corpses on stretchers covered by glittering red or yellow shrouds, waiting their turn. Burned rags and bones are tossed from time to time into the river, to float along the sacred current in company with flower petals, feces, and everything else which gets dumped into the river.

We saw none of the really odd sights of Benares, unless you count the funeral of a very old saint who, because of his special sanctity, was carried to the funeral pyre sitting bolt upright in a palanquin, looking waxy and over-decorated with marigolds. But we heard a lot about them. A French artist who says he has adopted Hinduism and who lives in a big palace above the river assured us that he himself had seen holy men pull their stomach and intestines out through their mouths, wash them in the Ganges, and put them back. Another man, he said, swallows a string and asks you to pull it out through his navel. The Frenchman said that he had indeed pulled a string from the holy man's navel, and had felt the tug of it as it came out of the stomach. Still another holy man is reputed to lift eighty-pound weights with his penis. Vincent Sheean, whom we ran into at breakfast one day, told us about that one.

I left Benares in a state of tremendous emotional confusion. Some of the most thoughtful and enlightened human beings I know are Hindu philosophers and scholars. Talking to them, reading the theory and philosophy of Hinduism, and in particular that of the Vedanta school of thought, I am persuaded that their view of life is the most penetrating in the world today. Countless lives, in each one of which we are given a chance to learn and progress, makes more sense to me than streets of gold after only one little flickering life.

Yet much of what I saw in Benares made me feel that there must be something wrong with a religion which chains its masses in hideous superstition and degradation. It is all too intense, too hysterical, too rich with mystery. Incense and filth, mysticism and materialism, simple piety and priestly greed, passion and the throbbing drums—they are all mixed, to me inextricably. Even Mahatma Gandi condemned Benares for its dirt, its orthodoxy, its religious hysteria; after one visit (in 1918), he said he would never return. And he never did.

But perhaps I will. I hate this feeling of being baffled and beaten by something I do not understand.

"Never mind," says Bob Lubar, quoting the Hindus. "There are many paths to God."

And so, arguing pleasantly, we drove home again through the green-and-golden fields of springtime. And it is good, very good, to be home in the comprehensible Cecil.

Delhi ❀ February 27

But even here in the Cecil, or at least here in Delhi, we are confronted with the mystique of Hinduism. We returned to find that down by the banks of the Jumna, one thousand Indian sages, swamis, sadhus, and hermits are holding a peace rally. More are arriving every day, and the newspapers are going wild with spiritual messages.

I used to think, as do many Westerners, that an Indian holy man sat in a cave somewhere in the high Himalayas, thinking noble thoughts about Man and his Destiny, but completely unaware of where that destiny seemed to be heading. To renounce the world also seemed to mean to renounce all news of the world.

Not so, as I discovered last year in Dehra Dun. We were visiting Indian friends, and one day our host asked whether we would like to see some sacred carp in a forest. Of course we would. We rode about five miles in a jeep through wild country, then got out and walked two miles into a deep forest. Finally we climbed down a cliff and found a round pond in which, indeed, were carp. Gradually I noticed a holy man standing silently at the door of a cave. His twisted hair was smeared with ashes, his body naked except for a small breech-clout, his skin daubed with sacred markings of saffron, crimson, and white paste. Startled, we bowed.

"Good afternoon," he said in perfect English.

"You speak English?" I asked in surprise.

"Certainly. I used to be a clerk on the railways in the days before I became a philosopher. But it is much pleasanter here. People bring me food; I have the fish to watch; and I can sit and think."

I noticed a pile of books in the cave behind him. No doubt the Ramayana, the Mahabharata, the Upanishads, I thought. But anyway, I asked him what they were.

"The complete works of Aldous Huxley," he answered brightly.

Other swamis may not be quite so *au courant*, but there is no doubt that by and large the holy men have been saddened by the lack of spiritual content in the governments of the world today, and have decided that the time has come to act. Clad in the orange robes of Indian sainthood, carrying their begging bowls, their mystic staves and banners, and the golden figurines of their manifold gods, they have been traveling for weeks from the holy Himalayas, the caves of the High Karakoram, and the temples of the sacred Ganges. And now here they are, camped one thousand strong outside the walls of India's capital—representing, they claim, several hundred thousand other holy men of various sects, all eager to save the world from disaster.

In a message issued a few days ago, Swami Shantananda Maharaj, who calls himself "the Great Yogi and Philosopher of Kashmir," called upon the leaders of the world to follow Indian ascetics in their efforts to establish world peace.

"The worldship, overburdened with ignorant sinners," he said, "has been wrecked in mid-ocean, sinking. Hue and cry of the destitute, desolate sufferers has awakened the Great Angels of Peace from their spiritual slumber of Ecstasy in the Himalayan Caves.

"They are now rushing down to Delhi to rescue the drowning mankind, leading them to right, from pride, greed, and might.

"India, ever the torchbearer to the universe, the temple of God, and abode of seers and sages, will guide the suffering world. The whole world, excepting India, being intoxicated with pride of man and material power, is preparing for death and destruction. I beg the lunatic children of God to come to their senses."

The sponsors of the rally, the Sarvabhaum Sadhu Mandal, or Organization of Ascetics of the World, have also issued a statement:

"Earthly affairs of the human family have progressively passed under the guardianship of our sharp-witted energetic cousins of the West during the last three or four centuries. In their quest for mastery, in which they imagined lay the key to happiness of all, they ravaged the seas, pulverized the earth, lashed the skies, and worked miracles with the atom and the gas. But happiness they have nowhere found. On the contrary, today the world is cloven into two mighty warring camps and 'the masters and the monsters,' both terrified, stand shivering on the brink of death and destruction. It is clear Western weapons and ways cannot secure peace and happiness for mankind.

"It is as well as admitted, after the debacles in the gorgeous United Nations, that a new source of power must be discovered and invoked to intervene if the human race is to be saved from extinction."

This source of power is, of course, "the spiritual force residing in the altruistic asceticism of India." What they really want to do first is to convince the government of India that great benefits would follow if the government would only make fuller use of seers and sages—as both administrators and advisors. But the sad truth is, as even the holy men agree, that today the wandering ascetics are not as highly regarded as they once were.

"In Bharat [India] itself, the sadhu community in general has apparently lost its pristine glory," the organization has admitted. "It is regarded with contumely by a large section and hated by others. It is disrespected in government circles and even regarded as a social disease demanding purgation."

This, one would gather from a visit to the noisy encampment by the river, is probably true. Today gurus (or spiritual teachers) are a dime a dozen in Delhi, but nowhere among the visitors who are flocking to sit at their feet, to listen to the prayers and lectures, does one see any Westernized, government-type Indians, or anyone at all of the upper classes. Here, at least, the devotees seem to be entirely peasants from nearby villages, peons, and coolies. Even Bhag Singh, a fairly devout Hindu, is contemptuous of India's so-called "holy men." "Maybe one hundred sadhus," he says. "Maybe two good men. Rest thieves."

The holy men gathered by the Jumna understand this prevalent attitude and believe that a great deal of the responsibility for the situation is their own fault. One of their foremost problems is the hordes of beggars without religious or philosophical pretensions who have discovered that a sure way to the heart and purse of the reverent Indian masses is to don the orange robes of sainthood. Nowadays the public, unable to distinguish between bogus and real, continues to give alms "just in case," but looks with increasing suspicion on all self-proclaimed men of God. It has been estimated that two million such men live entirely upon the charity of the Indian public.

This conference is supposed to cost $35,000. A few days ago Swami Majaraj said that the sadhus didn't have anything like this amount of money, but that they were "confident that vibrations always bring money." So today they are concentrating on vibrations, and tomorrow there will be an all-day recitation of the names of God and an all-day worship of the sacred fire. These efforts, says the Swami, should certainly bring money for the bills and peace for the world.

What is one to think? Are they humorous, with their smearings of sacred cow dung, their little, naked, rib-showing bodies, and their pompous pronouncements? Are they typical of Indian arrogance, ignoring the horrors of Indian poverty and disease and yet daring to preach to the West? Are they profound sages, speaking wisdom which we should heed?

None of these, and yet a little of all of these, I think. Truth in India is never absolute, is always somewhere in between.

March

Delhi   March 12

A M going to have a baby in October. We cele-
brated this joyous news by going dancing at the Tavern Grill of
the Imperial Hotel. To my intense annoyance, Eric insisted that
I drink milk all evening.

Dr. Mary Thomas, who gave the definite assurance, is a very
charming Indian Christian with a background of training in England and America. I am always astonished at the casual aspect of
India—although Dr. Thomas is a fully qualified, practicing doctor, her office is a bedroom in her large and handsome bungalow
in New Delhi, and her examination table is a string bed. She
seems to have little medical equipment, and she takes notes on
the backs of old envelopes.

Neither of us knows whether I'll go all the way through with
her. The government, she explained, owns most of the hospitals
and allots beds to various doctors for the use of their patients.
She hasn't had any beds allotted to her, so she's not doing much
maternity work. But it's a long way to October, and maybe some-

thing useful will turn up. That is one thing that India does to you—you don't worry much about what is to happen. Peasant fatality, perhaps.

Right now it is enough for me to know that someday, in some place, my child will be born. *"Insch Allah!"* as the Moslems would say—or "God willing!"

Delhi ❀ March 15

Thank heavens I brought a medical textbook with me from America. Today I read through the section on "How to deliver a baby in an emergency." Very informative. Asked Eric to read it too, but he says he can wait until October.

Other things can't wait, though. Pat Lubar, who had a baby in Bombay last year, says that I'll have to send to America for all those strange things babies need. You can't buy diapers in India (what *do* they use? I've never been able to make out), or little shirts or crib sheets, or those pretty little sets of bathroom bottles, or cotton swabs on sticks, or any of the gadgets American mothers seem to feel are so necessary. Perhaps they aren't, but when it comes to *my* baby, I find that although I'd theoretically like to do things the Indian way, I'm as American as the rest of them. I don't want to do any experimenting on it.

I hadn't thought of sending home to a mail-order house for a layette, as I have only faint memories of jokes about Sears, Roebuck catalogues hanging in New England outhouses. But Pat Lubar said she did, and that it came through customs all right, and was fine. So today I drove the six miles into New Delhi and went to the United States Information Services Library to look at catalogues. What wealth they seem to represent! Amid the scarcity of consumer goods in India, the pages and pages of cheap shoes and dresses and farm machinery and furniture looked opulent. We have so much, materially, and they so little; suddenly

I understood more clearly than before how jealousy and envy can be mixed with admiration.

All afternoon I poured over the layette displays, sitting among the Indian students and their books on chemistry and physics. A lovely afternoon, except that I felt rather silly when the nearby students craned their necks, as they always do, to see what I was reading. There I was with the pages spread open to bathinettes.

Across from me at the big table in the library sat two "coffee house types"—university graduates, probably, who, like so many others, haven't yet been able to find jobs and who spend their days gossiping and politicking in the Queensway coffee house. I wondered what they were doing in the library. Peeking furtively, I saw that they were absorbed in studying the bra and corset ads in *Mademoiselle* and *Vogue*. Occasionally they nudged each other and giggled. They left just before I did, and I happened to follow them down the stairs.

"Decadent people, the Americans," one of them commented.

"No spiritual values," agreed the other.

Delhi ❄ *March 16*

Sent off my order to Montgomery Ward (an eighty-one piece layette for $26.98. God Bless America!). Did a puja prayer to the statue of Ganesh, the elephant-headed good-luck god which stands on our mantlepiece, asking that everything may come through the customs all right. I am still struggling with a bottle of vitamin pills which was airmailed from New York last December, arrived in Bombay early in January, and is still there.

It is obvious that Bhag Singh knows. Between his duties of making beds, dusting, supervising the sweepers, carrying our clothes to the dhobi for washing, and running errands, he has taken to bringing me periodic, unsolicited glasses of milk throughout the day. Buffalo milk, usually, and boiled of course. Goodness knows how he has learned about milk for these times, as I don't suppose his wife gets any, poor thing. She's going to have her fifth baby next month.

Delhi ❈ March 20

Several nights ago the Soviet Embassy invited the press to see the movie *The Battle of Stalingrad*. Afterwards there was vodka and caviar, one reason Soviet invitations are so eagerly accepted by the press. There was the usual mingling of all the journalists one knows with the strange types who always appear at Soviet parties: scruffy young men in dirty shirts who turn out to be junior reporters for obscure vernacular papers. Mostly they get drunk very quickly and pass out under the Embassy shrubbery.

Subhan, one of our good newspaper friends, was talking to a young man who seemed typical of the strangers: grubby suit, frayed collar, no tie, a lean and hungry look. But his eyes burned with intelligence under a high, bony forehead. I wandered over, and Subhan introduced me to A. P. S. Ayyar. The young man looked at me for a moment, and his face twisted sardonically.

"And what does the decadent, white, capitalistic, imperialistic American press think of the film we just saw?" he sneered.

"I thought it was very fine," I answered, and walked away.

This morning I was sitting alone at a table in the coffee house when Mr. Ayyar walked in. He saw me, started to pretend he hadn't, changed his mind, and came over and sat down.

"We Madrasis have very good minds," he announced.

"Yes, I know." His name had already told me he was a Brahmin from Madras State.

"No doubt that is why I decided in the university to become a Communist," he continued, staring at me as if he expected me to get up and run. "It is, you see, an intellectual concept—a process of reasoning. I have read Lenin and Marx and all the Soviet dialecticians. The Russian Embassy makes these books available to students very cheaply—a few annas, that is all."

"Yes, I know."

"Why do not you Americans make books cheap?" he asked unexpectedly. "Once I wanted to read about your Thomas Jefferson, but the book cost ten rupees, and I could not afford. I am still unemployed but if I ever find work perhaps I can afford to buy."

"I have books you could borrow," I said. "If you come to see us at the Cecil Hotel I will lend them to you. And the United States Information Library has many books." The boy looked hurt.

"A Madrasi does not wish to be propagandized," he announced. "But I would like to find out whether Americans are really as decadent as the Russians say. Perhaps I will come to see you." He finished his coffee, paid but didn't tip the waiter, and rose.

"You are the first American I ever met," he said solemnly. He turned quickly and strode out of the coffee house.

I wonder if he will come? Really, I would not relish the job of trying to convert a Madrasi Brahmin to anything; their minds are far too intricate. "For every solution they can find a difficulty," says Eric. But this boy is very young.

Calcutta ❀ March 25

Outside the ramshackle building a poster in red and white advertised the "World Peace Congress" Eric and I had flown from Delhi to cover. Along the narrow bazaar street the flow of Calcutta life went on unheeding, but near the door a smooth little man, typical of the government intelligence agents to be found in the vicinity of Communists, looked at us curiously. Later we learned that within half an hour of our arrival the Central Intelligence Department in New Delhi had heard about our visit and from our descriptions had decided who we were—correctly.

The headquarters of the World Peace Congress was at the end of a long passageway, three flights up. The room was crowded with arriving delegates, propaganda pamphlets, discarded sandals, and tin trunks spilling forth clean linen. Everywhere there was a happy air of bustle.

Around the walls were various instructive maps of the Soviet Union, pictures of Stalin and Lenin, the inevitable ecstatic poster of triumphant peasants trampling on fat landlords, and quotations from the masters. "There are no fortresses that Soviets cannot take. Stalin, 1933" said one of them.

We were introduced to Mr. Dutt, an earnest young man in owlish spectacles, who said he was a lecturer in economics at a local college. Yes, said Mr. Dutt, they were expecting delegates from Russia, Communist China, and Indo-China to arrive at any moment. This was the day before the opening of the World Peace Congress, and for at least a week every interested person in India had known that the government of India had denied visas to all foreigners wishing to attend the congress. But yes, insisted Mr. Dutt, they will be coming "just now."

Mr. Dutt was very correct, although he knew that we represented the decadent white press. He told us the conference had been called by the All-India Trade Union Congress, the All-India Progressive Writers and Artists Association, the Indian Peoples' Theatrical Association, and several other Leftist cultural organizations—but not the Communist Party of India. He then gave us a copy of the "Call of the Peace Preparatory Committee," and politely made it clear the interview was over.

The leaflet, which was in English, read in part: "The owners of monopoly capital in America are hatching to bring about another war—they are out to grab the whole world.

"While the American imperialists are providing a mounting evidence of their barbarous war frenzy through a systematic undermining of the foundations of the United Nations and through the Atlantic pact and the atom bomb, the Prime Minister of India . . . proclaimed the friendship of the Indian government with those bloodthirsty warmongers. Against the rude repudiation of our national interests and popular will, we are determined to organize a powerful protest, whatever be the obstacles thrown in our path by the government's policy of repression."

In the case of the World Peace Congress the government's policy of repression did not seem excessive. Evidently it was felt that the wings of the meeting had been clipped by the ban on foreign delegates, and in any case there are indications that the congress had been called to give opportunity for behind-scene stock-taking, rather than to provide occasion for violence.

Deshpriya Park, where the congress was held, is a quiet green space in South Calcutta, surrounded by old pink and white three-story houses. When we arrived at 1 p.m., the hour when the congress was scheduled to begin, the crowd was just starting to collect and workmen were still erecting a shamianah, a kind of large tent. Later much bitterness was expressed because the congress was not allowed to have a pandal, another kind of tent. We spotted several intelligence agents in the crowd, but not a policeman was in sight.

While we watched, workmen finished tacking up a painting of Picasso's dove. On one corner of the dais was a pleasantly smiling poster of Paul Robeson, who presumably was to be with the conference in spirit.

Under the shamianah, about one thousand Indian delegates, men and women, sat quietly on the grass, and out in the sun several hundred young men milled about while others relaxed in groups under the waxy leaves of the frangipani trees. We tried to talk to some of them, but they heard our Anglo-American accents, and after a few moments of politely uninspired conversation, turned away.

On the steps of a Victorian bandstand, a bookstall had been set up to display pamphlets in Hindi and English, some of them published in Moscow and one of them issued recently in Bucharest. Wandering nearby we saw the Russian correspondent of *Tass* who had traveled on the same plane with us from Delhi.

Promptly at 2:30 the conference opened with a rousing song by five members of the Indian Peoples' Theatrical Association, one of the most accomplished drama groups in India. For the next four hours, while the crows cawed and the laden oxcarts trundled by in the streets, the meeting proceeded as scheduled: reading of messages from foreign "peace" organizations; a speech in favor of peace and Russia by the president of an important union; the adoption of a resolution greeting the peoples of Russia, the "peoples' democracies" of Eastern Europe, and the "peoples of Freed China"; the adoption of another resolution condemning the reactionary Nehru government for its action in denying entry visas to the Soviet and other delegations. The afternoon was very hot and long, and sitting on the steps of the bandstand among the propaganda pamphlets, I grew sleepy with heat and boredom.

The second day was much the same as the first. When Eric and I arrived at the park a rapid-speaking young lady in a purple cotton sari was giving a speech in Bengali, from which occasionally emerged such English words as "democracy," "liberty," and "oppression" for which there are no exact Bengali equivalents. When we left, an intense young man was speaking in Hindi, but we could distinguish only such words as "radio," "hysteria," and "Uncle Tom," the last repeated several times. As we walked out of the park, we passed a group of small boys playing cricket with improvised bats.

The third day—today—the meeting shifted, with police permission, to the Maidan, which is to Calcutta what Central Park is to New York. The crowd was bigger this time, and perhaps three thousand persons had collected around the foot of Ochterlony Monument, an immense pillar put up years ago by the British to commemorate a Scottish general who fought a successful campaign in Nepal.

From time to time, processions of workers from the jute mills and from various railway unions arrived waving red banners and shouting "Down with Nehru and the West!" On the platform a speaker declaimed: "Take any weapon you can! Make yourselves free!"

"Who are these people?" we asked our Sikh taxi driver, wanting to see what he would say.

"They are just poor coolies and mill workers who are hungry," he answered.

We wandered on the outskirts of the crowd, and asked the same question of a village boy, who had been busily selling handfuls of hotly-spiced grain to the delegates. "It does not reach my understanding," he answered humbly.

We asked a water-seller, squatting on the ground amid his earthenware cups and jugs. "They are people who want more bread and rice," he said.

It was Sunday on the Maidan, and the Communist meeting was evidently only one entertainment among many to tempt the passerby. A huge crowd nearby had collected to watch a wrestling match; another was entranced by two dancing monkeys; beyond it a performing bear attracted the attention of several hundred laughing coolies. Other amusements scattered about the huge area included a story teller telling tales of Rama and Sita, singers and drum-beaters, a fortune-telling cow, a holy man discoursing on the *Gita*, a pundit leading a prayer meeting, a boy loudly proclaiming the virtues of a foot ointment compounded to order on the spot, and a cricket match.

The class distinction was never more evident. Easily recognizable by their clothes, their spectacles, and their general air, the young intellectuals, students, and other members of the middle class were gathered en masse at the World Peace Congress. In rags and tatters, the proletariat were having an even better time watching the dancing bears and the monkeys.

Today, more than anywhere else at any other time, I have been conscious of the great shock-absorber quality of India. It doesn't fight back, it merely tolerates, ignores, blankets, and encompasses the opposition. This is one of the qualities of India which makes the task of the Communist so difficult; the water-seller and the taxi driver are beginning to believe that the Communists are offering them more bread and rice than they are getting, but the belief is not yet very strong, and the attractions of the bears and monkeys are stronger. And yet, the Communists play a long game, the only kind you can play in India. Subconsciously, did the village boy listen to their words and absorb them, while he watched the antics of the monkey, and laughed?

Calcutta ✿ March 26

Always, in Calcutta, those irritations which are minor to me in other Indian cities become major. Then passionately I hate doors that stick and keys that won't work and having to wait twenty minutes for a telephone call which shouldn't take two minutes. And I hate the stupid taxi drivers who never know where any address is, but pretend they do, so that you are lost and miss your appointment. And I hate the heat baking your brains and making you cross to simple people; God made so many of them in Calcutta you're cross all the time.

I hate rusty water in the bathtubs, and showers which dry up just after you have soaped your burning body. And idiot boys who make appointments for you with the boss, but forget to tell you the boss is coming to see you, not you to him. All because the poor boy can't speak proper English, and you can't blame him for that, can you? That makes it even worse.

But it isn't just the boy. I rage up and down the room under the unworkable electric fan, screaming silently to myself at Calcutta: the flies and the ugliness, the hopelessness, the lying, the cruelty, the dung and the dead on the streets! Then, exhausted, I collapse on the hard hotel bed and dream of brooks flowing among beds of mint and forget-me-nots, of strawberries ripening gently, of people who are kind in a way I understand. I don't understand Indians; they don't understand me. I'm tired of feel-

ing guilty and seeing ugliness and despair, and of feeling like this.
I'm *homesick.*

Kalimpong ❀ *March* 27

Well. Obviously, I should *never* go to Calcutta. It is the
only place in India which I really cannot abide. I am always conscious there of the Bengali worship of Kali, goddess of destruction.
It is a city suffused by the consciousness of death, of destruction,
and of hatred.

I hate Calcutta because I feel *most* guilty there, guilty of completely losing my temper and making dreadful generalizations
about India on the basis of one benighted province. I can well
understand why the early bomb-tossing revolutionaries were almost all Bengalis; the atmosphere of Bengal made me want to toss
bombs, too.

It seemed better, however, to get out of Calcutta. So, on im-
pulse, and knowing that I could at least find a background story
for the paper, I flew yesterday to Bagdogra at the foothills of the
Himalayas and hired a car to drive me three hours up winding
mountain roads to Kalimpong. Every minute the air grew cooler,
so did my head. The chauffeur and I drove by frothing and
tumbling mountain streams. We passed under great ferns as high
as trees. We saw tea plantations and flocks of coolies with happy
Mongolian faces. We drove up a last high peak, down a hill, and
came at sunset to this crazy little Himalayan Hotel.

We are so close here to the border of Tibet that the atmosphere
is more Tibetan than Indian. The lounge where everyone gathers
is hung with Tibetan banners; the famous MacDonalds who run
the hotel are Scottish-Tibetan. In the evening all kinds of people, most of whom seem to be specializing in one phase or another
of Tibetan life, drift into the lounge, fix their own buttered rum
at the bar, write their own chits for the record, and sit around a
central charcoal brazier—talking of Tibet, of course.

Last night there was a thin, bearded young Scotsman who says he has just returned from a year in eastern Tibet. He went there as a missionary for one of the more primitive Christian faiths, and in the course of his travels became an expert on demonology. He told fantastic stories of "oracles" possessed by demons and, therefore, able to twist bars of steel into bowknots which no one else could even bend. And he was eloquent on the subject of the secret solicitation of demons, which he sharply distinguishes from propitiation. This takes place, he says, in the innermost recesses of the Tibetan lamasaries where "evil is palpable."

"Do you really believe in demons?" I asked him. He looked at me in astonishment.

"My dear lady," he said finally. "It isn't a question of believing; it's a question of knowing. Frankly, angels and demons are far more real to me than you are."

The two lady managers of the hotel, who had been listening, broke the silence into which I had evaporated by announcing that they were Nestorians. One of them added, however, that although they were both hardheaded businesswomen, whenever they traveled in Sikkim or Bhutan or Tibet, they were aware of strange forces and invisible beings.

"Honestly, dear Madam, when I went into Bhutan and saw the flickering lights at night on top of the lamasaries and heard the trumpets calling, I swear I could feel a rushing in the air!"

Kalimpong is on the old trade route from Tibet; the little bazaar wandering over the hillside is periodically filled with mule teams and Tibetan muleteers just in from the high Himalayas, unloading their furs and hides and bricks of green tea. Since the new communist rule in Tibet will shortly cut off this trade, and it may be years before we see the Tibetans again, I went up to the bazaar today to take some photographs.

Tibetans don't like being photographed, because they believe the little black box takes "soul force" away from them. However, if you do it quickly enough and smile at them, they don't make much objection. My first subject was a beauty: a tough muleteer in rough leather boots, a black robe with a silver dagger stuck through a red sash, and a furry black cap. He was squatting in a cloth-dealer's booth and happily draping himself in yards of rose-sprigged blue silk.

I walked up a narrow alley and came upon a group of men sitting on bales of wool which they had apparently just unloaded from their mules. Two of them looked rather more ferocious than the others, and they were wearing what looked like Soviet Army caps. I quickly raised the camera and took their pictures.

As I turned away, I heard a howl behind me which sounded like an enraged bloodhound. Looking back, I saw that one of the group—the blackest, dirtiest, wildest Tibetan muleteer in all the Himalayas—was rushing at me with a dagger raised in his right hand. With his teeth drawn back in a hideous snarl, his eyes blazing, his face black with the smoke of many charcoal fires, his matted pigtails dancing wildly, and his knife gleaming, he looked like every demon I've ever seen in nightmares.

Terrified, I stood there as he leapt to my side and stopped, his right arm with the dagger poised above me. All I could think to do was to smile at him weakly and make a kind of apologetic grimace, trying to look as innocent and feminine as possible. Simultaneously, I realized that there was no one in the alley but the muleteers and me.

Suddenly the Tibetan lowered his arm and burst into spasms of the most demoniacal laughter I've ever heard, great bellows which sounded like the devil laughing in hell. Still laughing, he stooped down and picked up a dirty piece of fur strip lying on one of the bales of wool, and threw it at me. With as much dignity as possible, which wasn't much considering my weak knees and urge for haste, I walked away. I could still hear him laughing as I rounded the corner.

Later, the Scottish missionary told me he had heard Tibetans laugh like that while they watched a companion hacked to pieces for some minor offense.

Darjeeling ❀ *March 29*

No use coming this far without taking a look at Darjeeling, I told myself. So this afternoon I hitched a ride in a jeep and rode for two hours across the mountain roads, under towering green ferns through which, from time to time, I could catch a glimpse of the big mountains, the High Himalayas. But this evening they were hidden by clouds, and after a short walk around the hilly, unremarkable town, I found there was nothing much to do but retreat to the bar of the Planters' Club, where I am staying the night. And there I met Bill, perched like an eager owlet on an adjoining bar stool. Eager not for girls, it developed, but conversation.

"Wonderful people, these Tibetans," he mused aloud as he unwrapped a paper parcel revealing two small brass tigers. The tigers, although he doesn't know it, are made by Hindus for fifty cents a pair in Calcutta, and sell for five dollars in Darjeeling as Tibetan curios.

His name, he told me, was Bill. He was a tea planter. And he liked Tibetans, who are often to be found in this area. His pinched young face, yellowed from his most recent bout of malaria, glowed for a moment. "We had a dance on the tea garden the other day," he said, "and I waltzed with a Tibetan lassie. A wizard popsie!"

In a corner of the bar a month-old copy of the London *Times* crackled reprovingly, and the old planter behind it peered sternly for a moment at Bill. If only we had been introduced, he would have been able to make some pungent remarks about the dangers of mingling socially with the natives, but since we had not, he contented himself with a glare. You still find a few of them like this left about undusted in odd corners of India.

Bill was oblivious of the old planter, as he is to many drawbacks of his life such as pythons, malaria, and labor trouble on the gardens. Bill, the new generation of British tea planter in India, is living a new life to the hilt and loving it.

"Been out here two years and have another two to go before I see the folks again on my six-months-home leave," Bill said. "But meantime, I don't mind so much, you know.

"One thing was kind of bad at first—bunch of us young English assistants came out together to our garden and found that all the other white people there were Scottish, and kind of upper class if you know what I mean. Well, for a year they wouldn't more than speak to us. We'd sit at our end of the company bar, and they'd sit at theirs, and we'd all get drunk, but not together."

He looked solemn for a moment, and because he was obviously as friendly as a puppy I shared his unhappiness at this exclusion. But then he grinned. "It's all right now though," he said. "We teach them English songs, and they teach us Scottish ones. And believe me, they know a thing or two!

"Life isn't half bad on the gardens," he said after a long gulp of whiskey. "We had a dance at Christmas and one on New Year's Eve. And the rest of the time there's cricket and tennis. And I've got me three little dachshunds for company.

"And all sorts of exciting things happen, like the time I found a krait (that's the most poisonous kind of snake there is, don't you know?) curled up in my desk drawer. Or the time a wild elephant ripped the steering wheel out of my pal's car. He wasn't in the car at the time, luckily. And then there was the time I got my legs covered with leeches, and I didn't know how to get them off. That shows what a green chappie I was in those days. Now, of course, I always carry a bag of salt with me to sprinkle on them, like everyone else does."

Bill laughed, and called for another drink. "I tell you, life in Tottenham Court Road wasn't like this!" he said.

It was cold in the little bar, and we moved over by the electric heater and thus nearer to the old planter behind his *Times*.

"Labor troubles?" answered Bill in reply to my question. "Yes, some of the gardens up here have been having trouble here and there. Don't know much about it myself. On our garden mostly seems to be some personal matter, like the coolies not liking the head clerk, or something. But I do hear that on some of the gardens there've been strikes and such.

"But you know, I like these Indians. Seem like pretty good chums to me, although they're all wacky, of course, and their whole religion is based on sex, or so I hear. But just the same, I like to go along to their festivals, and the kids are just as smart as our kids in England. They like to learn anything you take the trouble to teach them."

The *Times* descended abruptly, and the florid face of the old planter rose above it like an apoplectic moon. "Young man," he thundered, "don't talk about teaching these people anything! Why, the whole trouble with this country is education! We British made the greatest mistake of our lives when we started giving them education." He threw down his paper and stood up in order to thunder more effectively.

"These Americans!" he stormed. "They talk of resisting Communism by educating the people and improving economic conditions. Why, who are the Communists in India today? The half-educated Indian middle classes! I tell you, all India needs is a strong frontier and enough police to keep the people quiet!"

"Isn't it a little late for that, sir?" asked Bill.

"But it isn't too late to stop making all these idiotic concessions to our coolies, like higher wages," rasped the old man, shifting ground rapidly. "The more you give them the more they want! I tell you, they were much better off in the old days, before they had shoes and umbrellas and all the fancy things they buy now; and wanting to send their children to school, too."

"Well, I don't know about shoes and umbrellas, although I rather like them myself, sir," said Bill apologetically. "But when a little chappie comes to you and says he hears the world is round and not flat like his daddy says, what can I do but haul out the old orange and explain it to him? Seems to me a bright chappie deserves a little education, doesn't he?"

The old planter sat down again heavily, and suddenly he looked rather crumpled and tired.

"Everything's changed," he said. "Wouldn't recognize this country now from the way it was when I came here thirty-six years ago as a young man. Came down from Oxford and out here because my uncle owned a garden, just the way everybody else comes out here."

"Not everybody now, sir," Bill said politely. "My father was a factory hand. I had to leave school at fifteen to go to work. Then my plant closed down, so I just answered an advertisement for a mechanic on a tea garden, and here I am."

The old planter, ignoring the interruption, droned on more to himself than to us. "There are still more than two thousand of us here," he muttered. "But nobody knows how long we can hang on. The Indian tea garden owners treat their labor worse than we Britishers do, yet the government is trying to squeeze us out, not them. They make us buy rice for twenty-five rupees a maund and sell it to the coolies at five rupees, and they weigh us down with all kinds of restrictions.

"We still have the power to throw thieves and troublemakers off our gardens, but I don't know what we can do with these Communists when they get to work in the gardens, as they're beginning to. Once our workers get affected we can't throw them all off the estates! And the government won't help. It almost looks as if they wanted us to go, just because we're white."

Bill and I sipped our drinks in respectful silence. The old planter stared at his cigar smoke. A waiter padded barefoot through the room and turned off a light.

"Tell me, sir," Bill asked at last. "Do you think there's a future for a young chap like me out here? Can I make a life career in Indian tea?"

"If you die young," the old planter answered sourly, and retreated once more behind his month-old copy of the *Times*.

56 ✤

Darjeeling ✤ *March 30*

Yesterday when I arrived it was foggy, and I could not see the mountains. But this morning at dawn I walked out on the club verandah, and there were the snows—a magnificent range of Himalayan peaks covered in eternal snow. The highest, at the center, was Kachenjunga, over 28,000 feet high. Left and right stretched other peaks, none of them less than 20,000 feet. Across the valley from Darjeeling, they seemed to float in the sky above a sea of cloud, remote, mysterious, almost holy.

As I watched, the clouds swept up from the valley, and the mountains were gone.

Reluctantly, I turned away and began the long trip back to the steaming plains.

April

❧

Delhi   April 4

WHEN I returned, I found that Bhag Singh's
wife had had her baby—a boy. To celebrate the event Bhag Singh
has asked us for two hundred and thirty rupees advance on his
salary—more than two months' worth to buy his wife a gold
nose ring. We were both aghast at this fantastic expenditure contemplated by a man earning one hundred rupees a month, but
Bhag Singh won't listen to reason.

"You know how it is, Sahib," he says. "When your wife really
wants something, you can't deny it to her." Eric gave what
amounted to a snort and told Bhag Singh firmly that no matter
how much I wanted something, he was damned if he was ever
going to spend two months' salary on my whims. Bhag Singh
smiled politely and repeated that he wanted two hundred and
thirty rupees to buy his wife a *big* gold nose ring.

It's the same story all over India, of course. And who are we to
begin changing the customs of our poor bearer? In this land of
sudden famine and unforeseen catastrophe, a wife's jewelry has
always been the peasant's form of security. During the riots, I saw

thousands of people who were reduced to living on grass and tree bark, but whose women still clung tenaciously to their heavy silver bracelets or sparkling diamond nose rings. Portable jewelry is really the only form of insurance for the mass peasantry, but it makes me sad to think of all those fine millions (billions, I guess) of potentially productive rupees tied up in golden nose rings and silver anklets. Anyway, this evening Bhag Singh got his two hundred and thirty rupees and went off to the jewelry bazaar, salaaming and beaming.

Delhi ❊ April 6

In the joys of travel and return, I had almost forgotten A. P. S. Ayyer, the young Communist.

One evening, when the sky was growing smoky and dim outside our open living-room door, he appeared on the doorstep looking like a hungry and inquiring crane. After a moment I remembered him and asked him in, groaning inwardly at the thought of the diatribes to come.

But he looked changed. His hair was combed, and although he still wore no tie, he had a new suit and shirt. And his manner was no longer arrogant. He was polite, almost diffident.

"What has happened to you?" I asked.

"I have had a conversion," he answered solemnly. "I could no longer stay away from a place where there were books, so I went to the United States Information Library. I found Wendell Willkie's *One World*, and I read it. It was convincing, so I now believe in the Western point of view. I have therefore found it possible to go to work for an English-language newspaper in Delhi which also supports the Western point of view."

Since then, he has dropped in several times to see us, usually around five in the evening when we are having tea. He wishes, evidently, to discuss democracy in all its aspects. I enjoy him and feel more relaxed with him now that I have discovered that he does not resent being asked to leave after several hours, if we have other things to do. We have even discussed this matter, and he tells me that Indians always expect to stay until they are asked to leave.

Thanks to him, I have finally learned something about Indian names—or anyway, south Indian names—and how they are constructed. And I now see why so many Indians find it more convenient to use initials rather than their full, or fulsome, names. (The economist V. K. R. V. Rao, for instance, whom we usually refer to as "Alphabet Rao.")

Sesh's full name is Attur Pattabhi Seshadri Ayyar. Attur is the town he comes from. Pattabhi is his father's name. Seshadri is his own given name. Ayyar is his caste. Seshadri may or may not mean anything; he's not sure. And Ayyar can also be spelled Ayer, Ayar, or Iyer. Sesh uses any spelling he wishes and frequently varies the spelling.

"Spelling in roman letters is only a phonetic approximation of the sound in Tamil," he explained. "So it really doesn't matter, does it?"

Delhi ✽ *April 10*

The hot weather is upon us, alas. All over the city the *khus-khus* tatties are going up over doors and windows—scraggly, scratchy screens of twigs which must be wet down every hour or so by a *beestie* carrying a goatskin of water on his scrawny shoulders. They make the rooms cool, but dear me how I hate splashing through the great puddles of water which lie all summer in every doorway!

The chatty-sellers line the roadways now, selling the earthenware jugs which retain the coolness of water so marvelously. Indolence is upon the city, even the cows move more slowly; people lie motionless in any patch of shade they can find. Funeral processions wind more frequently through the streets, the escorting band incongruously playing "Marching Through Georgia," the body wrapped in red or yellow or white, lying on a charpoy, and borne on the shoulders of several men, while others trail behind, sweating and melancholy. Deaths always increase when the hot weather comes.

Today, our desert cooler was installed in a bedroom window. Much shouting and confusion on the part of the six mechanics, much imperious commanding by Bhag Singh, but at last it is working. It blows air through wet burlap and straw so that the air in the bedroom is cool and wet and smells a little of burlap and new mown hay. Much better than an air conditioner, at least in this dry heat before the monsoon breaks.

In the living room the big, overhead electric fan whirls perpetually now, and except for the times when we try to read newspapers in its blast, I bless it.

The growing heat is at last bringing the social season to a grinding close. This winter, like all the others, has been very formal—a cocktail party almost every evening, a dinner afterwards. Never would I have dreamed, in my American days, that I would someday own twenty-three evening dresses and feel the number inadequate! But the trouble is that most of the parties are diplomatic and that we see the same people over and over again—Americans, British, Swedes, Foreign Office Indians, journalists of all nations; their wives know my clothes as well as I know theirs, and we all know each other's conversation, too. Yet we must go to these endless parties, "to keep up our contacts," "to pick up news." This is the way foreign correspondents are supposed to operate. But how remote the glitter and the chatter seem from the real India.

Sometimes, at these parties, we forget for a little that this is not a country like any other. Over the martinis and the manhattans, Indian government officials, speaking with perfect Oxford accents, discuss their stay in Washington, and their wives chatter of department stores and escalators. Foreign diplomats murmur the same things their colleagues will be murmuring later in the day in Rome and London. Stormy, cultivated Nehru moves from group to group, looking bored.

The subject of American aid comes up in a little knot of Indian journalists, and one of them, angry and proud, exclaims: "I'd like to throw every grain of wheat back in America's face!"

But then an old man enters the room and stands in the doorway, gazing with kindly abstraction over the heads of the other guests. The party suddenly hushes; the band plays India's national anthem, *Jana Gana Mana*, which means "Rulers of the Hearts of the People." And looking at Dr. Rajendra Prasad, President of the Republic of India, one senses a new element in the room. One remembers suddenly, in the midst of the diplomats, the cocktails, and the canapés, that this, after all, is India. The room fades, the fellow guests melt from consciousness like creatures of a dream, and there is for the moment only the face of the President of India—a kindly face, a humble face, a care-worn face, the face of India itself.

He has always been close to the heart of India, this simple old man. He has gone to jail for his fellow countrymen; he has been hungry and alone. Even now, when he is President of India, he lives a life of village simplicity in the ornate palace of the viceroys which is his official home. His face shows all this, for it is patient and dedicated, a mirror of his life.

It is, above all, evocative.

There was a boy, a goatherd we met in the fields not far from Delhi. We asked him what he ate every day. A handful of lentils, he said, cupping his small brown hands together. And what else? we asked. Nothing else, he said. Only the lentils.

There was a baby, his stomach swollen, his face pinched, lying in a tattered fruit basket on a railway station platform in Calcutta. He had been born on that station platform eight months before, because his mother was a refugee and had nowhere else to go. Now she had no more milk to give him, and each day they shared a small pot of gruel given them by a harassed charitable organization. That was all.

There was a student in Allahabad, squatting with his books late at night under a street lamp. There was no money at home, he said, for light to study by. He had tied a lock of his hair by a string to the lamppost, to keep his head from falling forward in a doze over his chemistry books. It was hard to stay awake, he said, when you were always hungry.

There was a gaunt old woman, crying in the dust of a Bihar village. Her husband had died some years before, and since then she had lived on the charity of her neighbors. But now there was drought and starvation in Bihar, and the old woman fought with the stray dogs for dry bones.

The anthem ends, and everyone relaxes. Again the barefooted waiters slip between the guests, offering their trays of martinis or tomato juice. Cigarettes are lighted, and the band plays a waltz.

"Why should America force us to be beggars?" asks the arrogant journalist. But now there is hesitation in his voice.

"How can we make sure that India is sufficiently appreciative of American aid?" whispers an American diplomat to another American. But somehow there is a note of doubt in his tone, as he is not quite sure that the question is pertinent.

For the old man with all of India in his face has walked into the room, and moves among us, as close as hunger and need, as simple as undemanding generosity.

Delhi ❀ April 12

A strange sort of revelation came to me tonight.

We went to a small party given by an Indian journalist in a Connaught Circle restaurant, and afterwards, a few of us went up to his hotel room to talk and drink a little longer. We all knew each other very well, so it was easy to relax, to sit on the floor, to kick off the high-heeled sandals. One of the boys began singing Indian folk songs, while the rest of us clapped a soft accompaniment. In a corner Eric was teasing his best Indian friend about

"Indian spirituality" and "moral superiority." Eric is the only Westerner I know who feels perfectly free to slap an Indian colleague on the back and say: "Oh, come off it old boy!" And they love it and laughingly admit that they *were* being a bit stuffy. Like most people, Indians enjoy being teased, if it is done with amiability and affection.

The room was filled with a warm yellow light and people. Most of the faces were brown, for Eric, another American, and I were the only Westerners. As we sang, my eyes ranged at first unconsciously, and then with deliberation, over the brown faces: wheat, honey, café-au-lait, rich cream, earthen, sun-ripened.

"Why, brown is the proper shade for a skin to be," I thought suddenly. I contemplated the American. He looked sick—unfinished. I looked at the Indians again. They looked healthy and absolutely right, as if Nature had finally found herself when she at last came to use the brown pigment.

On the way home I told the American that I had decided brown skins were more beautiful than white. He looked at me strangely. "So you've discovered that too," he said. "I've known it for a long time."

Delhi ❀ *April 20*

The days grow hotter and hotter. But there is consolation: the knowledge that for the next six months there probably will be no high-powered visitors from abroad. For a while, we correspondents shall have a rest from the parties "to meet Mr. X"; from the intimate dinners, designed to enlighten Mr. X on India, at which Mr. X tells every one at great length just what is wrong with India; from the newspaper reports and comments on Mr. X's latest speech, press conference, or lecture; from the distressing rumors of what really happened when Mr. X had dinner with the Prime Minister, and finally, from the reports of what Mr. X said about India when he reached home.

In the last few years a lot of non-embassy Americans have come to India. Some have come as tourists, to be milked, bilked, and ridiculed after they left, but at least to see and enjoy the Red Fort and the Taj Mahal, and move on. Others have come for a year or so, to work. The scholars, scientists, and agriculturalists work quietly and effectively, and no one pays the least public attention to them.

Then we have the touring Congressmen. Their study tours of this complicated land never last more than three or four days, but during that time, things are a bit tense.

They see Mr. Nehru, of course, and the Foreign Secretary, and two or three ministers whose names and jobs they can never get quite straight. They go on sightseeing tours, and there is always a big party at the embassy for them. None of this does much harm, nor does the fact that they often show up at formal receptions wearing Hawaiian sports shirts and hound's-tooth checked jackets.

It did seem unfortunate, however, when one Senator told a high Hindu government official that he had just visited a Hindu temple, and asked the official whether he didn't agree that the Hindu gods were "kinda repulsive?" "Oh quite," answered the suave but famously devout diplomat.

But even the Congressmen don't make as much of a publicized racket in the capital as the touring big-shots: magazine and newspaper editors, publishers, columnists and correspondents so eminent that they are always known as authors.

Some of them have done a fine job. Stewart Alsop, Walter Lippmann, Marquis Childs, and John Gunther have all acted here like intelligent men anxious to learn something. Vera Micheles Dean managed to present the American position incisively and dispassionately without antagonizing anybody; Mrs. Roosevelt was magnificent. David Lilienthal was popular before he came and more so after he went home and told Americans they should worry less about the Oriental mind and more about the Oriental stomach. Those of us who worry a lot about the Oriental mind nevertheless, think this remark should be inscribed in large type (perhaps in a montage of wheat grains) on a placard to be hung in the bedrooms of every American visiting India.

But then there are the others, the really awful ones. These men usually arrive in a flurry of publicity, either from Japan where they have put the Emperor on the right track, or from the Middle East, where they managed to reconcile Arabs and Jews. They stay with the Ambassador or (if he can't help it) the Prime Minister. They are all convinced that one talk with Nehru will "fix up all this neutralism business."

The first item on the agenda is the talk. Sometimes these talks are harmless, sometimes not, but Mr. Nehru has never been known to change his foreign policy after one of them. Sometimes it ends up with Mr. Nehru pounding a table in response to being told that "India must sign up with America or take the consequences." Usually, Mr. Nehru takes the opportunity to make a particularly anti-American speech the next day.

If our big-shot is a serious scholar, he will ask to see "the real Indian people." This means he will spend half an hour walking through a village and a week-end shooting tiger with a maharajah.

Then there is usually a lecture before the Indian Council of World Affairs. For this, the authority often decides to "give it to them straight from the shoulder." So he tells them India can't expect any help from America unless she commits herself immediately to an all-out battle with communism. This idea, when presented as an ultimatum, arouses instant antagonism.

But now thank heavens, the weather is hot, the brain-fever bird is chattering, the visitors have disappeared, and summer is here.

Simla ❀ *April 25*

To escape the heat, we have come up to Simla for a few days of blessed cool air, pine trees, and mountains. And today, as a professional excuse for this tiny vacation—and also because it sounded like fun—we went to the annual Sipi fair, far up along the road to Tibet.

Because no automobiles are allowed on the narrow Simla roads, we had to travel in rickshaws. Each is handled by four men because of the steepness of the roads and the generally well-fed condition of Sahibs and *Mem-sahibs*. For any sensitive white person, riding in a rickshaw seems a guilty method of travel, but with four men on the poles the guilt is lessened, and we traveled merrily enough along the twisting road which winds eventually to Tibet.

In two hours we reached Mashobra, a tiny hill town perched on top of a high mountain. Here we dismounted, and led by a guide, began walking down the forest trail to the grove of Sipi, two thousand feet below. All through the woods, Indians were leaping from rock to rock, running down the beds of streams, or passing us on the trail, heading for the fair. Above our heads, swinging from tree to tree, monkeys seemed to be making in the same direction.

The grove of Sipi, we found, was an immense stretch of green grass and pine needles surrounded by towering pines. At one end was a wooden temple of Sipi, or Shiva, decorated with arches of paper flowers. At the other were the booths of the traders, who had walked for days over the Himalayas to come here. Most of the booths offered only cheap wooden toys, glass bracelets, pink plastic barrettes, and old bars of American candy; with the exception of a few Tibetan knickknacks there were (alas, as usual) no handicrafts.

In times past the festival at Sipi was a huge affair, part religious, part business, part fun. Many thousands of villagers used to come to it, for it was considered the high point of the year throughout the whole countryside near Simla. But this year everyone was complaining that there weren't as many people as usual, that business was bad. The after-effects of partition, the new India—there were a dozen theories.

"It certainly isn't like the old days," sighed an itinerant photographer. His canvas backdrop, a gaudy painting of Indian palaces, leaned invitingly against a nearby tree. But people only stared at it and moved on.

Despite the changes, there was still a lot of noise and fun. At the center of the grove, two men were beating a gigantic drum in varying rhythms, surrounded by an admiring group of onlookers. When they tired, another team ran in and began pounding out new rhythms, and they in turn were replaced by another two men, all laughing, dancing to the staccato drum-beats, showing off, and having a wonderful time.

Another group patronized a crude wooden Ferris wheel or watched some dancing bears and cavorting monkeys. Through the grove sounded the flute of a snake charmer, and by peering through forests of brown Indian legs, we could see the old man squatting on the ground, his cobras weaving rhythmically to the music of his clay pipe.

The power of the local prince is now only nominal, but he is still a deeply respected figure in these parts, and his presence at the fair is more or less obligatory. To make the bucolic event bearable for His Exalted Highness, an immense amount of paraphernalia had been transported over the mountains on the backs of coolies and set up backstage-center of the grove. Carpets had been spread over the grass, and above them a striped canvas open-sided tent was stretched. The Rana and his guests sat on an overstuffed green couch, and members of his court occupied big living-room chairs. Beyond the tent was a long heavy table complete with china of every sort and a silver service. I also noticed at least one hundred straight chairs, more tents, several door mats, fifty small tables, and two Victorian hat-racks, their scrolls already adorned with top hats.

The Rana himself looked to me like an ageing roué who would have been more at home in the Stork Club than in this sylvan retreat. In a bright-blue, Western-style suit and a pink turban, he sprawled on the divan, yawning occasionally and looking at his large gold-and-diamond wrist watch. His Prime Minister explained to us, in a whisper, that His Exalted Highness was worrying about the future of India.

With a swirl of drums and flutes, the people of Theog, a neighboring state, arrived in the grove and danced in a great circle on the cleared space before the Rana's pandal. The men, in white trousers and short tunics, waved purple-and-orange handkerchiefs as they danced. The women, in flowing hill skirts and pantaloons, brandished silver-gleaming swords. The Rana looked tired.

The men formed another circle, and one of them ran to a far end of it, dancing to the accompaniment of drums, flutes, and bells. A second man appeared at the near end, carrying a bow and rubber-tipped arrows which he began shooting at the dancing man. When he finally succeeded in hitting the elusive dancer, another team took their places. The Prime Minister explained that the dance game was an allegory of the panther hunts in the mountains. The Rana looked bored.

A matronly hill-woman, obviously adorned in her most glittering finery, seated herself at the Rana's feet, and bowing her head modestly, began to sing a peasant love song of the hills. It was haunting and sweet, I thought, but halfway through the Rana stood up abruptly and walked out toward a pine tree, where he stood until she was finished, moodily twirling his waxed mustaches.

Oh well, the Rana's Prime Minister loaned us hill ponies to carry us back up the mountainside to our rickshaws. And now we have another night in these blessedly cool mountains where, in two days, my prickly heat has disappeared. Tomorrow we go back to Delhi for a few days. Then we'll set off on another trip —this time a long one to areas more remote than Simla. It seems reasonable to get in as much traveling as possible before I have to retire to the contemplation of the book on babies which has just been sent me from the States. It's by a man named Spock and looks useful. But right now I'm more interested in the political and social explorations which await us in Bihar.

May

❀

Muzaffarpore, Bihar   May 4

T HIS is the kind of trip I like—
traveling in a remote area of India, with Indians. At last one almost has a chance to accomplish the impossible, to merge and
identify. Putting up with what seems hardship to a Westerner,
but is normal (or even luxury!) to an Indian traveler, diminishes
the sense of guilt at least for a little while. A meaningless way of
diminishing it, of course—like flagellation, I suppose. But it's
more fun.

The Socialists, who have a peasant "self-help" program going
in Bihar, invited the foreign correspondents to come along and
see the program in action. Eleven of us accepted, but at the last
minute nine others thought it was too hot, although the temperature hasn't been over one hundred and two for the last week,
or made other excuses. So Eric and I came alone—and felt bitterly ashamed for our profession when we were met at the Patna
airport by a delegation of amiable Socialists bearing eleven
flower-garlands for the expected group. Most of the garlands
were hung around my neck, for lack of anywhere else to put

them, while the lean young men tried bravely to conceal their disappointment.

Because the train to the hinterlands didn't leave until morning, we were dropped off at the Grand Hotel to spend the night. Patna was once a big British center, and I imagine that the hotel used to live up to its name in an Empirish way; now it looked like some forlorn cinema set used once in a film about Ali Baba and then forgotten on a back street of time. Laundry stretched across the fretted first floor balcony; the Victorian stone pinnacles above had become roosting places for crows. Scrubby palm trees, their leaves gray with pre-monsoon dust storms, indicated that once there had been an effort to make a garden here; now the ground was bare beneath the trees, bare and brown, littered with banana peels and scraps of dirty rags.

Our young Socialist guide, immaculate in white homespun clothing, led us into a dark little lobby. A stained couch and three chairs, all with their springs broken, leaned against the walls. Several dusty etchings of Dutch windmills and English river scenes hung askew behind the reception desk. A fat clerk, looking somehow as if it had been many months since he had received the last guests, dozed with his head on the desk. The young Socialist tapped him on the shoulder, and the *babu* awoke and looked at us in surprise.

"You have reservation?" he inquired.

"We sent telegram reserving room for the Sahibs," said our friend.

"We have received no telegram for many days," the clerk said, and turned away, shrugging his shoulders. After we had all stood there for a moment or two in silence, he glanced at us again and relented—especially after we smiled at him encouragingly. Bluster gets nowhere in India.

"I shall see if we can let you have a room *Sahr*," he told us portentiously. After carefully scanning the rows of empty letter boxes, each accompanied by a key and each denoting an empty room, he seemed satisfied with the ritual at last. We signed a dirty and tattered registration book (noting that the last guest to sign in, an Englishman traveling in machine tool parts, had preceded us by three weeks) and were led to our room by the *babu*, two peons carrying our two bags, and the young Socialist.

The room was like all the others in remote British-Indian hotels: a coconut matting rug; a gigantic bed in the middle of the room, with mosquito net curtains to be tucked in at night; a great mahogany armoire; two wooden chairs with only shreds left of their cane-bottom seats; peeling walls about twenty feet high; an overhead electric fan; and a twenty-five-watt light bulb hanging from a cord.

"It is comfortable, I hope?" asked our new friend, looking anxious and eager to please. I don't think he had ever met any Westerners before, and obviously he was worried about our mysterious needs and desires.

"Oh marvelous! Perfect!" I exclaimed, gushing in that exaggerated American way which makes Indians and Englishmen nervous.

"Quite all right," said Eric. Reassured, the young man, the manager, and the coolies all departed.

The main feature of the bathroom, I soon discovered, was a long porcelain tub, completely filled with cold water. The bottom was covered with sand, the sides were slimy and green. No water came from the taps when I tried them experimentally. Obviously one was expected to bathe Indian-style, sloshing water over the body with the brass vessel which stood on the floor beside the tub. The wooden seat of the toilet was cracked, but it was at least a flush, even if it only worked every fifth try.

Whitewash, gray with time, was splashed on the edges of the windows and had dripped, long ago, onto the concrete floor. Turning to go, I noticed the cobwebs covering the panes of the sweeper's door leading to the hotel backyard. There were two small lizards basking in the late afternoon sunlight which fell against the door jamb. Black grease from a hundred hands stained the once white paint. "My God!" I thought, "Why can't they

clean it up? Why don't they even *notice* the mess in the front garden, the filth of this bathroom?" And then, for surely the thousandth time in India, I wrestled with anger, fought it down, finally breathed calmly again: Look, this hotel isn't their culture at
all, it's Western culture. The British are gone now—why expect
Indians to maintain something they don't understand and don't
like, such as bathtubs? Water poured over the body *is* a cleaner
way to bathe, isn't it? And as for the general mess, well, would
you feel like scrubbing and raking in this temperature? And so
on over the familiar arguments, none of them ever quite convincing, but somehow lulling in their repetitive familiarity. The
Scotch I found waiting in the bedroom (no ice, of course) was,
however, even more effective.

The dining room was lighted by one dim bulb. The plaster was
chipped away from the stained green walls; there were heavy black
sideboards with dim glass and broken pinnacles; and all the other
tables were empty. The only picture on the wall advertised Ever-
ready flashlights: a small boy kneeling by his bed, praying. The
seat of his trousers was, inevitably, only half-buttoned. Hastily, we
ate as much as we could manage of our thin tomato soup, fish
cakes, boiled mutton, cabbage, and stewed canned apricots covered with a gooey custard. Then we retreated to the mosquito net
and the Scotch. "Damn the British and their hotels," I thought
as I fell asleep. "I'm glad to be going back to India tomorrow."

Early the next morning, after crossing the Ganges by ferry, we
discovered that we were among the fortunate; we were to travel
first class on the train from Patna to Muzaffarpore, a matter of
some eight hours. In third class, which is the way most Indians
travel, the seats are hard wooden benches. Travelers, with their
babies, chickens, baskets, miseries, and diseases are jammed in until there is little room to breathe.

But in the first-class compartment, which extends clear across
the train, there are two long, leather-covered benches, another
bench at right angles, two planks suspended from the ceiling by

chains, and a sign which says: "This compartment to seat twelve, sleep five." First-class compartments also boast a tiny bathroom where the water runs warm and rusty, and electric fans. The switches for the fans had been stolen, we saw as we climbed aboard, leaving only the ragged wires sticking out of the sockets.

"No matter," said a passing train guard. He fiddled with the wires and in a few moments the fans were whirling merrily. See, I reminded myself. It *didn't* matter. There's an Indian lesson in this, and someday I shall see it in all its purity.

Sharing the compartment with us were Jayaprakash Narayan, the Socialist leader who was going to Muzaffarpore to make some speeches and encourage the Land Volunteer Army; an unblinking character in the far corner who looked like a belligerently retired police officer; and a middle-aged man in a dhoti and checked sports shirt. In the informal way of India, he had already made himself at home on his bench by removing his shoes and unbuttoning his shirt down to his navel. It was a hot day, and the wind blew warm through the open windows as we sped through the fields of sugar cane.

Cradled on the middle-aged man's knees was a small girl, her eyes outlined with kohl, her ears pierced for tiny gold earrings. She lay quietly throughout the journey, apparently indifferent to her father's caresses. Indian children, I often notice, seem much more subdued than American children, or even Japanese children. Tiny babies lie silently in their swinging cradles, and normally active four-year-olds seem to move slowly and carefully. I have often wondered if it was a matter of training, or of climate or, alas, of malnutrition.

A young boy crouched on the floor at the feet of the lolling little girl, and occasionally he made shy efforts to amuse her. Neither she nor her father paid any attention. I wondered why the boy didn't sit on a bench, as everyone else was doing, and after awhile I asked Jayaprakash about it.

"The boy is a servant, and thus is naturally never allowed to sit on benches," he explained with an apologetic smile.

"Where you going?" abruptly asked the middle-aged man. We told him.

"Why?"

"What you work for?"

"How much salary you earn?"

"You married?"

"Any children?"

"Why?"

"How long are you in India and how do you like?"

His curiosity satisfied by the answers to these polite and, to us, perfectly normal questions, he turned his attention to a long scrutiny of Jayaprakash, and finally fell asleep, snoring softly in rhythm to the rocking of the train. The rest of us looked out of the open windows at the palm trees and sugar-cane plantations.

In an hour we drew into Sonepore, a large market town famous for its annual horse fair.

From the far end of the station we heard shouting, and then a band of about one hundred young men, bright in the red caps of the Socialist party and waving the red Socialist flag with its white emblem of a cogwheel and a plough, appeared outside our compartment.

"Jayaprakash is our leader, he will show us the way!" they shouted.

"Socialist Party *Zindabad!* Congress Party *Murdabad!*" they chanted.

Jayaprakash, tall and cool in his white dhoti and shirt and his gay red cap, stepped to the open door and raised his hand for silence. "*Zindabad* is a good word," he said, "for it means victory, and we all wish victory for the Socialist party. But *Murdabad* is a bad word, for it means death, and we do not wish death to anyone. Do not use that word again in your slogan." The boys looked chastened as they garlanded him with jasmine, but they smiled and shouted "*Zindabad!*" as the train moved off.

"It is difficult to teach these boys," said Jayaprakash, settling back into his seat. "They have heard so much about the Communists and their violent methods that they think we Socialists should use the same methods of revolution—throwing bombs and burning streetcars. It is hard to make young people understand that our revolution must come slowly, through education, through the conversion of men's minds, through work with our own hands."

The middle-aged man, awake now, spoke up. "But even so, you Socialists want to move too fast." he said. "You want to take all the land away from the landowners right away, for instance, without payment, and give it to the peasant. But I am a Congressman, and I follow the way of Gandhiji. And Gandhiji would say that it is wrong to deprive any one of his property without paying him for it."

"The landlords have already received their payment by years of exorbitant rent," said Jayaprakash. "It is time they suffered as they have made the peasants suffer."

"No," said the Congressman, "the majority must not profit at the expense of the minority. And ends do not justify means."

The train chugged into the next station, and the argument jerked to a stop. Down the platform came a young Sikh carrying a doll-size bed and on it what looked like a welter of blue rags. Climbing into our compartment, he placed the bed on the upper rack and reverently bowed to it. His crinkly black beard was tied up in a little net, and he wore a white turban sprigged with blue roses.

"This is the holy book of the Sikhs I am carrying," he told us severely. "Please not to smoke only outside." Obediently we put out our cigarettes, knowing that any form of tobacco is anathema to a member of the Sikh religion.

We chugged into another station, where a red-topped delegation, brilliant as a poppy field, awaited their leader, this time with an offering of a basket of bananas. Jayaprakash thanked them quietly, with folded palms, but he made no speeches and kissed no babies. For the next five miles, every one, including the small girl and her servant-boy, munched bananas. We all tossed the peels casually on the floor among the welter of shoes, luggage, and cigarette butts, knowing that at Muzaffarpore an untouchable would come aboard and sweep the compartment so that the whole process could begin all over again.

The policeman-type roused himself from meditation and spoke for the first time. "The trouble with the Socialist party," he said ponderously, "is that it has no sense of discipline. What India needs is not a lot of young students filling their minds with crazy ideals, but disciplined youth who do what they are told, who know how to drill, who could take over India in defense of our ancient way of life when occasion arises."

"Like the Rashtryia Sawak Sevak Sangh?" asked Jayaprakash, refering to India's version of the storm troopers.

"Exactly," said the policeman.

"But isn't that basically fascist?"

"What matter that?" asked the policeman.

As if in comment, the skies, which had been growing dark, suddenly began to howl with rage. In two minutes the outdoors was obscured by swirling dust in which only the nearest palm trees, bent almost double, could be seen. The little train ground to a stop. Above the roar of the wind we heard a ripping sound and a crash. The train shuddered slightly.

Hundreds of third-class passengers piled out of their carriages and made for a safe distance, their heads ducking into the wind, their shawls flapping. The policeman jumped out onto the road bed, and in a few minutes was back with information. Nothing much had happened, he said. It was just that the roof had blown off the engine cabin. Craning out of the windows, we watched some energetic male passengers and the train crew (who seemed accustomed to the job) hoist the roof back into place and wire it down. In half an hour we were on our way again.

At the last station before Muzaffarpore, a small delegation of schoolboys awaited Jayaprakash, cheering. As the train came in, they threw handfuls of fragrant frangipani flowers through our compartment's open windows, and when we stopped, they garlanded all of us with jasmine and roses. Jayaprakash turned to a small boy with a red cap balanced over one ear.

"What does a good Socialist believe?" he asked.

"That poor people should be fed and clothed and that everyone should be treated with justice," said the boy promptly.

"You see," said Jayaprakash happily, as the train pulled out of the station. "Even the children are coming to understand Socialist ideals."

"A Congress child would have given the same answer," said the middle-aged man.

"And an R.S. S. boy," said the policeman.

"Or a Sikh boy," said the Sikh.

Or an American boy, I thought to myself. Who does not believe in food, clothes, and justice? But this is something about India which I have noticed often, this tendency to announce the obvious in a tone indicating that the thought must seem unique to a foreigner. Indian philosophy may be the most profound in the world, but Indians also seem to think they have a corner on even the mildest of "good" thoughts. "God is love," a swami will intone, his eyes boring into yours to see if you can possibly understand this idea. "Our message to the world is that we should love each other and be kind to one another. Please to convey this in your newspaper," says a sadhu. I always want to tell him (but I never do because he would not believe me) that we too have been repeating these thoughts for many centuries, but that we are still faced with the problem of how to put them into practice. Like us, Indians seem to suffer a certain division between what they say they believe about love and kindliness and what they practice between themselves. I think there is more loving-kindliness within a family (and perhaps within a caste) in India than there is in the West, but less between strangers and out-family people.

Slowly the cane fields gave way to mango groves, then to the clustered collection of mud-and-thatch huts which were the outskirts of Muzaffarpore. In thoughtful silence we began to extricate our luggage from the coverlet of frangipani petals, wilted garlands, dust, and banana skins. Ahead of us, as we drew into the station, we could hear the roar of the crowd which had come to welcome Jayaprakash. The little girl woke up and began to cry.

Muzaffarpore ❀ May 6

We are staying, for a day or so, at the Muzaffarpore Club, once the center of social life for British planters in North Bihar, but now only a ghost of its old self. Our room is one of a series opening out onto a wide verandah, a little stretch of grass, and a magnificent "gold mohur" tree, now in full bloom.

Oh, the flowering trees of India, how glorious they are, the flame and the jacaranda and the "gold mohur"! In the evening we sit in the verandah's big chairs, the arms built out in the old style so that gentlemen may extend their legs. And we sip our *chota pegs* and gaze upon the "gold mohur" and the black crows in the sunset, and listen to the gentle plaints of old servants: "Sahib, when is government coming back? Sahib, was better in old days. Sahib, was many Sahibs here, was polo and dancing and much money. Now only Indian gentlemens come, drink lemon squash, Club not got money. Indian gentlemens not bring wifes, not dancing, not having parties, not giving baksheesh. Now maybe Club having close, what happening to us, we here maybe twenty fifty hundred years? Sahib, why government go away?"

Poor bearers, poor old men. First, in their youth, they had to learn all the strange ways of foreigners, with knives and forks and spoons, glasses and dishes and napkins, seven-course dinners, sheets and pillow cases, and toilet paper, soap, and shoe polish. They learned well (provided they were always allowed to follow the routine they had first been taught), and they earned far more money than they would have earned working for Indians. Most of them took little interest in the freedom fight, for who were they to want their source of income to leave India? Then too, there was pride, in those days, in working for a British General or a big sugar planter, and sometimes even affection and respect. But now? Now, for reasons most of them do not understand, the Sahibs are gone, their world collapsed. One by one they will return to their villages, or adapt themselves unhappily to Indian employers, notoriously harsh on servants. In the great welter of India, their tragedy is minor and temporary. But it is sad.

Last night we attended a political meeting—a form of activity which, in India, sometimes seems a substitute for all the Western lower and middle class pleasures the Indians don't have. For a man who can't rub two annas together, or who has already seen the local movie, or is tired of his wife, a political meeting is a fine and familiar entertainment. The sponsors of the meetings don't really matter. There is always a kind of electric excitement which comes when five or ten thousand people gather on a big open plaza, the men sitting cross-legged on the dirt, packed close together in endless waves, the women and children, a much smaller group, squatting quietly on tattered rugs in the background. There is always a raised platform bearing on its dubious boards the local dignitaries, and the delicious possibility of collapse. There is always the microphone which goes out of order with a high squeal which makes the men laugh and the women scream. Sometimes there is even Mr. Nehru shaking the defective microphone with rage—because to him its refusal to function correctly symbolizes the scientific backwardness of a great many Indians. And there are always slogans to chant and songs to sing.

"Long live Gandhiji!" shouted a young man from the platform, as our meeting began. "Long live Gandhiji!" echoed the crowd. "Jayaprakash is our leader; he will show us the way!" "Jayaprakash is our leader!" the crowd answered. "An hour a day builds a new village!" "An hour a day builds a new village!" At last they were getting down to the central idea of the meeting. This idea took about four hours and eight speakers to explain.

The thought is one which the Indians might grasp more readily if they had ever had the pioneering experience of Americans: if you wait for the government to build all the new roads you need and all the drainage canals, you'll never have the roads or the canals. But if people work together for the common good, they can make what they want, and everyone will benefit. The idea seems simple, but it is extraordinarily hard to put across in India—perhaps because the concept of general welfare (apart from family and caste) is unfamiliar; perhaps because the tradition of expecting the government to do everything is so deep-rooted; perhaps because a great many people are tired, hungry, and hot a great deal of the time.

Last night, Jayaprakash worked hard at explaining the Socialist's plan for creating land armies and work brigades in each village of Bihar. "Gandhi's idea of making extra income by spinning was fine," he told the crowd, "but it doesn't go far enough. It's not enough to stay at home and spin; you also have to come out and work together for mutual benefit. You mustn't wait for the government to help you; you must help yourselves. Even if you build just a small track, progress will come, new breezes will blow, and the goddess of fortune will walk down it. Even women can help. They can carry earth on their heads when you're excavating canals."

A young man in the front row jumped to his feet. "Let us go build a new town!" he chanted. "Let us build a new town!" roared the crowd. "Come, let us build a new village and a new society and a new order!" intoned the chairman of the meeting. "A new village, a new society and a new order!" the crowd shouted. Then the meeting broke up, and the push-carts around the plaza, selling hot cakes and steaming lentils, did a thriving business. Driving back to the club Jayaprakash told us that some people had walked twenty miles to come to the meeting and would walk home again that night. "But whether or not they will work on the roads and canals, I don't know," he sighed.

• • •

But they did, at least for one morning. Today at eight we started out of Muzzaffarpore in a local official's springless old car and drove for an hour out into the country. Finally, we jounced to a stop at a point where a narrow footpath joined the dirt road. Then we walked for a mile along the footpath to the outskirts of a village of perhaps fifty mud houses, like all houses on the Northern Indian plains, sun-baked, parched, and colorless. But today there was color in the bright red caps of the Socialist workers and excitement in the group of villagers who had gathered to begin building their first road to the outside world, a road along which bullock carts and maybe even trucks could come and go.

"*Jai Hind!*" ("Long live India!") said Jayaprakash.

"*Jai Hind!*" answered the villagers, beaming. Each of the men held a kind of mattock, each looked expectant and a little frightened. This was, after all, a very new idea, and the thought of untouchables and Brahmins working side by side—a point on which the Socialists had insisted—was revolutionary. On the flat rooftops the women stood immobile, watching. Jayaprakash took a mattock from the chief of the village elders and held it high above his head.

"I hereby begin the work of the new India!" he shouted, and started digging. "*Jai Hind!*" shouted the villagers, and their mattocks began churning the hard earth almost with frenzy. Drums beat, and bells clanged in rhythm.

Once started, they showed astonishing zeal, I thought, considering that most of them were thin as skeletons. An hour later, when we finally had to leave, they had churned up quite a respectable width of road-bed stretching between the last crumbling wall of the village and the narrow track leading through the dry grass to the outside world. And as we drove away over the rutted earth, I found myself with hands clasped in lap, praying in a sort of way that they would keep up the zeal even when the illustrious leaders had left, that they would build their road to the future, that they would not relapse into "pathetic contentment," which in India is another phrase for stagnation and sometimes for death. But they must do it themselves; they must understand that they must do it themselves, for the government is too harassed, too financially burdened, too lacking in trained personnel to do it—to build the roads to the outside world which are a key to so many village problems. Let them understand, I thought, please let them understand—no matter who teaches them.

For more than an hour we jounced along over dirt tracks, deeper and deeper into jungle Bihar. Palms grew around us, and camel thorn and tall trees. From time to time we saw a village far off, or a cow. But not people. It was hot, and there were flies in the car. Eric and Jayaprakash talked. I concentrated on the bumps in the road, which I didn't like.

At last, blessedly, we came to what seemed a smooth stretch, and here, it was evident, we were expected. Triumphal arches, tottering constructions of woven bamboo laced with wilted flowers, spanned the road. And by each arch stood two boys, each blowing an immense trumpet. What the trumpets were made of I don't know, but they were about six feet long, and wavy. Held upright against the sky, they made a tremendous impression and a tremendous sound, rather like a bull calf bawling for its mother. The boys looked proud and excited.

"The village of Chandrahatti," announced Jayaprakash. "A traditional reception." He had never been here before, but this is a safe remark. What American, greeted by a band of Rotarians marching out of town with tubas to welcome a foreign visitor, would not come up with the same sort of explanation?

Stopping the car at the ultimate triumphal arch, we got out and were met by a committee of elders. They bowed; we bowed; there were introductions which I didn't quite understand—but everyone looked beaming and important. We followed them under the palm trees to an open space where about 200 boys were seated cross-legged, waiting for us. In the background, sheltering among the trees, their parents and their sisters stood, silent and a little frightened in their withdrawal. It was all very formal—only the little children drew close to look at us. I smiled at them, but there was no response. This solemn reaction of Indian children is one of the disconcerting things in India; still, one always thinks that a child who is smiled at will smile back.

As we were lead to the seats of honor, I realized to my horror that this was no Socialist pep-meeting, but a meeting in honor of the eleven journalists who were expected: twelve chairs were set out under the banyan trees, one for Jayaprakash, and the others for us and our treacherous colleagues. Where did they get chairs in a remote village which never used them? At what great expense were they imported just for this occasion?

We three sat down, garlanded in jasmine and marigold, and there were the usual speeches of welcome by the mayor, or head of the panchayat, and other dignitaries. Then, a thin, consumptive-looking man in threadbare but shiningly white dhoti and shirt was led up to us. He held in his hand a scroll, framed and under glass. His thin hands trembled a little as he held it out, not knowing whether to give it to Eric or to me.

"I am village schoolteacher," he said. "I also teach boys English. I am not very good teacher maybe, but I teach best I know. I welcome talking you people speak English, first I ever meet. This is what boys selves have written you expressing what they thinking to distinguished journalists."

With tears blurring my eyes, so that the hand-written scroll surrounded by its ugly gold and black frame (and how far did someone have to travel to buy that proud frame?), wavered in my hands, I read what the boys had composed:

"In the pious hands of the observers of the world affairs, we respectfully present our winged feelings.

O, great onlookers of the world stage! Don't you see the great drama being enacted on the stage of India with our respected Sri Jai Prakash—the string-puller? We have great hopes in you. You unveil falsehood and worship Truth. We have firm faith that you

*will carry out every nook and corner of the earth his new pro-
gramme of new India, where there will be no caste-system, no
rich, no poor, no high, no low.*

O, great pioneers!

*Humanity looks to you to strike on the note of social, eco-
nomic, and political freedom. You will please bridge the gulf of
geographical boundaries and lean your pen for the establishment
of the work of equality.*

We,

The Students of

Chandrahatti Kamtaul H.E.

School,

Muzaffar Pur,

are ever yours."

This scroll will hang over my desk forever, wherever I have a
desk. To a journalist, what more chastening words have ever been
composed? From anyone else in the world this would be irony,
but from these boys, these backwood elves whose entire knowledge of the Western world comes from Shakespeare painstakingly
deciphered, and perhaps a stray copy of George Meredith, this is
devastating faith. All my life I would like to think that a bunch of
boys in Bihar, eighty miles from the nearest railroad, really believe
that I personally unveil falsehood and worship truth. Of course,
the really meaningful thing to me is that in my heart I would like
to think that their faith is not displaced—only, what Western
journalist can go around saying: "I unveil falsehood and worship
truth"? This is one of the things I find so charming, so relaxing,
about Indians. They can say things like this without any self-con-
sciousness whatsoever; not just these country boys, but the most
sophisticated Indian student will demand: "What is life without
morality?" or announce, "My search is for spiritual meaning," and
not feel embarrassed as the Westerner, who might agree with him,
would feel. Yet they feel embarrassed at the sight of an American

girl in a sleeveless, sunback dress. Odd. Is their embarrassment
sexual, ours spiritual? Why?

Heat shimmered over the plains. White dust from the dry dirt
roads billowed around us and seeped into the car despite the
tightly closed windows. We coughed and sweated, dozed and
bumped, and drove on and on and on. I didn't know where we
were going, or much care, as long as it was somewhere cool, clean
and quiet. For the first time, I had to admit to myself that the
process of having a baby *does* seem to affect one's capacity for
rugged traveling. And this wasn't really rugged travel, just hot
and bumpy.

In delicate-minded India, nothing can be said to a man about
my "condition," so I do not know whether Jayaprakash suspected
I needed a rest, or whether he had planned to stop. But at length,
to my great relief, we came to a garden, a house, and a cool verandah. Our host, a thin elderly gentleman with steel-rimmed spectacles was, we were told, a retired lawyer and a Socialist sympathizer.
In good English he welcomed us warmly, led us to seats on the
verandah, and told a servant to bring lemon squash. It came and
it was good, but it was not what I wanted just then. To voice my
need directly was, of course, out of the question, for the Indians
would be horribly embarrassed. Within the house I could hear the
voices of women, and from time to time I caught one peeping at
us through a window—but too far away to be of any help. Finally,
I managed to catch Eric's eye and silently communicate my
plight. He turned to our host.

"I wonder if my wife could go somewhere and wash?" he asked.
Our host looked startled.

"Dinner will not be for some time yet," he answered. "But if
she wishes I will have a place made ready." He shouted something
in Bihari; a woman's voice responded from the shadows of the
house. For the next mysterious and seemingly interminable half
hour, I could hear whispers in the background, scurryings, and the

swishing of saris, occasionally an excited command. Half the irritation of living in India, for a foreigner, is that much of the time
one doesn't know what is really going on—or why a request which
seems simple to us does not seem simple to other people.

"You may now wash," our host announced at long last, and
rose to lead the way. I followed him into the now apparently
empty house, up the stairs, down a hall, through a bedroom, and
into another, smaller room. He beamed happily, and pointed.
"Here you wash," he explained. I looked around. The room was
entirely bare of any furniture or appurtenances except for a small
wooden stand on which rested a brass pitcher full of steaming
water, a brass bowl, some soap, and a towel. Sighing, I washed,
while our host stood by and chatted amiably about the inferiority
of Indian-made soap. Anyway, I was at least clean again, I
thought morbidly as I followed him downstairs.

But Eric saved the day, for during my absence he had done
some investigating of his own. He nodded at a low baked-mud
building across the courtyard, and while the men resumed their
politics I slipped away. The room, needless to say, contained no
flush plumbing. But that didn't matter.

An hour or so later, we were led through the house and onto a
verandah surrounding an inner courtyard. Our hostess, a plump
woman in a white sari, gray-haired and smiling, greeted us with
folded hands and motioned us to be seated where we liked at a
row of small tables. On each was a large brass tray covered with
little brass bowls, each containing food—vegetable curry, pickled
cauliflower, dried chilis, peppercorns, and lentils. Very Indian,
very hot, and very good. While we ate, the courtyard and the verandah were full of movement—servants, children, young men
and women, old men and women, all of whom seemed to belong
there but none of whom were explained. They came and went;
they smiled or did not smile; they drifted in and out of the sunlight and the shadows like phantoms, like birds, like both.

And then a gentle young girl was leading me down a dim corridor and into a room green with the mango-reflected light of after-

noon. She motioned to a high, hard bed, covered only with a smooth straw mat, cooler than bedspreads, cooler than sheets, quiet, delicious. She picked up an Indian fan from a table—a small square of bamboo matting attached to a red wooden handle —knelt on the floor beside me and began fanning the flies away from my face. Her white sari fell in soft folds over her young body, soon, like mine, to bear a child.

I asked her if she spoke English, and she said yes, she had learned it at high school in the nearby town. Right after graduation her parents had made a marriage for her with the old lawyer's youngest son, and she had come to this house as a daughter-in-law. And yes, all the other people I had seen in the courtyard were relatives—daughters-in-law, sons, young daughters still unmarried, grandchildren, cousins, and old aunts. They were all very good to her, she said. She was happy here. Her husband was kind to her and so was her mother-in-law, that important and sometimes ty-rannical figure in every Hindu joint family. The girl's voice was soft and warm as she spoke of her husband, and I could smell the spray of jasmine she had tucked in the folds of her braided black chignon.

"Where will you have your child?" I asked at last.

"Why here," she answered, in some surprise. "Where else?"

"Who will help you?"

"The woman from the village, of course, and my mother-in-law and the other ladies. This is my first baby, so I do not know any-thing, but the other women know all about it."

"No doctor?"

"No—why should I need a doctor? I am well."

"And how will you learn how to take care of the baby?" This time, contrary to the rules of all well-brought-up young Indian ladies, she looked at me as if I were mad.

"What is there new to learn?" she asked. "Babies have been born since forever, and women naturally know how to take care of them. The other women in the house will show me whatever I need to know, just as their aunts and mothers showed them when they had their first children. And when I am old I will show *my* daughters-in-law, and when their children are old . . ." She lapsed into silence, dreaming into the future. After a few moments she rose to her feet in that swift, fluid gesture of lithe young Indian women, and with a shy smile, slipped out of the room.

After she had gone, I lay quietly, thinking about her and about myself. Not of our feminine similarities which theoretically should make it one world for us, but of the cultural attitudes which separated us. Take just the matter of the two babies. For her, having a child was a perfectly natural, easy process, an episode which she knew little about and didn't need to know about until the time came, when the older women would instruct her. They, of course, knew everything there was to know.

For me, childbirth also should be a perfectly natural, easy process, but I believe this not because of my tradition, but because I have read *Childbirth Without Fear*, and I believe what it says. I have also read medical books, pamphlets on various methods of anaesthesia, and a nurse's textbook on the delivery of babies. I approach childbirth with confidence because I feel I now know quite a lot about it; if I did not know I would be terrified. She approaches it with confidence because she knows nothing; if she did know, she would be terrified. But is her confidence deeper than mine?

And take the matter of caring for babies and bringing up children. To her, this is not even a question of tradition, it *is* tradition, and therefore right. In the cities, perhaps, sophisticated Indian women may laugh pleasantly at the ways of their mothers and chatter self-consciously of child psychology. But this family, like so many middle-class country-town families, is isolated from the cities and the restlessness of Western theorizing. And it is restless: we in the West now take it for granted that each generation will rebel against the ways of the preceding generation, that what was good for mother will not be good for daughter, or at least desirable to daughter. Every twenty years we have a new school of baby feeding, toilet training, thumb sucking, and developmental psychology. Most intelligent American mothers, trained from childhood to seek among the experts for knowledge, would be inclined to trust a book more than they would their own mothers. Mother would be "out of date." The thing is, in America, the expert is usually outside your own home.

"Out of date," I reflected, is a phrase one almost forgets in India. Sleepily now, I began making a list in my mind of all the topics of controversy in America, all the gadgets and conveniences which are constantly changing, all the material symbols of our life of which this Indian household is only faintly aware, if at all: Freud, theories of child care, television, competitive full-color advertising, new cereals, new soaps, detergents, automobile design, refrigerator design, whether cigarettes cause cancer, hi-fi, overpopulation, crowded schools, interior decoration, variety in food, housing developments, fashion trends, sexual adjustment, theories on male versus female, Communism, girdles, chlorophyll in toothpaste, deodorants, thruways, nuclear power, commuting, calories, servant problem, comics, guns, stocking runs, liquor, formal versus progressive education, geriatrics, nutrition, sibling rivalry, group adjustment, Sunday School and God, divorce, women's clubs, community responsibility, juvenile delinquency, electric appliances, cellophane, plastic toys . . .

Imagine, I thought, a life in which all of these words scarcely crossed the consciousness. An existence in which life does not leap lightning-like from the peak of each generation to the next, but flows smoothly down, in a pattern of continuity. A life in which one does not seek from strangers, those experts, the answers to questions, but trusts instead to the family elders and the old wisdom, or to an intuition which leads one inevitably back to tradition. How peaceful such a life might seem, how pure.

But no, I decided, turning over restlessly and swatting a fly. That kind of life would be blissful if it were really a Shangri-La, but it isn't. Ignorance and the old ways mean that millions of women and babies die in childbirth; that flies roost on the faces of sleeping children, bringing death; that women suffer disease and pain in stoic isolation, because they are unwilling to see a male doctor; that minds are closed to new ways of creating a better way of life for all people.

New ways, a better life—that is our search in America. The fact that we are eager to make that search and are unwilling to believe that it is ever achieved is responsible for our bounty and our ease. But it also makes us subject to exploitation in the field of the unimportant and the material: change your car each year, change your living room curtains, change your hobby, change your hair-do! And so we are buffeted and are restless, knowing none of the peace of this Indian home. Somehow, we (or at least I) must find a way of life between the two. And at last I slept.

Champaran, Bihar ❀ *May 8*

"We're the last," said Tom Purcell gloomily. "This is the end of our race, in India, at least." His blue eyes looked sadly through the twilight toward the old mango grove at the far end of the garden, where four generations of Purcells lay entombed.

Tom Purcell, one of Eric's old family friends, came to get us at the club yesterday afternoon, and bounced us over fifty excruciating miles of pitted road in his battered station wagon, for a visit with him and his wife Janet. So here we were in the evening, fifty miles from the nearest telephone, railway, or electric line, a few miles from the tiger-stalked jungles and the borders of Nepal, drinking whiskey and soda in evening clothes upon a wide verandah and talking of the days that were gone and the days that were to come.

A few years ago, Tom told us, there were more than one hundred British planters in North Bihar, most of them members of families which, like the Purcells, had been living in India for a century, growing indigo, and, when that crop became uneconomic, sugar cane and rice. Today the Purcells are the last ones here, and of their three big estates and their three thousand acres, only fifty acres and the old family bungalow are left. When these are sold, the Purcells, like the others, will go away forever.

"It's hard to say exactly why all the planters left," Tom meditated as he lounged under the mounted head of a snarling tiger he had shot in the old and happier days. His handsome lined face, with its R.A.F. mustaches, looked sad, not bitter. So too did his blonde wife Janet, fading but pretty in the soft gray light of a pre-monsoon evening.

"Of course we know why we're pulling out," he said. "The main reason is that all our friends are gone, and we're lonely. But the other planters? Well, it started just around the time we all realized that India was going to be free at last. Some of the big planters got the wind up—said we British wouldn't be top dogs any more, that the Indians would be prejudiced against us in any law cases that might come up, for instance, and that we better get out. So a lot of them left, mostly for South Africa. I understand they're quite happy there.

"Then somebody else reminded us of the anti-British riots in Calcutta in early '46, and said they thought that once the British police officers and army boys had gone, we'd all be murdered, here in this remote area as we are. So they pulled out, and many families were scared enough to follow them. As it turned out, they were wrong about this point, but in those days, nobody knew."

Tom clapped his hands and shouted *"Kohai!"* A barefooted servant, eyes deferentially lowered, appeared like a puff of smoke in the doorway. Tom ordered two more *burra pegs*, and the servant whisked off.

"It was a good life we had in the old days," he mused. "The roads were fairly smooth then, and we could reach the club in a couple of hours. Every Thursday afternoon there was tennis and every Saturday polo, with a dance in the evening. And, of course, cricket on Sunday.

"Then sometimes there was pig-sticking—our club was famous for its pig-stickers. And every Christmas a two-week shoot in the jungles to the north, with sometimes fifteen or twenty people and lots of elephants and a big bag of tigers. And other shoots during the winter, sometimes for black buck or sambar or leopard, as well as tigers."

He waved a hand toward the wall behind him, thickly hung with the antlers, skulls, and furry heads of dead animals. In the light of the one hurricane lamp on the porch they looked enormous, and the shadows of their antlers snaked to the ceiling like the witch's claws of a child's nightmare.

"And then in the summer," Tom remembered, "we went away from here to the hills where it was cool—Simla or Darjeeling—and stayed up there five or six months. Everyone's children, of course, went back home to England for their schooling as soon as they were seven, and every few years we could get home to see them."

Janet signed. "That's the only part I hated," she said. "Not seeing the children for so long really was a bit hard. But it had to be done, of course."

The servant appeared with the whiskies. There was no ice, for the electric plant was broken, and there were no spare parts in all India now with which to mend it. Beyond the verandah, in the darkness, a coolie pulled at a rope which in turn moved a large punkah back and forth above our heads to cool us.

"Well, that's all in the past," said Tom, drinking deep. "And you can't say that the Indians deliberately tried to destroy our old way of life, or that they even want us to leave. It's just, oh, a dozen small things that I suppose are inevitable when a young new government takes over—telegrams that don't arrive, trains that are always late now, nowhere to get the supplies . . .

"Take the roads, for instance. They haven't been repaired since before the war, and I don't think the government is ever going to get around to them. Why should they care about our cars when there are so many other things to care about, and most Indians use bullock carts anyway? But the road as it is now shakes a car all to pieces, and it takes nearly three hours to reach the club. And when you get there, there's nothing but ghosts and a few Indians who eat with their fingers and don't play tennis or cricket, don't drink, and won't bring their wives to dances. I try to talk to them sometimes, but we don't seem to have much in common.

"Then—well, the sugar mill has changed hands, and the new people are Marwaris, and everybody knows they like to make a quick profit and pull out. They owe me almost thirty thousand rupees for last season's sugar cane, and they won't pay me. Keep promising to, but never come through. And nowadays there's nobody you can complain to.

"And supplies! Once we got everything through the club, but now we're lucky if we can get a tin of marmalade now and then, or a tube of toothpaste, even ordering from Calcutta or Bombay. No more goods being imported from America or Britain any more; they have to save exchange, and besides, the Indians don't want the same things we do.

"We used to have a pretty good doctor only two hours away, but now the only man we've got, short of a day's journey, is an Indian veterinarian. Don't mind his being Indian, but I don't quite like my wife being treated by a vet!"

Tom was silent, while the hurricane lamp buzzed, and far out in the night a brain-fever bird called arrogantly. A jackal howled, and Tom said it was somewhere over near the little family graveyard in the mango grove.

"Well, I don't know," he said at last. "Maybe if we weren't so set on our own patterns and our old way of British life, we could fit in better with the Indians now they're running their own country. But somehow we don't fit in any more, and it's time we were leaving."

He swallowed the last of his whiskey and stood up among the shadows, tall and ghostlike in his white dinner jacket. "Shall we dine?" he asked.

Champaran, Bihar ❀ *Still May, and a Tuesday, I guess*

The days slip by, and I scarcely know where they go, so deep am I sunk in the *dolce far niente* of this dying British life in India. Over my anguished protests, Eric has gone off alone to Nepal, insisting that a three-day horseback-and-climbing trip over a rough mountain path was not likely to be much good for me or for the baby. I pointed out, quite reasonably I thought, that Molly Izzard had trekked into Nepal with her husband, Ralph, when *she* was pregnant. Eric answered that their case was entirely different, and besides, Molly was British, and everyone knew the British were far more used to walking than Americans, and therefore, their unborn babies were probably more used to it too. Not wishing to start any transatlantic argument, I gave in at last and have settled down at Champaran to await Eric's return. It is, after all, a good place to wait.

This Purcell bungalow, typical of the country houses of old British-India, would seem at first sight familiar to most Americans, for it is built more or less on the ranch-house style of our own Southwest—wide verandahs, a low-sweeping tile roof, and the high ceilings so necessary in any hot climate. The furniture is dark, heavy mahogany redolent of the Victorian assurance of the permanent Empire. The punkahs, too, suggest pre-electricity India; a heavy pole with its two-feet wide flounce of cotton moves rhythmically just above our heads as we dine or talk or sleep; the creak of the ropes is as steady as the quiet background sounds of a ship under weigh.

The Purcells had put aside their old punkahs, they thought forever, when the electric plant was installed twenty years ago. But when the plant broke down two months ago, they re-hung the punkahs (the little holes in the walls for the ropes were still there) and assigned several old coolies to the job of keeping them moving. The first afternoon, as I lay on my bed for a siesta, I saw the punkah begin to move, luxuriated for a moment in the cool breeze, and then rose to peek out the window and see who was pulling the rope. A very old man with a short white beard was dozing on the floor of the verandah, pulling the rope with a big toe. I went back to bed, but I couldn't sleep for worrying about the old man, the monotony and the weariness and the heat he must be suffering. Finally, I got up, put on a robe, went out on the verandah, and told him to go away.

"Oh *Mem-sahib*, please let me stay!" he begged. "It is my *job* to pull your punkah, and this is a very good job. I have nothing else to do, and I am glad to have this job. I am a very good punkah wallah, *Mem-sahib* will see! But if you do not approve of my work, I will be shamed. Please, *Mem-sahib*, please let me stay!"

So all right. Now I sleep calmly and firmly, with no troubled conscience at all about the old man. Or only a little.

Outside the house are lawns, a vegetable garden which was once a tennis court, chicken coops, pigeon cotes, servants' quarters which remind me a bit of the old slave quarters at Monticello, a fine avenue of teak trees, a few fields of sugar cane, and beyond all this, the river. At evening time we exercise the dogs along its sandy banks and look for crocodiles. We haven't seen any, but Tom says they are here.

Yesterday morning, after Janet and Tom and I had finished our several-days-old newspapers on the verandah, I asked them whether they could tell me how many servants and workers they employed to run the house and the few remaining fields. They looked at each other blankly, but after much argument and re-minding and several hours, came up with a list:

1 head bearer (same job as a butler in England)
2 other bearers
1 bread maker
1 sweeper (cleans bathrooms and takes care of dogs)
1 water-carrier (no running water in the house)
1 cook
1 dishwasher

1 dhobi (laundryman)
3 gardeners
1 electric mechanic
1 carpenter
1 driver (chauffeur, used mostly for errands)
1 grazier (for the cattle)
1 animal man (mostly takes care of chickens)
1 mahout (handles elephant)
1 mahout's assistant
2 punkah-wallahs
3 dak runners (peons, used for carrying messages)
2 office clerks
6 ploughmen

"I couldn't possibly ask the man who washes dishes to help feed the dogs," Janet explained, noting my expression of incredulity. "Or expect the cook to set the table, or ask a bearer to scrub out a tub. You know about the caste system as well as I do." And I guess I do. Also I see that when servants find it possible to live on an average of six dollars a month (food and quarters provided) it is probably a very good idea to spread the jobs around. The fact that the Purcells give employment to so many people, most of whom seem contented, is no doubt more important than my own unease at the thought that thirty-two Indians are necessary to the comfort of two Britishers.

It might all be wonderful, of course, but the trouble with all these iron-bound rules and castes is that they also put the masters into gentle but implacable strait jackets. For Tom it isn't so bad, because he has the estate to manage. But Janet, poor Janet, has absolutely nothing to do. I watched her today, and my final conclusion is that she is a gallant woman whose life would drive me mad.

Tom went off about his business directly from the breakfast table (kippered herring, fried eggs, cold toast, and tea) and Janet suggested that we finish our own tea out on the verandah. I rose and picked up my just-filled cup, but in an instant a bearer with a most reproving expression was beside me with a silver tray.

"The bearer will carry out the tea," Janet explained.

As we sat on the verandah talking and drinking tea, a middle-aged man in a dirty white dhoti and shirt came wheeling down the teak avenue on his bicycle and stopped before the verandah. From a canvas bag on his back he unloaded several letters and rolled-up magazines and newspapers.

"Oh, the post!" Janet exclaimed joyously. This was obviously the big moment of the day. Babu Ram, the mailman, put the mail carefully on the top step, looked at Janet with what I thought was a rather beady eye and began to talk to her in Bihari. Soon she was answering him sharply, almost desperately, and then in a voice of resignation. Later I learned what the conversation was all about.

"*Mem-sahib*, I have been delivering your mail faithfully for many years," announced Babu Ram.

"Oh yes, Babu Ram, you have, many many years."

"And you have never lost anything?"

"I do not know that I have lost anything, Babu Ram."

"Alas, the postal service is not as good as it was in the days of the British Sahibs." Here a heavy sigh.

"Well, perhaps it will get better, Babu Ram."

"I do not think so, *Mem-sahib*. Mail is sometimes lost at the office, now. And the road to your house is very bumpy—perhaps, sometimes, I might lose some mail on the way. You are very happy to receive mail, isn't it, *Mem-sahib?*"

"Yes, Babu Ram." A momentary and slightly mystified silence, at least on Janet's part, while Babu Ram's eyes strayed with apparent idleness over the property.

"Those are very nice chickens over there, *Mem-sahib*. And you have a great many."

"Why Babu Ram!"

"The road is *very* bumpy, *Mem-sahib*."

"Babu Ram, you are a government employee, and postal delivery has always been free. Besides, at Christmas there is always baksheesh."

"Times are different now, *Mem-sahib*. And the road is so bumpy perhaps none of your mail will ever arrive again. A little red chicken might help me to remember to be careful."

Janet knew when she was beaten. To whom could she appeal in Champaran, except Babu Ram's boss, who might demand two chickens?

"All right, Babu Ram, I will send a present to your family just this once." She called a servant and told him to see that one chicken was delivered to the postman. Babu Ram bowed deeply, palms together, and climbed back on his bicycle.

"The road will be bumpy for a long time, next week and every week and every month," he muttered, making sure Janet would hear him, and wheeled away toward the chicken house.

After Babu Ram had disappeared, after Janet had told me of the conversation, after we had both shrugged helplessly—knowing there was no other comment we could make—we opened the post. I began reading a day-before-yesterday Calcutta newspaper; Janet worked on a crossword puzzle but soon gave it up in favor of an English fashion magazine. It is not yet time for the annual visit of the darzee, who comes to live at the house for two months every fall and make dresses for Janet and shirts for Tom, but Janet enjoys planning her wardrobe months in advance. Most of her dresses are copied from American or British magazines and made of imported English material which she buys on her rare visits to Calcutta. They are so successful that she always looks ready for any English garden party, although there are, of course, no parties to go to.

Janet has plenty of time to examine the magazines, for one of the penalties of having many servants is that a *Mem-sahib* is expected to do no housework and no gardening. The head bearer, for instance, looks after all the household linen and would be deeply hurt if Janet ever so much as peeked into the linen closet. She may knit, but she may not mend, for mending is considered below her station. Once, she told me, she waited until all the servants were safely away on their afternoon siesta, and then furtively mended a little hole in the mosquito netting of her bed. But she felt so guilty and so nervous that she never tried it again.

Nor is gardening any outlet for her energies, for here again she is not supposed to do any real work. Last fall, she told me, she threw convention to the winds and went out to divide some iris rhizomes. "But the three gardeners stood right beside me, glowering," she recalled with a giggle, "and they embarrassed me so much that I had to give up and go back to my crossword puzzles."

Custom permitted her, she said, to pick flowers, but a boy must accompany her to carry the flower basket and the garden shears. No *Mem-sahib* in India is supposed to carry anything, not even a glass of water from one room to another.

Three years ago I would have had a typical American reaction to all this: "Well, why the hell not go ahead and do what you want to? After all, the servants can't hurt you!" But now I know that while in America such a gesture would seem a fine, brave thing, in India, if you make it, you also make a fool of yourself. I remember, for instance, the wife of a Scandinavian official who came to live at the Cecil Hotel. She was a brawny, jolly lady who enjoyed being active, and she wasn't going to change just because she was in India: so one day she went out and washed the family automobile. The servants stood around and watched her, at first in amazement, then in contempt. After that she found she could never get any service in the hotel; even the table bearers delayed serving her, and deliberately sloshed the soup they finally set in front of her. The lady and her husband finally had to move to a house where, it is hoped, she now refrains from washing cars.

"Is not good, she do that," Bhag Singh commented at the time. "Is losing caste, is taking work away from other people."

That's the key to it, I suppose. It used to make me cross that whenever I bought a newspaper or a magazine in a Connaught

Circle store, it was handed not to me but to a small boy. The boy then carried it out to my car, and for this service I was expected to give him two annas. "I'm certainly strong enough to carry a newspaper," I would mutter to myself. Yes, but the boy is not strong enough to survive without the food which his two annas here and two annas there will buy him.

Caste is really the strongest trade union in the world, and we white Western Christians are trapped (or protected?) by it as strongly as are the Hindus. One of the favorite stories in Delhi is about a former viceroy's wife who discovered one evening that the dog had made a mess on one of the marble floors of the viceregal palace. She called the head bearer. He reported to her that while there were some eighty-five servants still on duty in the palace, all of the sweepers, alas, had gone home. Since only a sweeper would do "dirty" work, the mess would have to wait until morning. The vicereine knew that not even the power of her husband's office or the majesty of Imperial Britain could change this situation. So she waited until the bearer had departed, tucked her long pearls into the bodice of her satin evening gown, and did the clean-up job herself.

How long is it since I have made a bed, washed a dish, or pressed a dress? I don't yearn for housework, but sometimes I feel a wistful, feminine urge to perform a few of these homely tasks. And so, evidently, does Janet.

But her only real housekeeping responsibility is to check over the food and other stores with the head bearer and order fresh supplies from Bombay or Calcutta. Vegetables come from the garden, milk and butter from their own cows, and rice, fish, and meat from the village bazaar. The usual meat is mutton or chicken for it is harder and harder for non-Hindus to get beef. India is supposed to be a secular state, but religious sentiment against cow-killing is very deep and, since independence, very powerful. Here, as in many areas of India, there are new local ordinances prohibiting what the Hindus call "cow-slaughter."

All other food comes by post, if it is not stolen en route, from

the big cities where some shops still maintain a special mailing
service for their customers in outlying areas. Janet depends on
this service for the marmalade, the canned fruits, the vitamin pills,
the cosmetics, the soap flakes, and the dozens of other things
which we Westerners find so necessary and which the Indian
bazaar has never seen.

"But it's getting so difficult," she mourned today. "Half my
orders arrive unfilled, because with the new import restrictions
the things just aren't to be had any more. Why, I had to write
six shops before I could get a new toothbrush!" (Indians use
twigs of the neem tree, and I must say their teeth are beautiful.)

To me, however, no shortages are evident, and I marvel at the
way the household seems to follow a pattern set in the days of
Victoria's rule: morning tea in bed, breakfast, "elevenses," tiffin
(lunch), siesta, afternoon tea, a stroll under the teak trees or
along the river, bath and a change into evening dress, drinks on
the verandah, dinner.

Dinner, served at half past eight, is the inevitable and formal
British feast: soup, fish, roast, sweet, savory, all consumed with
the aid of an enormous battery of silverware, the sound of the
punkah's soft swish, and the barefoot padding of the bearers.

"One must keep up," says Janet, vaguely.

Only at night does India seem to move closer to this little
British oasis. Around the oil lamp on the verandah the flying ants
buzz and dart, prey of the small lizards called Geckkos who live
on the bungalow walls. In the thatch below the tiles, the bats
stir at nightfall and emerge flapping into the darkness. Just before
bedtime, the sweeper goes through the house with a bucket,
collecting frogs from under dressers, chairs, and beds. Last night
he found twenty-seven.

These warm nights we all sleep on the verandah under mosquito nets. Lying in the dark, I look out into the moonlight and
see the flying foxes swooping toward the lichee trees on the lawn
and hear the hoarse shouts of the Indian family which has been

set to guard the ripening fruit. Rajkali, the elephant, trumpets
suddenly and wakens a brain-fever bird in a far mango tree. The
bird is silent at last, but then, inevitably, comes the howling of
the gathering jackals. Tom leaps out of his bed, grabs his shot-
gun, and bangs away at a moving, howling shadow. "Got him!"
he exclaims, and climbs back into his bed. The rest of the jackal
pack streak off toward the river, and finally, the night is silent.
I drift, at last, to sleep.

Champaran ❀ May 18

I have been shocked today, perhaps more deeply than at
any other time during several often-shocking years in India. And
the worst of it is that I don't really know whether I have a right
to be shocked or not.

This morning, as we walked out on the verandah after breakfast, Tom's office clerk, or *babu*, came running across the lawn.
He was almost incoherent with tears and rage, but finally Tom
managed to get the story from him: two days ago he had bought
a months' supply of rice, sugar, and other rations and stored them
in his house. This morning he found they had been stolen—by
whom, he did not know.

Tom, looking grim, set off at once with the *babu*. He returned
at lunchtime, tired but evidently satisfied.

"Did you catch the thief?" I asked him.

"Yes," he answered, taking a sip of the gimlet (gin and lime
juice) which the bearer had just presented.

"We summoned the local Hindu priest, or pundit," he said
after a moment. "Then I wrote the names of twelve people who
might have been guilty on little pieces of paper. I folded them
tightly and placed them in one of the pundit's shoes. Two men
knelt on the ground with the shoe balanced between their
fingers. Then the pundit began to chant prayers and to toss bits
of dust and sand into the shoe.

"The shoe began to turn slowly around, which meant that one of the papers in it bore the name of the thief. The pundit took out half the papers and repeated the prayers, but the shoe didn't move. This meant that the name of the thief was in the papers he had removed. So he took out the six in the shoe, and replaced them with three of the other six. Thus, by elimination, he finally came down to one name. It was the wife of one of our plough-men."

"Very amusing," I said. "And then did you call the police to find out who was really guilty?" Tom looked surprised.

"Oh no," he answered. "The police in Bagaha are no good, and nobody trusts them. We always call the pundit whenever we have a theft, and I've always been convinced of the guilt of the person the shoe indicated. If there wasn't something to it, what would make the shoe turn?"

"But Tom, surely you can't believe—"

"It doesn't matter whether or not I believe it," he said stub-bornly. "The important thing is that the *babu* and all the other people believe in it."

"But what would you do if the ploughman and his wife won't confess?"

"I should sack them. In any case, although they haven't exactly confessed, they have agreed to pay the *babu* the amount of the stolen stores."

"But Tom, you haven't any real proof!"

"This is proof, as far as the Indians are concerned," he main-tained. "After all, you have to think of the principles involved."

Well, that's exactly what I *am* thinking about, although I didn't say so to Tom. Despite the many failings of Western man, surely one source of his greatness lies in the thousand-year-old struggle to fight ignorance and superstition with logic, reason, and the scientific approach. Loving India does not mean that I can love the same kind of superstition which hunted witches at Salem. Nor does my reaction mean that I am anti-Indian; the edu-cated Indians I know are far more violent than I am in con-

demning the mumbo-jumbo voodoo beliefs which enchain the
Indian peasantry.

Tom is taking the pragmatic approach to this theft and feels
himself justified. *I* think he's throwing Galileo and Harvey and
Newton and all the rest down the drain.

Champaran ❊ May 19

This morning the head bearer reported that there was a
cobra under the house. We all went to look, and we couldn't see
anything, but the servants insisted the snake was there, all right.

"Call the snake man," Janet ordered. This man, she told me,
was an old man who lived in the village and who belonged to a
very special caste which performed only three jobs: luring snakes
from houses, getting honeycombs from trees, and training fighting birds.

Soon the old man arrived, wrapped in dirty cotton garments,
carrying a basket. He asked where the snake had been seen, and
then crouched near one of the low concrete pillars on which the
house is built. From out of the folds of his tattered robes he drew
a little flute and began to play. After awhile he put down the flute
and talked quietly, softly:

"Come, oh honorable snake," he whispered. "You shall have
milk and many frogs. You shall be treated with respect; you shall
be honored. You shall be treated kindly. Milk and frogs . . ."
Over and over.

And the snake slithered from the dirt under the house and came
to the old man. Sure enough, it was a cobra. Even at a very safe
distance we could tell.

The old man leaned over to pick it up. The snake coiled, rose,
and bit him. We gasped, but the old man seemed unconcerned.
From a little bag hanging around his neck, he extracted a small
black seed and placed the seed over the puncture on his finger.
"It will be all right," he said quietly.

From another little bag, he pulled out a piece of root which looked like ginger. He began to wave it slowly under the nose of the snake which he now grasped firmly in his uninjured hand. In twenty minutes the snake seemed sound asleep, and the old man wound it gently into his basket. Later, far away from the house in some distant field, he would let it go.

He showed me the hand the snake had bitten. The seed had swelled to four times its size. "It has absorbed the poison," he explained. "Soon I will take it off, and it will be as if the snake had never bitten me." But he didn't know, or he wouldn't tell me, what kind of seed it was. Just something his caste and his family knew about. Janet paid him five rupees—about one dollar—and he went away, snake, basket, and all.

Champaran ❀ May 20

Last night was my first elephant ride, and a strange, swaying kind of experience it is. But not frightening, really, for the thick cotton pad we rode on seemed as wide as a prize-fight ring; I mounted from a ladder and held on during the ride to a rope tied around the great belly and back of Rajkali. After awhile, I learned to roll with the ship and actually enjoyed the feeling of being up and above everything and able to look right into the second floor windows of the big village houses. Not that there is ever very much to see in those poor bare rooms.

Ponderously we proceeded into town and "parked" on the sidewalk of a narrow alley to watch a Hindu wedding procession on its way to the bride's house. Around us stood a crowd of townspeople, some of them jammed right up against Rajkali's legs. But none of them seemed to worry over their safety as much as I did, for already we could hear the music and see the procession advancing.

First came two little girls in blue satin pajamas, wearing tipsily tilting silver paper crowns. They were followed by a group of boys carrying sprays of paper flowers, and a ten-piece band in dirty red uniforms. The band, as it approached, was playing "The Maine Stein Song." Later, as the men of the band marched slowly down the long street, pausing every twenty steps, they also played: "Marching Through Georgia," "Way Down Upon the Swanee River," and finally, perhaps as a sop to the uncultivated masses, one song from an Indian movie. Why these little Indian bands play light American music for wedding and funeral processions, I don't know. But it always surprises and amuses me, particularly when it happens in a remote, out-of-the-way little town like this.

After the band came two gaily painted elephants and a riderless horse decked in purple and tinsel trappings, with a gilded bridle and bit. Then came the groom on horseback, a boy who couldn't have been more than sixteen years old. He wore an orange turban signifying his caste, of course, and a cream-colored tunic with a scarlet sash, white jodhpurs, shiny new English-rayon blue socks, and pointed gold slippers.

Last of all came an old blue jeep in which I counted twenty-seven children. All of them were yelling.

Right in the middle of the wedding procession our mahout decided to turn Rajkali around. Since the alley was narrow and already jammed with people and animals, this was an insane thing to do. We shouted at the mahout to stop, but it was too late: the whole thing seemed to erupt like a scene in *Alice in Wonderland*. The wedding horses panicked and began to rear and neigh. Then the crowd panicked into a shouting, whirling mass, and in thirty seconds, the gorgeous horse had lost all its purple and gold trappings; the little boys' sprays of paper flowers were smashed to smithereens; the little girls lost their silver crowns; the band instruments were knocked into the gutters. Only the groom seemed unaffected by the melee. Etiquette requires that a groom must never show any emotion even if confronted with chaos, and the strength of the tradition was demonstrated by this young man: throughout the uproar, he continued to sit rigidly upon his rearing horse, and not a muscle of his face even quivered.

In the mysterious way of India, it was all over in another thirty seconds. The crowd realigned itself, laughing and grinning. The riderless horse was redecorated with his purple and gold. The sprays of flowers were picked up and, somehow, stuck together again. The little girls found their crowns and put them on. The band dusted the trombones and drums, and stepped off smartly again, heading for the waiting bride to the tune of "My Old Kentucky Home."

There are two reasons why the mahout might have acted as he did. He is a Moslem and bitterly scornful of all Hindu marriages; he may very well have deliberately intended to wreck the pretty little parade.

On the other hand, perhaps he was nervous. For that morning his wife had gone into labor in the mud hut beyond the vegetable garden where they live. He had called a midwife, he told us, although midwives these days were very expensive: if the child was a girl he would have to pay the midwife five rupees (or one dollar), if it was a boy the cost would be ten rupees. He only earned about thirty rupees a month so either expense would be worrisome. Since he already had three boys, what did he want with another child, particularly a girl? Girls are nothing but trouble, and you have to pay a huge dowry when they get married . . . And so on and so on, grumbling and rocking and swaying all the way home.

This morning the mahout's wife had her baby, a girl. Tom tells me that even though the cost of the midwife is less, the mahout is disgusted and is thinking of drowning the child in the convenient river.

Champaran ❀ *May 22*

Today I met Dumri, a bright-eyed untouchable boy with a big wide smile and a deep dimple in his left cheek. Dumri's twelfth birthday was just celebrated, not with birthday cakes and extra sweets, but with a new entry in the government's official books: "Dumri Dome—a thief."

In three years when Dumri's sister Akali, now hard at work learning the ABCs of Hindi and studying *The Child's History of India*, reaches twelve, she will become officially: "Akali Domin—thief and prostitute."

All of this was expected by Dumri and his family, for they are members of the Magahaya Doms, a once-nomadic Indian tribe which long ago was classified as criminal. For more than sixty years now, the tribe has been settled, under close detention and supervision, at the Chautarwa Agricultural Settlement of Bagaha, which I visited today.

Throughout India there are scores of similar tribes, all of which the British government found it necessary to classify and control. Right now the Indian government is debating this necessity, and Parliament has appointed an inquiry commission to visit the different tribes and perhaps suggest a new way of rehabilitating them. No doubt the whole system will soon be changed, but in the meantime it is interesting to see the problem at first hand and study, even if superficially, a social experiment which failed.

The history of the Magahaya Doms is rather typical of most of the criminal tribes. Like the others, they were not always criminals, but were made so by a turn of history's wheel which threw them out of the inflexible, Indian social pattern. Once, the Magahaya Doms will tell you, they were a caste of the proud Rajputs, respected warriors in the deserts of Rajputana, fighting the Moghul invaders.

Three hundred years ago, however, their tribe, although undefeated, threw down their arms and fled the battlefield. For this sin they were expelled from their homes and their villages and sent into the wilderness. They wandered eastward and eventually settled in the forests of Bihar. For the next two hundred and fifty years the men made their living by burglary of nearby villages, swindling, and highway robbery, while the women generally became prostitutes. No other living, not even agriculture, was known to them.

In 1882 a Mr. E. Henry, then magistrate of Champaran District, rounded up all the Magahaya Doms—using a combination of cajolery and force—and settled them on the land under the supervision of a police detachment. This arrangement continued until 1913, when the Salvation Army took over the administration of the camp. In 1947, in accordance with the inevitable development of Indian nationalism, the Salvation Army was replaced by the Harijan Sewak Sangh, or Untouchable Service Society, a private organization founded by Mahatma Gandhi.

The new administration has not brought about many changes, perhaps because of meagre financing, perhaps because the only change the camp manager would really like to see is complete abolishment of the whole system.

At the center of the camp are the two prison blocks. The gates are locked each night at eight p.m. and opened again at five a.m. on the theory that the thieving Doms are thus prevented from nocturnal prowling. The blocks are simply high concrete and brick walls, enclosing a well, several *peepul* trees, goats, a few cows, some mongrel dogs, and a welter of four hundred and fifty human beings. Each family is allotted one of the ten foot by ten foot rooms built around the inner edge of the wall.

Each adult is given three-quarters of an acre of land, and half of that for each minor in his family, and is allowed outside the compound during the day to farm his land—usually planted in sugar cane or rice. If a man has a clear record for five years, with no charges against him, he is allowed to settle outside the gates.

Even Doms with good records must carry a pass whenever they travel to a market town and stay away overnight. These passes must be shown at the police station, and Doms away from home must sleep in police station precincts. A few, inevitably, run away every year; the rest are contented to remain at the settlement with their families and the only source of livelihood, aside from thieving, that they know.

The saddest record of the settlement is that of the little school attended by most of the children: in the sixty years it has been established, not one child has passed even a grammar school examination.

"They don't see any point in studying," said the camp director. "Take Dumri here—he was a good scholar when he was younger, but for the last two years he hasn't even tried." He patted the boy's thin shoulder with affection, and told him in Bihari what he had just said. The boy answered quickly, brightly, and the camp director translated:

"Why should I bother to study and improve myself when I know that I shall be called a thief even when I am not a thief, and that I will never be free to go out in the world to make my own way?"

Old Birwa Dome, the boy's uncle, spoke up scornfully from the shade of a nearby *peepul* tree: "These Gandhi people come and talk to us about the freedom of India," he snorted. "But what does that mean to us? We still live the same way. We haven't smelt freedom yet!

"Sure, they give us land to cultivate, and we're all well enough fed and well enough clothed. And maybe we aren't all good angels yet. We like a drink of toddy now and then, and maybe, once in awhile, somebody pinches a mango or a custard apple. But that's no reason for talking to us about freedom, and not giving us any!"

The camp director is not quite as confident as old Birwa Dome that the Magahaya Doms have been rehabilitated. In fact he has come to the conclusion that the criminal tribes settlements must be closed and the tribes settled freely on the land, separated from each other in different villages, for the simple reason that the semi-imprisonment method of reclamation hasn't worked.

"For more than sixty years these Doms have been cooped up here together, still outcasts from society, some of them still teaching their children the old tricks," he said. "They don't steal much any more, and the women are better behaved. But they're not happy; their children are psychologically warped.

"As long as boys like Dumri know they are automatically considered thieves, the temptation to become one is great."

I, for one, was certainly convinced that the time has come to fit the Magahaya Doms back into the society from which they were expelled three hundred years ago and to wipe Dumri's name off the official register of thieves. The fact that the Indian government, still so new and so preoccupied, is already considering this action certainly seems a cheering sign for the future.

Bettiah Raj Jungle, Bihar ❀ *May 24*

"Let's go up to the forest bungalow and spend a few days," Janet suggested one evening, as we sat with Tom on the verandah. "Maybe you could get in some shooting."

"Out of season," Tom answered gloomily. "Not that it matters now, of course."

The British, he explained, had cared a great deal about the preservation of Indian wild life, had instituted a wild life service which saw to it that open seasons and closed seasons were strictly observed. But this attitude, like so many others, was basically alien to India; since Independence, enforcement of the laws has been lax. The villagers, always looking for supplementary food, moved out into the jungles and shot deer whenever they felt like it. The deer were diminishing fast, Tom claimed, and would soon disappear altogether. On the other hand, tigers were increasing. Villagers were not interested in hunting as a sport but merely as a source of food.

"If a man-eating tiger is menacing their village, they'll call in a white hunter," he said. "But for the rest of the time, they just want to be left alone to kill anything and everything in the jungle."

"Well, it's still very pleasant in the jungles," Janet said pacifically. "And maybe you could bag a tiger."

"I've bagged enough tigers," grumbled Tom. "I'm finished with all that. Just want to get away to Australia or East Africa; that's all I want."

Nevertheless, it was finally agreed that the next day we would move up to the forest bungalow for a day or so. Not to do any shooting, unless we spotted a tiger, but just to look around and possibly see some wild life.

I had thought vaguely that the trip would be something like an overnight camping trip in America: bedding rolls and sleeping bags, mess kits and a few cans of beans. In fact, I rather looked forward to some rugged, do-it-yourself living. But I had forgotten the British traditions. Our "shikar" must have been but a pale reflection of the old days when two dozen Englishmen and a sprinkling of maharajahs would travel with an army of retainers for a two-weeks' shoot in the jungles. Still, it was a far cry from camping out with a tin of beans.

Before dawn, Rajkali the elephant was sent ahead with the mahout, in order to be at camp by the time we needed her. In the afternoon, the estate truck departed, filled with five servants and several straw hampers. Early in the evening, Tom and Janet and I took off in the jeep.

Within half an hour we were on a smooth dirt road rolling among scrubby trees. There were no villages—just endless miles of trees and bushes and grass.

"Often see tigers here," said Tom, who carried a rifle at his side. We saw no tigers. What we did see was another jeep loaded with Indians and rifles, with a man in uniform at the wheel. The carcass of a deer lay across the hood. The man at the wheel pretended not to see us, although Tom waved at him as we passed.

"That's the forest ranger and his family," he said. "Do you see what I mean about 'out-of-season' not meaning anything any more?"

The night came swiftly, and the headlights of our jeep probed through the dark tunnel of the road below the trees. In the darkness of the road just beyond the headlights I suddenly saw myriads of shining lights in the road, glowing and golden.

"Nightjars," said Tom. "They like to roost in the dust of the road at night."

Invariably, they turned their heads toward the sound of the approaching car, and the eyes, thousands and thousands of eyes, were reflected in the beams. Each bird would sit quietly until we were just upon it; at the last possible moment, with a whirr of wings, it would flutter out of the way. We didn't hit one.

At nine p.m. we pulled up before the forest bungalow—a two-story building with caretaker, which can be rented from the government by hunters and travelers. But this, I quickly discovered, was no sleeping-bag and open-a-can affair. The head bearer greeted us at the door, bowing respectfully. He led us into a living-room complete with comfortable furniture and a crackling fire in the fireplace. Soda siphons, glasses, and bottles of Scotch stood ready on a sideboard. Later we entered a small dining-room and sat down at a camp table covered with a white linen cover. The dinner which followed consisted of soup (with sherry), fried fish, roast lamb, peas, potatoes, apricot mousse, anchovies on toast, coffee, and liqueurs. The Purcell's china, glass, and silver, I noted, had been transported to the jungle for the occasion. For the first time, I began to believe in the legend of the Englishman and his traveling tin tub.

The bedrooms upstairs were rather stark, but on each charpoy a mattress had been laid and covered with linen sheets, blanket, and bedspread. And after all, why not? I thought as I sank luxuriously to sleep.

When I think of the word "jungle," I am evidently thinking of a forest in South America, or possibly Southeast Asia: huge green leaves the size of blankets, twisted vines which must be chopped with a machete, spongy earth and dripping moss, monkeys chattering and boa constrictors looped among orchids.

Certainly I have not been thinking of the jungles of north India. We spent today in the Bettiah Raj Jungle, and except for the fact that we were riding on an elephant, we might just as well have been in Bear Mountain Park in New York, or in any Connecticut forest after a summer of drought. Tall, reasonable-looking trees, scrubby undergrowth, a floor of dry leaves. A rather dull jungle, really.

But we did see some game. A great black buck crashing off across a low hillside. A herd of about fifty sambars—deer with manes and delicately curling antlers. And in a green forest glade, a group of the strange, gray animals the Indians call "blue cows." But I thought they looked like horses, even though they do not have the luxurious mane of the horse. Rather like a unicorn without the horn, except that a unicorn without a horn might be just a horse, I suppose.

Tom carried his gun, but we met no tigers, much to my relief. It was exciting enough to see the blue cows in the shadowed glade —so quiet, so self-contained, so eternal.

Champaran ❀ May 26

Eric is back from Nepal, looking brown and proud of himself, and filled with stories of the great contrasts in the country between the splendors of the temples and palaces and the degradation of the people. More striking even than in India, apparently. I gather that Nepal will never be Eric's favorite country.

Tomorrow we start the long trip back to Delhi. Not the way we came, which would involve that unbearable jouncing over the road to Muzaffarpore, but by elephant, country boat, bullock cart, train, and plane. The main point is to get across the

Gandak River to the rail head on the other side before the monsoon breaks, when the river may become impassable for days. The first rain is due any day now; one can almost feel all of north India holding its parched breath and waiting.

Staying with the Purcells has been a fascinating experience, partly because their way of life represents a dying period in India. When the Indians buy this house, they will take out all the furniture and use it for firewood, because they like to sit on the floor. They will remove the bathtubs and the commodes, for they bathe in running water and use the wide outdoors for their toilets. They will take down the left-behind tiger and leopard heads shot by past Purcells. They will plant the green lawns with crops right up to the verandah. They will remove the headstones in the little graveyard; already marauders have dug out the lead in the inscriptions. It will all be as if the English had never been here at all.

This last week I have been reading Trevelyan on fifth-century England when the Roman Legions were withdrawn. One by one, the great Roman villas in southern England, with their tesselated floors, their gardens, and their baths were abandoned by the "civilized" Romans to the crude Britons. I suppose at that time, too, the old Roman diehards muttered dire prophecies about "These people reverting to savagery," and "not appreciating the benefits we brought them." And so they didn't, and neither do the Indians. In the long run of history, it doesn't seem to matter a bit.

Delhi ❀ May 29

The Purcells told us that the five-hundred-mile trip would take two days, but they didn't mention the centuries and civilizations we would pass through on the way. One of the most absorbing things about India is the sense of time past and time present existing simultaneously; human beings representing all of the social stages of man, all of the rungs on the ladder of cultural evolution, live together in this land, sometimes separated only by a river or a forest. For the visitor, India is the nearest thing yet to a time machine.

North Bihar has an ancient and honorable role in Indian history. A little to the north of Champaran, across the border in Nepal, is the birthplace of the Buddha; a little to the south are the ruins of the temple where Mahavira established the pure doctrine of Jainism. In the sixth century B.C., Buddha and Mahavira roamed among the ancestor trees of the same jungle where we began our journey.

For two hours Rajkali crunched steadily through the dry jungle, occasionally stirring a herd of deer into fleet alarm or flushing a brilliant peacock from the tall grass. Once a barking deer showed its white tail, and another time we saw a black buck and doe beside a stream.

Our first village was a settlement of aboriginals deep in the heart of the jungle and connected to the outside world only by a narrow forest trail. The houses were of straw and mud; the children ran naked. Some of them had bones tied in their hair for decoration. The people farmed a little land around the village and gathered wild fruits, berries, and roots; they spoke no language any of us could understand, but they offered us homemade rice beer in earthen bowls. They smiled and gestured and made it quite clear they considered us honored guests from the land east of the sun and west of the moon.

Following the trail, we came back at last to the Gandak River, broad and gray beneath the smoky summer sky. On the banks of the river was a small fishing village of thatched houses and mud alleys. The villagers thought we were officials and followed us to the edge of the river, begging for help.

"The British Raj must give us money," one old woman wept. "Every year our village is swept away by floods, and then we have to build a new village somewhere else. O, honorable, powerful people from the government, please build us a new, strong village the waters cannot hurt. Today, tomorrow, the rains will come, and the waters will rise." She pointed a bony finger at the lapping waters and the crumbling sandbanks. We tried to explain that we were journalists, not government officials, and told them that now the "Raj" (or rule) was Indian, not British. But obviously they had not the slightest idea of what we were talking about; this little village was so remote that its people had never even heard of a newspaper or a radio. For them it was impossible to imagine a government which was not British, or a white person who was not an official.

While the whole village clustered mournfully on the river bank and watched us, we climbed into a leaky country boat which was waiting for us. Janet and Tom had sent a runner several days before to make all the arrangements. Our baggage was piled around us amidships, under the shelter of a curved roof of reeds. The four boatmen poled away from the shore, and when we were well out on the wide river, raised a tattered lateen sail. The boy at the helm began to sing softly, but we could not understand his words.

Halfway across the river we looked out from the reed shelter and saw, to the north, a sky blacker than any we had ever seen before. In five minutes a hurricane was upon us with lashing rain and howling winds. A pre-monsoon storm had broken.

Quickly the men pulled down the sail and headed the boat into a nearby sandbank. We settled down to wait out the storm while one of the men bailed steadily against the rising water level, and the rest, soaked and shivering, crept under the shelter with us. For an hour, while the rain and the waves pounded against the boat, they crouched there silently, staring at us with large, fawn-like eyes.

The storm over, we reached the other side of the river safely and found on the banks a bullock cart waiting to take us across the muddy fields and through the village to the railway station. The animals were miserable beasts, their ribs showing, their hides covered with dirt and scars. While we wondered, as often before, at the contradictions in India, where a cow is simultaneously worshipped and tortured, the driver twisted the tails of the animals to make them pull, occasionally breaking a joint, as is the custom. One of the animals collapsed with a low moan in the mud, and only much prodding made it rise again. We decided to walk the rest of the way.

This was evidently a large village, for it boasted a school: a one-room mud building and an open courtyard where thirty solemn little boys sat in a circle on the ground, listening to their school teacher in the center. We were not yet near enough to civilization to expect schooling for little girls.

Under a nearby *peepul* tree, a holy man sat cross-legged in contemplation, his body daubed with white ash, his hair matted, his eyes unblinking. Almost all the villagers who passed by him dropped a copper or two into his begging bowl.

The railway station, because of the floods, has to be moved every year. Thus the waiting-rooms and the stationmaster's office were flimsy affairs of bamboo, stretching along the tracks at the end of the line. Politely the stationmaster opened the first-class waiting-room for us. We were evidently the first such travelers he had seen this season. No one was ever quite sure when the train would arrive, he said, so in the warm little room smelling of green reeds and sunlight, we picnicked leisurely and afterward slept on the hard benches until the train came.

It was a Toonerville Trolley of a train, and it stopped at every tiny village to take on a new load of peasants and their wives, the men colorless in white shirts and dhotis, the women brilliant in red-and-silver saris. When the train became crowded, a man and wife climbed into our compartment, slipped off their sandals, and curled up on the long bench beside me. After half an hour, the woman looked at me shyly, and then in an inquiring tone asked me something in a dialect I could not understand. I smiled, spread out my hands in the universal gesture of hopelessness, and shook my head. She made a motion of rocking a baby, pointed to me, and again asked her question in an inquiring tone.

I shook my head, pointed to my stomach, smiled, and made a gesture of rocking a baby. She smiled, pointed to her own little round stomach, and made a gesture of rocking a baby too. We both nodded to each other happily and rode the rest of the journey in companionable silence.

At the main junction Eric and I changed trains and had our first "civilized" meal—a pseudo-British affair of soup, fish, and meat, brought from the station restaurant to our compartment on trays, with elaborate flutterings of almost-white napkins. Then the trays were cleared away, and shortly we were off on the long, over-night journey to Lucknow. We pulled up the wooden shutters which protect compartments from thieves, locked them, unrolled our bedding rolls, and went to sleep.

In the morning two plump businessmen from a provincial town joined us in the compartment. One of them said he was going to Lucknow to induce an official to give him a larger gasoline ration. The other said he was going there to get his son a job in one of the ministries where he had a "connection." Then he would have two connections, he remarked happily.

The conversation settled down, as it often does in the provinces of India, to a lengthy denunciation of the Congress government and its failure to achieve Utopia in the few years since independence. The trouble was, the two businessmen agreed, that there was too much corruption and neoptism.

After the backwoods of India, Lucknow, with its taxis and telephones, seemed like a pulsing metropolis, and the Royal Hotel, for all its peeling walls and rubber plants, a near-Waldorf. In the lobby we met a friend of ours, an idealistic young Congressman.

"All of India is awake now," he informed us over a glass of warm pineapple juice on the terrace. "The people are throbbing with new life, conscious of freedom, progress, and democracy!"

Politicians talk like that in India, even in private conversation. It is one of their most endearing characteristics, if you are feeling strong.

We booked our air passages and went out to the field in the
company's new American station wagon. The plane came in on
time; the steward was efficient, the flight so swift that before we
had finished lunch we were circling above New Delhi. Rajkali
seemed a long way back.

June

N o w starts the business of maternity clothes. What a bother, when, really, I should be thinking about serious things like Indian politics and religion. But this is a serious matter too, I guess. How I long for New York where I could simply walk into any store's maternity shop and buy what I need in a couple of hours! New Delhi has one shop which sells ready-made clothes. But this morning when I timidly asked the haughty Englishwoman who runs the store if she sold maternity garments she looked horrified and quickly answered "Oh deah me no, naturally not!" So I shall have to page through old magazines and find some pictures for the darzee to copy. Started off with V*ogue* this evening and discovered that V*ogue* women apparently do not propagate the race.

As I was leafing hopelessly through the pages, Sesh Ayyer dropped in. He looked more Westernized than he did a month ago, and he even wore a tie. As usual, I offered him some pineapple juice.

"As a matter of fact, I'd rather have sherry," he said, lounging in his favorite chair. I looked at him in amazement, for somehow I had always assumed that he was one of the pure young Indians who shudder at the very mention of alcohol.

"What have you been up to?" I asked as I handed him his glass.

"Oh, nothing much. Been seeing some Americans."

"Do you ever have dates with Indian girls?" Sesh looked a little embarrassed, as most Indians do when the subject of sex is even faintly implied.

"You know how it is here," he answered finally. "No well-brought-up girl ever is allowed to have a date or even talk to a man outside her own family. Of course there are a few emancipated ones, college girls usually, who defy their families. But the defiance seems to make them neurotic, or something . . ."

He smiled unhappily and asked for another glass of sherry. Our dachshund, Jimmy, came wagging into the room, and Sesh leaned down and patted him absently.

"As a matter of fact," he said at last, "I've been seeing something of a girl up at the university. She's very intellectual, very brilliant. We have talked a great deal about political philosophy and have arrived at similar conclusions." He stopped abruptly.

"Well?" I prodded.

"Well, the other day for the first time I tried to hold her hand. I had thought that maybe later I could kiss her. In about a month, perhaps. But she snatched her hand away as if I had burned her and scowled at me ferociously. Then she went right on talking about Hegel."

"You should be married, Sesh. You are of an age."

"Yes, I should be married," he admitted, looking miserable. "But I will only marry a woman of my own choice. I will never, never submit to an arranged marriage! My parents wish to pick a wife for me, but I have refused. I have told them I will pick my own wife, in the modern manner. But how can I, if I cannot meet Indian girls?"

Delhi ❀ June 6

Yesterday I telephoned a Mr. Naba, the government drugs controller, to see if he could help me get my layette through customs. Today he called me: "In view of the circumstances we think you may not have to pay any customs duty." This is absurd. He told me I have to get a "No Objection" certificate from the Reserve Bank of India. So I wrote for it.

June 7

A Mr. Benjamin of Imports Control called me and told me my packages won't be allowed into India as they are on the prohibited list. "Too bad you had them sent by air instead of regular post," he said.

"But they *are* coming by post!" I exclaimed.

"Ah well, then you can bring them in. But of course you'll have to pay customs duty."

He says I don't need a "No Objection" certificate.

June 8

A letter from the bank, saying yes, of course I'll need a "No Objection" certificate and please, what is the value of the goods?

Delhi ❀ June 10

A big Pakistani dinner tonight at Davico's, one of the Connaught Circle restaurants. As is usual at these affairs, particularly these Moslem affairs, I sat among the ladies, gorging on curry and spiced chicken and listening to the gentle chitter-chatter. But this time I didn't mind, for I sat next to a charming lady who talked about having babies in India. She had her first child when she was fifteen.

"You don't know anything then, or know what to expect," she said. "Girls aren't told about these things. Marriage just happens to you, when you're around fourteen, so you learn about *that*. Then when you start to have a baby, things just happen to you whether you know about them or not. And then of course there are always a lot of relatives and old nurses around; they take charge and do everything for you."

She was a big woman, tent-like in a glaring orange-and-gold sari, and very placid, very complacent. And no wonder, for although she was only twenty-five, she had already borne her husband four sons! With any luck, she might even be able to equal the feat of her mother-in-law, who had produced nine sons.

"Before two of them were born," she informed me, "my husband's mother read medical books, and those boys grew up to be doctors. Before another two she read law books, and they became lawyers. And before one of the boys, an engineering book; he's an engineer." ("What a well-read Indian lady she must have been," commented Eric, when I told him of this later.)

We went on to talk of child care, and I found her ideas of Western theories on the subject about twenty years out of date, as they usually are among Indian women who think they know what the Western child psychologists are saying.

A few of her friends, she said disapprovingly, are bringing their children up "Western style." This means, she indicated, that they leave their babies all alone and don't go to them when they cry. With great horror she told of a Westernized friend of hers, a woman who prided herself on keeping up with her husband, being modern, and going to cocktail parties. "And one night she gave a party, and the baby started crying in the next room, and a friend asked her why she didn't go to it—but she said the 'modern' technique was to leave it alone. And late that night they found the poor little baby nearly scalded to death by a burst hot water bottle!"

No Indian child of the "better" classes who follow the old ways, she said, is left alone in a room for even one second until it's at least seven years old. Babies sleep with their mothers, and later on they always sleep in the same room. If the mother must go out during the day, which she rarely does, a nurse or a bearer is always with the child.

"I think our old Indian ways are best," she ended primly.

I tried to tell her about the "new" thinking in America, about cuddling and comforting being back in style, and I even tried to give her some idea that not all American mothers spend their time at cocktail parties, but she wasn't interested. Her eyes began to glaze, her sweet motherly face to droop with indifference. It is always this way; Indian women love to tell us all about how they do things, but I have never had anyone ask me anything about our lives in America. Oh, yes—once an Indian woman in Bombay asked me incredulously: "Do American women *love* their children?"

Anyway, it was probably presumptuous of me to try to tell the Moslem lady anything about child-raising. She seems to be bringing up four boys to her own and her husband's satisfaction. And here am I, several years older than she, just beginning on my first!

Delhi ❀ June 13

Dr. Mary Thomas is going away for the rest of the summer. So is the English doctor whom most of the *Mem-sahibs* use when they have babies. Both of them had recommended a Dr. Passricha, and today I went to see her.

I was appalled. Her office is on the second floor of an old building in New Delhi, above the ground-floor offices of the Associated Press and the United Press. Narrow, filthy steps lead up to a verandah where there are a few battered settees and a great many odd Indians. Inside, there is some kind of dispensary full of men. Dr. Passricha's office is nothing but an examination table set behind a canvas screen. The screen is full of holes. There is no bathroom and practically no privacy. Dr. Passricha apologized, and explained that there were simply no private offices available in New Delhi—a result of the influx of refugees, probably.

At first I was really frightened at what I'd gotten myself in for, but by the end of the consultation I was completely reassured. Dr. Passricha was trained in Bombay and London, and I must say, she was more thorough in her examination and her questions than either of the other doctors I've been to before. Pelvic measurements and so on. She's a Parsi, and the Parsis are among the most intelligent and modern communities in India. Also, she's pleasantly homely, middle-aged, has soft hands, and she wore a spotless cream-colored sari with white lace edging which reminded me of the blouses my mother used to wear when I was a child.

Meantime, we're acquiring some of the things a baby seems to need. When we go to diplomatic parties at the Delhi Gymkhana Club, one or the other of us always slips away and hastily scans the bulletin board for notices of things for sale by people leaving India. I'm in luck: one American couple had for sale a huge pram, a playpen, a baby cot, a highchair, a bathinette, and two hundred and ninety-eight tins of strained baby food. I went to their house this morning and found they were asking five hundred rupees—about one hundred dollars—for the lot. This seemed pretty stiff, so I offered three hundred rupees. The gentleman accepted with alacrity. The same principle as bazaar haggling, but quicker.

All of the things were delivered to the front of the hotel just at the noon hour, when everyone was sitting on the terrace, and I had to go out to receive them. So now there should be no doubt in anyone's mind. Obviously, we weren't buying a pram for the dachshund.

Bhag Singh and I stored everything away in a garage under the servants' quarters while six puffy-bellied Indian children—none of whom have ever ridden in a pram or tasted strained baby food—looked on wonderingly. The bathinette and the playpen are a bit broken, but I'm still jubilant.

Delhi ✻ *June 14*

The monsoon is in full flood. Every day it rains and rains and rains. The Jumna, no longer a narrow blue stream, laps at the foot of the Red Fort and disappears on the other side into the horizon in a vast gray expanse broken here and there by the tops of trees. Occasionally, a bloated cow or a human corpse swirls by and is quickly gone. All over north India the floods are spreading across the land; all over north India engineers are working to build dams and canals, but it will be many years before their work is completed. I think of the old woman we met beside the Gandak and wonder how it is with her and her village. Gone now, probably.

The temperature has dropped from the hundreds to the nineties. The air is humid, and our desert cooler no longer works. In the night we lie in pools of perspiration, and in the morning we discover new patches of prickly heat on our skins. Indians don't get prickly heat; Anglo-Indians sometimes show off their white blood by mentioning casually that they do. I keep our sheets and pillow cases in the refrigerator in the bathroom and rush them onto the beds just before we retire, but it does little good. Our shoes, my purses, and Eric's belts are covered with mold unless we keep an electric bulb burning in the closet.

Yet Indians long for this season. It is, to them, the time of poetry and love, as spring is to us. Between the showers, they put up rope swings under the trees and rock their children or their wives back and forth, reciting poetry. The mangos, the glorious mangos, are ripe now. Everyone debates the qualities of the various varieties—and always ends by agreeing that the *Alphonso* is really the best.

In the streets, everywhere, one can sense the exquisite relief of the monsoon—the assurance from the heavens that the glaring heat breaks at last, that water comes to cool hot skins and feed the parched crops. In the relief there is joy, and in joy there is time for sentiment. The Indians call June "the time of love," and that is why so many children are born in March.

At the moment, however, my personal joy centers in the fact that ahead of us lie two weeks in Kashmir. Eric left three days ago in the car; tomorrow at dawn I will fly to Srinagar to join him.

Srinagar, Kashmir ✿ *June* 17

The first time I came to the Vale of Kashmir I was disappointed. Perhaps I had subconsciously confused the words "Vale" and "Veil." I had expected a lush ravine with great ferns, towering pines, and soft veils of rainbow-glowing mists from the sprays of waterfalls.

Kashmir is nothing like that, at least in the valley. It is a wide, gently-rolling plateau—five thousand feet high—set about with bare and craggy peaks. Back in the mountains there are indeed the kind of ravines and vegetation I had pictured, but unless one goes trekking one does not see them. One sees instead the bare mountains all about, the great stretches of artificial lakes near Srinagar, and the tumbling wooden town itself.

Gradually, during many visits since then, the quiet beauty became powerful in my eyes; the enchantment of Kashmir penetrated my heart. Now, sitting on the flat roof of our houseboat and staring across Dal Lake at a sunset-reddened range of noble peaks, I wonder how I could ever have thought them ugly that first visit, that time which has now become almost legendary in my mind. And now, peacefully, I wish to re-live that fevered time.

It was October, 1947. The great partition riots, which took

perhaps a million lives and made twelve million people into homeless refugees, were barely over. We had seen too much murder and bloodshed in both India and Pakistan to be able to take sides any longer; we were weary of refugee problems and talk of revenge. Perhaps when you have spent many months looking at the mutilated corpses of murdered babies you reach a point beyond an understanding of revenge, when only an emotion of universal grief seems appropriate. We needed a little time for peace and restoration, and so, because we were in Rawalpindi, we went to Kashmir. There had been no riots in Kashmir. Kashmir, everyone said, was quiet and beautiful. The Hindu Maharajah had not yet decided whether to join India or Pakistan, but no one seemed to be hurrying him.

At that time the only road into Kashmir from the Indian subcontinent led from Rawalpindi in Pakistan up past Murree, through the mountains of Western Kashmir up onto the plateau, and past Baramula along the Jehlum River to Srinagar.

Still on the Pakistan side, we drove along beside a river which formed the border of Kashmir and saw hundreds of people crossing the river toward us, riding on logs or crude rafts. One young man lay on an inflated goatskin and paddled across with his hands and feet to the bank where we had stopped the car. Dripping, he climbed up the rocks and spoke to us.

"We have been driven from our homes by the Maharajah's troops," he announced. "We have brought our women and our children to safety in Pakistan, but we are going back to fight. I myself have only come over here to get a gun and ammunition."

It seems strange to me now to think that this little rebellion in the western district of Poonch has been so completely forgotten in the surge and confusion of later events. It was certainly a small wave of history swallowed almost immediately by a larger one.

On the Kashmir side of the bridge from Pakistan we had to stop the taxi and go through customs. Although the population of Kashmir was largely Moslem, the Maharajah and the ruling class were Hindus and, therefore, worshippers of the cow. Our baggage was carefully searched for forbidden beef as well as for firearms. The officers finished with us quickly and then turned to two large wooden boxes which an old Moslem in the front seat was taking to a doctor in Srinagar; the young clerk pried open the lids and recoiled when he discovered both boxes contained live leeches.

"Search them. They might be hiding guns," ordered the customs officer. The clerk picked up a stick and began poking unhappily among the leeches. The customs officer, a thin Hindu pundit, leaned against a railing above the river and, in the way of all educated Indians, talked politics.

"We Kashmiri pundits are the third most intelligent people in India." he said. "Only the Bengalis and the Madrasi Brahmins are smarter than we are. That is well known.

"If Kashmir joined India there would be two other peoples ahead of us. But if we joined Pakistan, we would be able to dominate them, because we would be more intelligent than anybody else."

Wondering how democracy is ever to succeed in Asia, we drove on another hundred miles, through the Jehlum gorge and up into the Vale. Once, we stopped beside a field of early winter wheat and spoke to a peasant boy. He was wide-eyed and shy, and he spoke softly.

"No, there is no trouble here, Sahib," he said. "All is peaceful. I do hear in our village gossip that the government is fighting with itself, but what is that to do with me?"

On the outskirts of Baramula, a pleasant little town at the edge of the Vale, a crowd was massed near a stone bridge. A haggard young man was auctioning off clothes one by one. While we watched he sold a pair of pink-satin Punjabi trousers for three rupees.

"Those belonged to his wife who was murdered," explained an old man standing nearby. "He, like so many others, is a refugee from the West Punjab, without money and forced to sell every-

thing. Hindu refugees have come here to Kashmir because they
know it is peaceful and they will not be persecuted, although
most of us are Moslems."

Within a week, the customs officer, the peasant boy, and the
young refugee were probably all dead.

For three days, we found the peace and the enchantment we
had sought. Our houseboat, the *New Dera*, was moored far out on
a distant bank of Dal Lake. The air was still warm, but the chenar
trees—rather like plane trees—were crimson and gold around the
lakes. In the afternoons we traveled to town in a gondola-like
boat called a *shikara*, reclining on spring seats covered with pillows and Kashmiri embroidery; the boatman used a heart-shaped
paddle and sang Kashmiri love songs. In the cold and moonlit
evenings we rode home again in the *shikara*, a blanket covering
us and a small charcoal brazier tucked at our feet.

All morning we lay in deck chairs on the sunlit roof of the
houseboat, watching dragonflies dart above the lotus blossoms on
the lake, watching the brilliant blue kingfishers dive for fish,
watching the hoopoe bird ruffling his crown of feathers, listening to the sound of a far-off paddle on the waters, the sound of
a distant flute, a song. We drank cold beer; we ate huge curries;
we slept.

But there were shadows, too. I had been warned before I came
that I would be saddened by the bitter contrasts of Kashmir, and
after a few days I was.

There is fruit in Kashmir in abundance; there are rich forests
over the mountains and minerals in the earth; there are good
possibilities for silk industries and viticulture, and there are
horizon-stretching lands for sheep grazing. There is water, that
most precious of possessions. Above all, there is the native artistry
of the people, who can weave the finest woolens in India, embroider the most delicate flowers, paint the shyest bird down to his
most exquisite belly feather.

Yet the people of Kashmir, who should be strong and prosperous and happy, are among the poorest, the most depressed, and the most subservient in all India. Many children had only little scraps of cotton to cover them, even on the chilliest of autumn nights. In Srinagar, the houses were picturesque, but in reality they were tumbling tenements, rabbit warrens, hovels. Dirt and disease were conspicuous. There were fourteen people living in the two-room cookboat attached to the stern of our houseboat. Every night I watched an old woman crouching in the bow of a small scull, her arms plunging into the icy waters in search of weeds, her feet blue with the cold.

Which comes first, the hen or the egg? Personality or history? Are the Kashmiris cringing and spiritless because they have been dominated by outsiders for centuries, or the other way around? The historians evidently disagree. Some of them think that the Kashmiris' miserable fate was due "partly to the cowardly character of the population, which invited oppression." Even the Emperor Akbar, they say, who loved the scenery and climate of Kashmir, raged at the men: "You Kashmiris have stomachs to eat but not to fight! Men? Faint-hearts, not lion-hearts." And in contempt, he ordered that the men of Kashmir should wear long robes like women, which they still do.

Not so, say other historians. The Kashmiris were once fearsome warriors, but due to a thousand years of misadventures, of conquerings and oppressions, they have lost their martial qualities and become craven. Akbar, say the historians, ordered those robes because he still feared the fighting spirit of the Kashmiri and knew that a man could fight less well in skirts than in trousers.

Ah, well. Perhaps the important point is that through the centuries the Kashmiri has survived invasion after invasion, allowing the conquerors to do as they will while he continued to cultivate his mustard and his wheat, to paint exquisite flowers on paper boxes, to smile and cringe, and to stay alive.

But for how long, we wondered? For decades the whole economy of the Vale of Kashmir had been geared to the tourist industry; hundreds of thousands of boatmen, shopkeepers, crafts-men, and servants made their living from the Europeans who came here on vacation or who retired here after their long years of service on the hot plains of India.

But few people had come to Kashmir in 1947, for the riots discouraged travel, and in any case many of the British had left India after independence came in August. Indians, by and large, go on pilgrimages or to visit distant families; the idea of a summer resort is alien to them.

In the shops of Srinagar, stacks of pretty papier-mache boxes lay undusted and unsold, while on the streets the merchants gathered to talk of impending bankruptcy. The flowered housecoats, which sometimes take six months to embroider, were marked down from one hundred dollars to fifty dollars and then to twenty dollars. In the countryside thousands of peasants who cut the timber for Kashmir's characteristic wood-carvings and grow the wool for the soft pashmina shawls were out of work.

On the quiet waters of the river which winds through Srinagar and around the border of Dal Lake, hundreds of houseboats lay empty. During World War II, when Kashmir was a rest center for GI's, the scrolled boats among the lotus blossoms rented for ten dollars a day per person. Now, for two dollars each, we lived in a four-room houseboat complete with five servants and meals of wild duck, quail, and teal.

Each day the merchants gathered in coveys of *shikaras* around the houseboat; each day their fruit, their flowers, their Tibetan jewelry was marked down a little more. The flower-seller offered his whole boatload of African daisies, zinnias, dahlias, and roses for one dollar. "Take them," he said bitterly. "I am finished with this business, for there is no one to buy flowers any more. For one rupee more you can have my wife's silver bracelet too."

But that first year of desperation everyone tried to keep up ap-pearances. It was the wedding season in Kashmir, and Ramzana Dubloo our houseboat owner, was marrying off his son Mahamdu. In the cookboats behind the houseboat, the relatives and friends gathered on the night before the wedding, feasting and singing and admiring the presents for the fifteen-year-old bride.

In the smaller cookboat, the women, their heads heavy with silver ornaments, knelt on the floor, singing:

> "Oh ho! So you're going to be married tomorrow!
> Then stay in the garden tonight and be cool.
> Or better still, drink some soda water!"

In an adjacent cookboat the men tried to outshout the women, but their songs were more dignified, telling of the exploits of Alexander the Great, praising the Prophet Mohammed or the joys of Kashmir:

> "What fortunate people we are!
> We, of all Indians, live in the Vale of Kashmir,
> The beautiful Vale of Kashmir!"

The Maharajah, that happy repository of most of Kashmir's wealth, was secluded behind the white walls of his immense palace on Dal Lake, playing politics. There were no signs that he was worried about the desperate condition of his people. No doubt he too was keeping up appearances.

So were the few score British who had chosen to remain in Kashmir. In Nedou's Hotel, almost deserted now, eighty-year-old Lady James dressed every evening in black velvet and lace and continued to enjoy her after-dinner cigarette. At the Srinagar Club on the Mall, that last stronghold of Empire, four elderly couples danced on Saturday night to the music of a gramophone. Beside the empty bandstand, an old colonel waved a hand in time to "The Blue Danube," and tapped a reminiscent foot. While the records were being changed by a gloomy Hindu in a yellow turban, the colonel's gray-haired wife came over to us, smiling.

"It's so wonderful to see fresh young blood in the club!" she exclaimed.

On our fourth morning in Kashmir, we walked into the Club for an early beer and heard the news: raiders from the tribal hills of Pakistan had invaded Kashmir and had cut the road to Rawalpindi, the only way out of the state. There was a small airfield at Srinagar, but there were no commercial air flights. The only road to India was a narrow track over a high and dangerous pass. We had planned to return to the plains that day, but it rather looked as if we better wait a day or two until the raiders were chased away.

It seemed, that first day, a comic war, with the emotional impact of a Gilbert and Sullivan operetta. We still didn't feel much like working, and the story seemed unimportant, but dutifully we went to call on the newly-appointed Hindu Prime Minister of Kashmir. He lounged in the sun near a bed of flaming red zinnias and waved his hand airily at talk of the raiders. "A mere two or three hundred," he murmured. "Our brave men of the Maharajah's Army are fighting like lions."

At the Srinagar Club, old Britishers in monocles raised toasts to "His Highness's Troops" and celebrated "V. K. night" when a rumor came in that the raiders had been surrounded and annihilated.

Victory in Kashmir, indeed! That night the raiders captured and wrecked the power station fifty miles from Srinagar, and the city went dark. For the first time we felt a bit uneasy in the lonely darkness of our houseboat, thinking of the tough and ruthless tribesmen we had both seen among the barren crags of the northwest frontier. The next morning we moved to Nedou's Hotel, a great, solid, ugly, and beloved British institution near the Mall and the Club. For the rest of our time in Kashmir, we drank and dined by candlelight.

At noon we began to hear gunfire, and by nightfall it seemed to be coming closer. The town was full of rumors and almost palpable terror. In the white palace on the lake, the Maharajah conferred with a high official from the Indian Ministry of States. Obviously something important was about to happen, but we didn't know what.

The next morning at dawn, while we and most of Srinagar still slept, the Maharajah fled from his palace, taking with him the crown jewels, the Maharani, and a few favorite courtiers. They left, we heard, in a fleet of limousines and were going to try to make it on the dirt road which wound over the Banihal Pass and down into Jammu, where the Maharajah had another palace. They made it all right, but those of us without limousines—which meant almost everyone left in the Vale of Kashmir—felt rather bitter at the desertion.

No sooner had the people of Srinagar discovered that they had, in effect, no maharajah, than they found that all of the government seemed to have disappeared. The news spread that within a day the tribesmen would enter the city. For a few hours there was panic, milling about, bewilderment.

And then, when it seemed that chaos was inevitable, Sheikh Abdullah took over. A Moslem, Sheikh Abdullah had for years been a friend of Nehru and Gandhi and an ardent fighter for Indian independence. For years, also, he had opposed the Maharajah's autocratic rule, and for this he had spent much time in jail. As a man he is simple and direct, sometimes to the point of naïveté, and his eyes are as friendly as those of a gay child. Like a child he refuses to hate other religions—a virtue, but not always considered so by his co-religionists.

And yet they followed him. Through the city that afternoon, bands of schoolboys and college students marched in singing groups, reassuring the citizens, telling them that Sheikh Abdullah, the Lion of Kashmir, had taken over the government and would protect them. Later in the day, at a great outdoor meeting, the Sheikh told them so himself.

But the raiders kept coming, heading for the rich plum of Srinagar. Where were the Maharajah's troops, those brave lions?

Gone, evidently, for now we were beginning to hear gunfire over the low hills just outside the city. The incredible, the sacking and looting and firing of this gentle city, seemed about to take place.

The next day officially started all the trouble. And now, with the mind clouded by hindsight, how hard it is to remember *exactly* how we felt! Only later, months later, did the probing political questions swarm: "Did Pakistan really support the invasion?" "Why did Mountbatten think Kashmir's accession to India was a necessary preliminary to India's sending troops to fight off the invaders?" "Had all of this been planned weeks before?" Now I brood over these questions, but not then, not that day. All we knew then was what we saw or heard directly.

We woke to the sound of close gunfire. It was a blue-and-gold-and-scarlet day, like all the others. Roses were blooming in the hotel garden. There was kippered herring for breakfast. Someone told us the raiders were only five miles away. I was frightened, but not terribly. Bad things happen to other people, not to oneself.

Then the news came, first through the bazaar and into the servants' quarters, and then to us: Kashmir had acceded to India; Indian troops had flown in at sunrise and were already in the field, fighting off the invaders.

All day while we worked, talked, and questioned, we heard machine-gun fire; that night in Nedou's bar we learned from Indian officers that the tribesmen were only four and a half miles from the airfield when the Sikh troops landed. Another hour or two and they would have been in Srinagar, have held the airfield. But now, evidently, everything was fine, and the danger was gone. We wrote cheerful stories, and the pilots took them back to Delhi for us.

But it wasn't that easy. As the days went by we realized that the tribesmen were not the disorganized rabble of fanatics we had first thought. They had howitzers and machine guns; they fought back; they kept coming. The Indian troops were fighting valiantly, but Srinagar was still endangered.

Every night the Club was full of elderly Britishers who had come in from outlying houseboats to hear the news. None of them seemed very worried.

"If the tribesemen enter the city," an ex-general's wife assured me, "we shall simply all collect at Nedou's and run up the Union Jack. No one would *dare* to attack us then!"

Eric and I were not so sure. And we felt much happier when one morning the Royal Air Force flew in a flock of rescue planes. A meeting was called that afternoon on the Club verandah, and about seventy-five Britishers showed up to listen to a stern young Major describe plans for the evacuation of the Europeans. The situation, he warned us, was very serious. Indian troops had been pushed back, and once again the tribesmen were only a few miles outside the town. They might arrive in Srinagar in a day or so. His Majesty's government urged all British subjects to leave at dawn tomorrow on the R. A. F. planes. His Majesty's government could not be responsible for their lives if they remained in Kashmir. Were there any questions?

"I presume we will be permitted to take our dogs?" asked a gouty old gentleman in tweeds. He was applauded by a murmur of anxiety from the audience.

"R. A. F. regulations forbid the transport of animals on planes," said the young Major firmly. "There can be no exception made in this case."

"Outrageous!" thundered the old gentleman, pounding his cane on the verandah planks.

"I won't go if my dog can't go too!" shouted a middle-aged lady with a dachshund clasped in her arms.

The Major fled, and the meeting broke up in disorder. There was talk of protest to the government, outrage, inhumanity to animals, the dastardly behavior of His Majesty's government in deliberately jeopardizing the lives of British citizens by not allowing them to take their dogs on the planes. One stalwart young Amazon offered to take fifteen dogs in her station wagon and to try to make it over the trail across the Banihal pass. The offer was eagerly accepted, and she later made the trip successfully with sixteen dogs, one of whom was a bitch in heat. "It was a bit of a strain," she told me when we finally met again in Delhi.

But the middle-aged lady and her husband decided to stay with their dachshund and move their houseboat to a far reach of the lake where they hoped the tribesmen would not penetrate.

"We'll be all right as long as we have enough rice and enough blankets," she said cheerfully. "We really couldn't leave our dog, you know."

After a night exploding with the sound of gunfire, most of the Britishers changed their minds, and so did we. I have never cared much for front-line corresponding, which seems to me, like poker, to be one of the few exclusive provinces of men; I should not care for it at all when there wasn't even a front-line and when the "enemy" was a mob of half-crazed primitive tribesmen who had never heard of the press, let alone the sanctity of the press. Eric agreed with me: as correspondents we wanted to stay; as sensible human beings we knew that we better get out while we could. Who knew whether the Indian troops could hold against ten thousand zealous tribesmen? Who knew whether there would ever be any more troops? Or when?

At dawn we joggled out to the airport in an old bus full of disconsolate Britishers and bulging bedding rolls. In the cold wind of sunrise we stood on the field and listened to the sound of machine-gun fire. It seemed very close. And who knew anything about the Indians as fighters—then?

Those R. A. F. planes warming up looked mighty reassuring, and with a sigh of relief we stowed our bedding rolls and typewriters in the belly of one of the planes and stood by with the Britishers for the order to climb aboard.

When the first plane appeared in the sky to the south we thought it was another R. A. F. rescue plane. But then there were more—and more. And as the first plane circled and landed, we saw that it carried the colors of India.

From one of the planes came Unni Nayar, our good friend who

was then a press officer for the Indian Army. He was twinkling with excitement.

"You can't leave now!" he exclaimed, when we told him we were just about to take off with the R. A. F. "Lots of soldiers, lots of good stories, lots of fun!"

Eric and I looked at each other and grinned. We hadn't wanted to leave Kashmir anyway. We ran to the British plane, which was just closing up before taking off, and pulled out our bedding rolls and typewriters.

Ah, those were exciting days, those weeks before we knew what a tangled and impossible issue Kashmir was to become. The future, we thought, would be simple. The Maharajah had acceded to India, but Nehru and Sheikh Abdullah had promised a plebiscite after Kashmir was peaceful again. There was no doubt in our minds that the vote would go to Pakistan, but at that time there seemed a clear distinction between the wild tribesmen—inspired half by religious frenzy and half by greed for loot—and the established nation of Pakistan. The presence of the Indian army seemed only temporary and highly desirable.

Kashmir was beautiful with autumn, and we were the only correspondents on the spot; Bill Sydney-Smith of the London *Daily Express* had managed to get himself captured by the tribesmen, and the Indian Air Force was far too busy transporting troops to bring up any of the newspaper boys clamoring in Delhi. The telegraph lines had of course been cut long ago, so we filed our stories with the friendly Air Force pilots in Nedou's bar. Not one of them ever failed to deliver our copy to the telegraph office in New Delhi after his flight back to home base.

We have come back to Kashmir many times since then, but it has never been quite the same again. We have seen the wild iris flowering over the meadows of spring, the fields of yellow mustard stretching beneath the blue sky; the gardens of Shalimar and the even more beautiful gardens of Nishat Bagh are timeless dreams of marble arches and green lawns; the kingfishers still dash above the lotus blossoms. But war has come, and an uneasy cease-fire; there has been clever bickering in the United Nations to which there seems no end. And between the proud rancors of nations, the humanity of the living Kashmiri has been bitterly crushed.

Once, in winter, we traveled to Pakistan and went up to see the war from the other side. We drove all day by jeep through wild country, visited hospitals and army camps, talked to the "cabinet officers" of Azad, or Free, Kashmir, slept in front of a fire in an old dak bungalow full of mysterious officers.

In the morning the ground was white with frost; the wind was high and icy. An old man and two children were huddled near the fire, shaking so with cold they could hardly hold the mugs of tea they had been given. All of them were in rags, and the two little girls, about three and five years old, were barefoot.

"They are the only ones left of my family," the old man said. "The others have died, for we have been wandering ten months in these mountains. Once I had a farm, and I was well-to-do and proud. Then the war came, and we had to leave our home. Now we are beggars."

"Do you know why the war came?" I asked.

"No, I do not know at all," said the old man. "But I am a very uneducated man, and I am not supposed to understand these things." He looked apologetically at the army officers who stood about in their warm uniforms, staring at him.

"Please forgive me," the old man said.

These are my present memories of Kashmir, as I lie on the sundeck of a houseboat in this year of uneasy truce, remembering. It all looks the same, the shimmering lake and the lotus leaves; it all sounds the same, the high, sad, love songs and the buzz of dragonflies. But it is not the same.

This year our houseboat is the *Teal*, a snug little boat ornamented on the outside with curlicue carving, on the inside with dark wood paneling. The living room, at the front of the boat facing out into the water, contains the usual carpets, easy chairs (with sagging springs), and coffee tables, and some mediocre water-colors of Kashmir executed by the old English lady who once owned the boat and who left most of her belongings to Ahmed Sher, the present owner, when she died. There is also a large old-fashioned, wood-burning stove which fortunately we do not need at this time of year.

Beyond the living room is the dining room, very correct with a polished oval table and a sideboard complete with neatly arrayed silver and glassware. The principal features, however, are a massive orange-silk and green-beaded lamp hanging directly over the table, and on one wall an enormous 1910 photograph of the deceased English lady, which we at first mistook for a picture of Lily Langtry.

Down one side of the boat runs a narrow corridor, and off it are three bedrooms, each containing a bed and dresser. Each bedroom has its own bathroom with a commode and an enamel basin and pitcher. Every evening a large tin tub is hauled into the room and filled with a few inches of lukewarm water. Sometimes one feels that a Kashmir houseboat is a combination of a hunting lodge and the Petit Trianon; in the bathrooms it seems more like a child's tree house.

For a few rupees, we found, we could have the boat moved to wherever we wanted to go. When we hired it, the boat was moored on the noisy river, so we decided to have it moved to the quiet waters of Dal Lake. The trip was instructive, for it showed us that in the city at least, nothing has changed very much in Kashmir.

While four men poled the heavy boat, the sahib and the *memsahib* (us) lounged at ease in deck chairs on the flat roof, drinking gin and lime juice, and waving to children along the shore. Like little mountain goats, the children leapt among the clay banks, salaaming and crying the traditional greeting of the children of Kashmir: "Salaam, salaam! We are your servants! Salaam, salaam!" Below us, on the fore and aft porches of the houseboat, the polers kept up a rhythmic chant: "*Mohammed! Ei-Ai! Mohammed! Allah! Ei-Ai! Allah! Secunder! Ei-Ai! Secunder!*"

Secunder is Alexander the Great, whom all Kashmiris seem to think of as great grandfather.

We came in sight of the huge white palace which the Maharajah had built for himself and abandoned at the moment when his people most deeply needed his presence; opposite it, the riverside was lined with the rotting tenements of his subjects. As we passed along the narrow canal leading to Dal Lake, we looked directly into the nightmarish little shanties empty of everything except haggard women in gray rags and great silver earrings, and dozens of thin babies.

But moored at last at Gagribal Point, the electricity connected to the shore, and only a view of lake and mountains before us, we were isolated from the misery of Kashmir, as the white sahibs have always been, as we always are when we come here. And now we live in the usual luxury of houseboat life, cared for by Ahmed Sher and his scurrying sons.

Ahmed Sher means "Ahmed the Tiger," but there is nothing very tigerish about Ahmed these days. A meek little man, he is beaten down by the adversities of Kashmir, and lives now on his memories of the days when the good English lady was alive and life was secure. He showed us his bank book: five years ago he had nine thousand rupees or about three thousand dollars on deposit; today he has just eighteen rupees, or six dollars. He shrugged his shoulders helplessly when we asked him what he was going to do.

"My father was a houseboatman," he said. "I am a houseboatman. I shall teach the business to my sons also, for I know nothing else to teach them."

This year, as before, we follow the usual pursuits. We sunbathe on the roof. We read old copies of Kipling from the houseboat library. We picnic in the gardens of Shalimar or Nishat Bagh, traveling there in the little gondolas called *shikaras*. When we leave the gardens, the boatmen still carry our baskets and blankets, the gardeners still present us (for the expected few annas) with great bunches of flowers and garlands of marigolds.

This time, as always before, the houseboat is visited daily by anxious tradesmen, their *shikaras* piled high with wares which they haul into the living-room or up on the roof and spread out to show us. An old man, his dyed red beard indicating that he has made the pilgrimage to Mecca, smooths a white cloth over the carpet and lays upon it a display of uncut jewels, Tibetan jade, and Chinese curios. None of them is very good, and he nods understandingly when we do not buy. "Nobody comes any more to bring us good things to sell," he says, "and nobody buys any more." He goes quietly away.

A young man comes to sell embroidered scarves, but his mind is not on his selling. He wants to talk politics. Indifferently he accepts our price for an antique paisley, climbs back into his *shikara*, and paddles furiously back to town, where a public meeting is scheduled.

Yes, they all want to talk politics. But Kashmir is virtually a police state now, and secret agents are everywhere. The voice must be lowered, the words quickly spoken: "We want to join Pakistan . . . everyone wants to join Pakistan!" But these are a special class, these men who have always lived on the foolish bounty of foreign tourists. We must look farther, question more deeply, travel more widely, before we can make up our minds on the Kashmir Question.

Srinagar ❀ *June 18*

One of the reasons Eric and I came up to Kashmir this time was that we hoped to get permission to visit Ladakh, the Easternmost part of Kashmir, which some people still call "Western Tibet."

Before the cold war and the Kashmir war, there was no particular news excuse for going to Ladakh; now there is. In 1948 Pakistan soldiers came within eight miles of Leh, the capital, and were only prevented from capturing it by the arrival of a stronger force of Indian soldiers who had marched over the fifteen-thousand-foot passes to the south. Subsequently, flyers of the Indian air force pioneered an air route through the mountains, cutting the traveling time between Srinagar and Leh from two weeks to one hour and ten minutes. Now the Indian army, aided by a locally recruited militia, maintains a firm watch over the cease-fire line to the north and the passes to Communist China. The government of India seems well aware of the strategic importance of Ladakh —and not solely because of its proximity to Pakistan. All of which makes it well worth visiting, added to the fact that it is always interesting to find out how far the twentieth century has penetrated into Central Asia.

Naturally, we've been having the usual troubles. In Delhi we applied to the States Ministry of the Central Government for permission to go to Ladakh, since there is no way to get there except in an Indian air force plane. We were told to ask for permission from the Kashmir government. We did. Days passed. Up here we were told to apply to the air force in Delhi. We wrote Delhi. Since then we have heard nothing.

Srinagar ❀ *June 19*

Today, an Indian Colonel from the air force arrived at our houseboat and informed us that permission had arrived for Eric to visit Ladakh. Not for me.

"It is a very difficult trip for a lady," he explained blandly. "Besides, everyone knows that your husband probably writes your stories for you."

Srinagar ❀ *June 20*

Eric left for Ladakh at dawn. I sat up on the roof of the houseboat, cogitating while I watched golden orioles flit through the fig trees on the river bank. Finally I went downstairs and drafted a telegram protesting Indian favoritism to British correspondents and discrimination against American correspondents in the matter of travel to Ladakh. This afternoon I sent copies to Prime Minister Nehru, Madame Pandit, the United Nations, Krishna Menon, the American Ambassador in New Delhi, the Secretary of State in Washington, the head of the Indian Air Force, the Secretary of the Indian States Ministry, and the chief of the Kashmir government.

It will be interesting to see what happens, if anything.

Srinagar ❀ June 21

Today the Air Force Colonel arrived at the houseboat, looking a little crestfallen.

"It seems there was a mistake somewhere," he said. "Permission has just arrived for you to fly to Ladakh immediately after your husband returns tomorrow. Unfortunately, there is only room for one visitor at a time."

Which telegram, I wonder, bore the fruit? Probably the one to Nehru.

Leh, Ladakh, Kashmir ❀ June 25

Without doubt, it was one of the most terrifying flights I've ever made. Landing in Hong Kong in a fog is bad. The flight to Gilgit last year, when I really felt the plane would have to turn sideways and fly on its wing-tips in order to get between the mountains, was a heart-in-mouther. But this one belongs with the worst of them. We flew at twenty thousand feet in an unpressurized plane, using oxygen masks, and still we had to hedge-hop over rocky ridges, seemingly missing them by only about ten inches! All about were the great peaks of the Karakorum Range; it seemed as if I could have leaned from the plane wings and touched the mountains on either side.

We landed, amid an uproar of monstrous mountains, on a rocky plateau beside the black waters of the Indus River. Outside the plane, the first sign of civilization I saw was a signpost: "China 190 miles. Tibet 200 miles. Russia 600 miles. India 400 miles." Considering that the Indian Army was in control of Leh, and that India firmly intended to hang on to Kashmir, that last bit showed a nice sense of delicacy, I thought.

I am staying at the former British Residency, the guest of the Indian armed forces. It is a typical old Residency with spacious rooms, heavy Victorian furniture, and a lovely view over gardens, the flat roofs of the houses of Leh, the sweep of the plateau down to the Indus, and the great mountains beyond. My hosts are officers and gentlemen and have already put me in touch with all kinds of odd and interesting people and all kinds of odd and interesting Ladakhi lore. And also, with considerable military information which, alas, I am not allowed to use.

After Tibet, Ladakh is the best place to study demons and other interesting matters at first hand, for the Ladakhis are Tibetan in race, religion, custom, and dress, although their country has for more than a century been part of Kashmir and of India. I have picked up more exotic information here in the last two days than I would ever have thought possible.

Yak tails, for instance, make the best Santa Claus beards in the world, and are exported from Ladakh for that purpose. A few yak hairs tied across the eyes make very effective sun glasses.

Also, if you breed a yak and a cow, you will get a dzo, which is a beast somewhat like a St. Bernard, only larger and considerably more useful in farming.

Avalanches, landslides and high winds, as well as chilblains and soured wine are all caused by demons. One of the many gods worshipped here is named Omamaranidziwanteyesawhaa.

Yesterday I visited a lamasary, or *gompa* as it is called here, and for the first time I really understood what that Scottish missionary in Kalimpong had been talking about: I felt the presence of demons. Partly it was the isolation, I suppose—the great rocky pile of buildings atop a little mountain eight miles out on the plain. And the climb, scrambling like a mountain goat up crazy flights of stepping stones. And the shadowed temple rooms, their walls covered with murals of bug-eyed demons performing outrageous tortures. And the lamas chanting their prayers and staring at us with opaque eyes. And finally, in the darkness behind a hidden shrine, a great tub of black oil silkily lighted by one candle. "The eye of God," whispered our lama guide. But I thought it looked like the eye of the devil himself.

Atop one battlement, in a bare and airy room, we found a young artist kneeling on the floor and painting tankas, the Tibetan prayer banners. They were charming—full of soft little animals and sprays of flowers, more Chinese than Tibetan. "I only like to paint the beautiful things, the things the Buddha loved," he explained. "I am very happy up here, painting and thinking. I do not think of demons at all."

Aside from the young artist, everything and everybody else we saw made me shudder. I think I like the Ladakhi people better than I do their powerful lamas.

To anyone who has never been in Tibet, Ladakh seems authentically Tibetan. Down the sandy Leh valley blow winds that feel as if they had slipped off the shoulders of Everest. On some days there is a sixty-degree difference in the temperatures of sunshine and shadow. The Ladakh plateau is at eleven thousand feet and there is said to be one third less oxygen in the air in Leh than in the plains of India. Judging from the way I panted up those *gompa* steps I can well imagine that this is true.

Until the air force pioneered that awful flight, it took a lot of time and a considerable amount of climbing ability to reach Ladakh. This is probably why very few people, except traders from China and Tibet whose business required the exertion, made the trip, and why Ladakhis have been able to continue roughly the same life they were leading 1,000 years ago, supremely confident that the camel represents the latest development in locomotion. When the first airplane arrived they tried to feed it hay.

Most of the people wear Tibetan clothes: gray, red, or black robes, worsted boots with turned-up toes, and velvet caps with turned-up ear flaps. Many of the women wear a gaudy headdress of turquoises and coral which must weigh at least eight pounds. They also wear filthy goatskin capes turned inside out. A friendly, cheerful people, men and women greet each other and any foreigner they may meet with a happy-sounding *"Julay!"* This can mean "Good Morning," "Good Evening," "Goodbye," "Thank you," "I've had enough," and probably many other things.

Ladakh is a woman's country, for here, as in parts of Tibet, polyandry is practiced by Buddhists, apparently in an unconscious effort to keep down the birthrate. When a girl marries, she takes on the eldest son of a household, and also the next two brothers, if he has any. A fourth brother is out of luck, and either becomes a lama, a landless laborer, or a *"magpa."* A *magpa*, whose lot is not a happy one, is married to a woman of property, but subject to dismissal without notice at any time.

Polyandry and polygamy meet in Ladakh, as about a third of the population are followers of Mahomet, who permitted a man to marry four wives. Intermarriage sometimes takes place, and as neither side likes the other's ideas on marriage, the tendency is toward monogamy. Polyandry was officially banned some eight years ago, but this would be news to most villagers.

Ladakhi villagers live in houses of mud and stone with flat roofs of peeled poplar trunks covered with more mud and stone. Their food is mostly barley and a barley wine called chang. They begin taking chang before breakfast, and keep on nipping at it all day, which may possibly account for their cheerful reputation.

Right now, late spring ploughing is going on in the fields. One brother-husband walks in front of the two dzos which pull the plough, apparently to encourage the beasts. A second brother-husband stands by as relief, sipping chang. The third wrestles with the wooden plough and chants instructions to the dzos: *"A leuu, yong do! Yong do! Eh chin lien, Hey leeay! Ah! Ah!"*

The wife walks behind, sowing the barley seeds from a bag tied to her waist. Last of all, smoothing the ground over the seeds, come the children, all of whom are considered offspring of the eldest brother.

Ladakhis always try to plough their fields and walk around all obstacles clockwise. This is an ancient superstition derived, it is thought, from the direction the sun seems to move around the earth. One of the Indian officers reminded me that the custom still lingers in Europe and England, where wine is always passed clockwise around a table.

Ladakhis still believe the old folk tale, first recorded or invented by Herodotus, about the ants as big as men who dig gold from the ground. They also believe that donkeys walk faster at night because they think the sky is going to fall on them.

Great believers in mechanical devices to ward off evil, Ladakhis daub their houses with red paint to keep the demons away and tie prayer flags to their roofs to waft a prayer over their heads with every flap of the flag in the wind. The roads and the fields are bordered with tumbled stone walls, each stone carved with the mystic words of Tibetan Buddhism: *"Om Mani Padme Hum"*— "Oh God, Thou Jewel in the Lotus." Carving these stones is a favorite spare-time occupation, for it is a sign of devotion much favored by the gods. I long to take one home with me, but I am warned by the Christian missionaries here that it is very bad luck indeed to take a stone. It must be given as a present.

I have seen a lot of the missionaries and have come to admire them and sympathize with them. One may doubt the wisdom of their being here at all, but one cannot doubt their courage or their faith.

About one hundred years ago, Moravian missionaries from Germany came to this part of the world, hoping to go to Outer Mongolia, either through Russia or Tibet and China. But then, as now, these countries were closed to them, and they settled first in northern India and in 1885 in Leh. This was as close as they could get to the borders of China, and what they still hope is the ultimate destination.

The Moravian mission over the years became one of the odd features of Ladakh, first under a series of German missionaries, and now under the Rev. Mr. Norman Driver, of Yorkshire, England, and his wife, Dr. Mary Driver. Mr. Driver has been in Ladakh for seventeen years, which he thinks of as nothing, since he came here for a forty-year term.

After almost seventy years of labor, the mission can now count one hundred and twenty converts among Ladakh's two hundred thousand population. Considering the staunch adherence to Buddhism in Ladakh, this is thought to be quite a respectable figure. To a people convinced that the demons to be met around every corner can only be propitiated by a hierarchy of lamas armed with an elaborate paraphernalia of bells, gongs, drums, and banners, the Moravian beliefs and practices are unappealingly simple.

The Wednesday afternoon prayer service which I attended was the antithesis of the bell-jangling, cymbal-clanging ceremonies of the lamasaries. About eight men and eight women, the bare-headed men in Chinese-style dark gowns, the women in peaked velvet caps, ankle-length robes, and goatskin capes, filed quietly into the whitewashed little building which is their church.

The square room inside was empty, save for brilliant Tibetan rugs on the reed floor, a harmonium, and a small desk with a bare wooden cross on the wall behind it.

The men seated themselves on the left, the women on the right, and the service opened with a German hymn, translated into Tibetan. Then Mr. Driver read in Tibetan from the Bible, and delivered in a soft voice a short sermon on "God's Universal Presence."

When the time came for general prayer, the women threw themselves forward on the rugs; as they did so the goatskin capes slipped almost over their heads. The men knelt and bowed deeply. After the prayer ended, two men in the audience spoke in turn on the subject of the sermon, their voices so gentle it was difficult even in the small room to catch the rhythmic Tibetan syllables. Then the Lord's Prayer, a final German hymn, and everyone rose and slipped away smiling into the noisy bazaar outside.

There are now eighty Ladakh Christians in Leh and some forty in outlying areas. A few years ago there were more, but some were lost when the lamas organized a boycott against the Christians in retaliation for what they considered unjustified expansion of Christian activities in the villages. For a year no one would sell milk or other food to any Christian; the Driver child acquired rickets during this period, and the Drivers themselves various other ailments. Eventually the boycott was called off as a failure.

Recently there have been some organized demonstrations against Ladakhi members of the Christian community who have worked out and are now advocating a system of simplified spelling for the very difficult Tibetan language. The lamas claim that if this system is adopted they will have to re-write the "A" and the "N" in "Om Mani Padme Hum"—and this, of course, is unthinkable.

Once again, I realize forcefully that there are many passionate issues in Asia which have nothing in the world to do with "communist instigation." How often must I learn this lesson?

By and large, however, relations between the Buddhists and the Christians are friendly. The dispensary and hospital operated by Dr. Mary Driver is well patronized, handling about two hundred and fifty patients a month in summer, and five hundred a month in the winter season when people have time to be sick. Because the mission is desperately short of funds, a small fee is charged for medicines and operations: about four cents for any kind of medicine and two dollars for a cataract operation.

Their greatest material achievement, the missionaries feel, has been the introduction of three new things to Ladakh: knitting, which has provided the women with a profitable pastime; potatoes, which were unknown and which are now widely cultivated; and a German method of preserving vegetables for the winter in underground holes, which has vastly increased Ladakhi consumption of vegetables.

Leh, Ladakh, Kashmir ❧ June 26

The missionaries introduced me to Mr. Gergen, forest officer for Ladakh and a fellow Christian. Today Mr. Gergen asked me to tea. His house was on the outskirts of town; stony paths meandered there through sloping fields where farmers in pointed caps sang to the sturdy dzos that pulled the wooden ploughs.

"Gergan Sahib?" I called to one of them inquiringly, although I had little hope he would understand the Indian word "Sahib." But he grinned and waved at a nearby, flat-roofed house, where a flowering apricot tree lifted pink branches above courtyard walls.

At this moment Mr. Gergan, a gentleman of jovial size and disposition, wearing the usual Chinese-style robe and an unusual gray felt hat, popped beaming from the courtyard door and escorted me into the house.

Against one wall of the living-room was a long, low window looking out over the great sweep of the sandy Leh Valley, with the Indus River a silver snake in the distance, the great peaks soaring above it. There was no furniture in the room save piles of brilliant Tibetan rugs on which we sat, some low tables painted in bright Chinese designs, and a bookcase full of English books on Buddhism, Christianity, agriculture, and Mongol history.

The walls were covered with photographs and chromos; one of them showed a young man in the uniform of World War I, kneeling with a girl in a great glow of ethereal light. Next to it was a faded photograph of a dignified old gentleman in a cutaway coat, Mr. Gergan's father.

"My grandfather was a Buddhist," said Mr. Gergan as he settled comfortably into the soft rugs. "But when he died he left his small son to the Christians to be educated, with a message that he had always wanted to become a Christian, but had not dared.

"That son, who became my father, also became the first Ladakhi minister of the Moravian Mission here in Leh. He was a great scholar and among other activities collected one thousand

Tibetan proverbs. Tibetans—and we Ladakhis call ourselves Tibetian although we are Indian citizens—always talk in proverbs."

Mr. Gergan patted his stomach and laughed. "One appropriate proverb is: 'Indiscretion in eating produces all belly above the knees' " he said. "Another I like is: 'The pattern of the tiger is on the outside, and that of a man on the inside.' "

A servant came into the room and placed before us two jade cups, each set in a silver saucer and covered with a silver lid. He lifted the lids and from a wood and brass pot poured an odd-smelling, cocoa-colored liquid.

"Ladakh tea," said Mr. Gergan happily. "If you were English, I would probably serve you regular English tea, but as you are American, I thought you might be interested in our local customs."

Ladakh tea, he explained, is made by boiling black tea for three or four hours with a teaspoonful of soda, adding a spoonful of yak butter, salt and milk to taste, and churning the mixture until smooth. The only polite way to stop a servant from pouring more tea after each sip is to gulp down an entire cupful and put the cup down empty. It wasn't too bad; at least I managed to get down a cupful.

"The English have taught us much," continued Mr. Gergan. "I, for instance, studied at an English-taught school in Srinagar, and there I learned many useful matters, such as how to be a forest officer in this barren land of mine where only the application of science to our problems can imrpove the lot of our people.

"I have also found consolation through my reading of English history. For instance, a century ago English farmers opposed the steam engine because, they said, it frightened their horses and ruined the crops. We have the same kind of problem here— peasants who resist progress because they think it will anger the demons. But remembering the English, I go ahead with our plans."

Mr. Gergan's sister, an apricot-skinned young matron with gay black eyes, came into the room to meet me. Obviously, she was dressed in Sunday finery—a robe of black with a green sash, pink silk trousers and gold pointed shoes, a cape bordered in gold embroidery, and a stupendous *perak*, or Ladakhi hat. The *perak*, which Mr. Gergan claimed was the finest in the country, was a flat wide band extending from the forehead to the middle of the back, covered thickly with turquoises and coral. Intricate arrangements of false pigtails were attached to it, and from each side behind the ears jutted wings of black lambskin.

The sister spoke no English, but in compensation (a typical Asian courtesy) she carried a musical instrument called a *damsnyan* or, as Mr. Gergan described it, "a Ladakhi banjo." At her brother's request she began to play a tinkling little tune which sounded like toy horses galloping. After this had gone on for some time, Mr. Gergan waved her away. Smiling and bowing, she departed.

"Now as I was saying," Mr. Gergan resumed, "we must have progress even in this backwater of the world. We border on Tibet, China, and Russia, and that means that sooner or later our people, ignorant as they are, will hear about Communism.

"At the moment the Kashmir government is in the midst of a great program of land redistribution and of agricultural reform. We are taking the land from the big landlords and giving it to the men who till it, and we are beginning to try to help them grow better crops and in general lead a fuller life. This is being done not only because it is right, but because we believe it is the only way to keep our people from listening to the new doctrines from China and Russia."

The servant cleared away the tea cups and brought two little silver bowls, each filled with a pale yellow liquid. For the first time I tasted chang, the local drink. It tasted like the rather sour but pleasant wine amateurs used to turn out from grape arbors in Rockland County.

Mr. Gergan gazed into his chang, and sighed. "I don't know much about this cold war you're having in the West," he meditated. "None of us would like the Communist system here, but we can't quite see why we couldn't learn something about Russian agricultural experiments which might be of benefit to us, or methods of raising mass literacy, without adopting the whole system."

He was surprised and interested to learn that Russian technical experts were also Russian propaganda experts. He shrugged his shoulders and sighed again.

"Well, that's the problem," he said. "Here we are up in the remote highlands of the Himalayas where we have been untouched for centuries by any new ideas. But now there is change all over the world, and news of this is filtering through even our high mountain barricades. And sometimes we don't know how to sort out all this conflicting news."

Mr. Gergan finished his wine and smiled. "We Tibetans have a proverb," he said. " 'The times do not change; it is men who change.' "

Leh, Ladakh, Kashmir ✸ June 27

Today we walked down the road running between the stone walls and the rows of poplar trees, and looked at Leh's three *Yarkand serais,* the stable-inns where the traders from Sinkiang used to stay during their annual visit to Ladakh. But today the big mud-walled courtyards were empty; the Turkis in padded coats and high boots come no more with their yaks and donkeys and camels, their bales of wool and tea. Communist China has closed the borders.

The three-hundred-mile border—still incompletely demarcated —between Sinkiang and Kashmir runs through some of the wildest territory in the world. Most of the mountains are more than fifteen thousand feet high, and some rise to twenty-six thousand feet. The rivers are turbulent, the land barren, the landslides frequent. There are no roads. Yet for more centuries than history can remember, traders have been winding their way along the seven tracks leading from Sinkiang into Kashmir, sometimes traveling for months before they reach the first big Indian or Pakistan bazaar.

For the isolated people of mountain Kashmir, the arrival of the Chinese caravans every spring, with their fat packs and their gossip, was a time of rejoicing; not only did the traders bring goods to buy into villages which are almost self-dependent, but they brought rare and welcome contact with the outside world.

I remember last summer, when Eric and I saw this joy at first hand, we rode on horseback, walked, and stumbled some sixty miles along one of the traders' tracks—a narrow path which winds from Gilgit in northern Kashmir, along the Hunza River, and eventually over the fifteen-thousand-foot Mintaka Pass on into Sinkiang and to Kashgar.

No road from Pakistan led into Gilgit then, and the supplies from the outside world were mostly brought in by airplanes from Peshawar or Rawalpindi, in Pakistan. These goods were barely enough to feed and clothe the local population which, before the Kashmir war, had received supplies from southern Kashmir. But now the north and south were divided between India and Pakistan, and the bazaars were almost empty.

"Never mind," everyone said. "The traders from China will be here in a week or so."

Two days out of Gilgit, on the edge of a rocky cliff, we met the first traders—Moslems from Chinese Turkestan, or as it is now called, Sinkiang. The two men rode ahead on their donkeys, perched high atop bundles of cloth and fur. They both wore quilted blue coats and black caps with fur earflaps; they both bowed to us hand on stomach, Chinese fashion. Behind them rode two women in robes and soft fur boots, their faces modestly covered so that nothing could be seen but their bright, curious eyes.

At the next village, a tiny collection of stone huts in the midst of green fields and blue flax, the people were excited. "The first

traders of the spring just came through!" they said. "Their caravan is following, with many things for us to buy." Already children were running out into the fields to look in vain at the empty
trail zigzagging up the mountainside. (And, oh, how grim it was
to leave those enchanting villages and face the rocky cliffs again,
the trail only a two-foot-wide ledge one thousand feet above the
black and roaring Hunza River!)

The next day, as we rode at sunset into Baltit, the capital of
Hunza, we found the caravan setting up camp on a sandy bank
just below the ruler's palace. Donkeys were still arriving in long
trains; tents were being put up; everywhere there was confusion
and excitement.

"My people spend the winter drinking wine and playing
flutes," said the ruler, "but springtime and the arrival of the
caravans makes a nice change."

The handsome men of Hunza, who sometimes walk sixty miles
to Gilgit for their ration of salt, were already beginning to gather,
to exchange news with the traders, to examine the goods, to bar-
gain. Out of the heavy rug wrappings came bolts of cheap cotton
cloth, some white, some printed with crudely swirling red-and-
green designs. There were furs and boots, blankets and quilted
coats—all crude, all useful, all cheap enough for any peasant to
buy.

"Thank heavens they have come," said the ruler of Hunza,
watching from a terrace. "We don't need much here in Hunza,
but what we need, we need badly."

We walked down and talked to the traders—a difficult job
since everything had to be translated from Turki into Burushaski
(the language of Hunza), then into Urdu, and finally into English. Most of them said they had made the two-month trip from
Kashgar in Sinkiang to Peshawar in Pakistan many times before and expected to do it many times again. From childhood,
they said, they had known no other way of life, and they looked
it. They seemed stolid, quiet people, good business men, utterly
unaffected by the joy their arrival created.

Two days later we left Baltit on our return journey. Fording the first river, we came upon the caravan again, also on its way to Gilgit. The silver bells on the donkeys' necks jangled, animals slipped on the wet stones, whips flashed—and already the men and women from the next village were running down the steep banks to greet the traders.

All along the route we caught up to them, or they to us. Once, just ahead of us, four laden donkeys went off the cliff at a particularly nasty turn, dropping thousands of feet out of sight onto the rocks below. The men shrugged their shoulders and plodded on. The next village was expecting them; there were still plenty of cotton bolts and jade cups to sell.

This spring the villagers of the Himalayas and the High Karakorum are watching the trails again, listening for the jingle of the caravan bells. But the borders are closed, and the men with quilted coats and pointed caps, fat packs and gossip will not come this year, or for many years. Perhaps they will never come again.

The people of Ladakh, who provided ponies, porters, and other services to the caravans and derived a large part of their incomes from these activities, would have been in a hard way when the caravans stopped had it not been for the arrival of the Indian Army, which requires almost identical services. As long as the army is here, which may be a very long time indeed, the people of Leh will not starve. But this, of course, is a short-term help; for the long-term future they are now beginning to count on the program of land reform which the Kashmir government started here soon after the Army arrived.

Under the maharajahs of Kashmir, the Ladakhis had never heard the word "reform." For centuries they had been contented to pay half their crops to landlords or monasteries, to practice agriculture by ancient methods, to grow up and let their sons grow up illiterate because there were no schools. No one had bothered to tell them about the invention of the wheel, other than the prayer wheel. (In Hunza we met a young man who proudly showed us an invention of his own: it was a water wheel and could be used, he explained, to grind wheat to make flour; he wondered if the Western world would be interested in his invention.) This was exactly the kind of human soil which might have proved fertile to Communist agitators, had there been any.

Today the Ladakhis are slowly beginning to discover that their old way of life is not immutable. The land reform program, which is also being carried out elsewhere in Indian-held Kashmir, is going forward: of the thirty thousand acres of cultivated land in the districts around Leh, nine thousand acres formerly held by big landlords have been confiscated (with compensation to the landlords) and are being transferred to their tenant-cultivators.

A new high school has been opened in Leh, and other schools are planned, in most of which textbooks based on American theories of progressive education will be used. Over fifty thousand fuel trees have been planted and will eventually provide a substitute for the animal manure now used for fuel instead of land fertilization.

The greatest stumbling block in the way of progress is the reactionary hold of the lamas on the peasants. The monasteries, or *gompas*, own thousands of acres of land, and by and large extort exorbitant rents from their tenants. Yet so strong is the force of Buddhism among the people that the government has not yet dared to redistribute these monastic lands.

One indication that the lands must eventually be transferred is the slowly growing unrest among the *gompa* tenants, who complain that they alone are forced to support the thousands of lamas, while their brothers, who happen to be landlord-tenants, are free. In at least one case *gompa*-villagers petitioned the government for distribution among them of the *gompa* lands—a brave move for people who believe that any lama can call down a million raging demons upon their homes. For the lamas, I think, the writing as well as the demon-murals are on the wall.

It is here in Ladakh that I have understood for the first time what some people mean when they say a plebiscite in Kashmir on accession to India or Pakistan would be both infeasible and a farce. The land is primitive, and most of the people live in craggy, inaccessible villages, knowing nothing of the world beyond the Dalai Lama in Tibet. How can they know the issues involved; how could they vote intelligently? And in any case, the vote would be directed by the lamas.

Much as they dislike the progressive measures of the present government, the lamas would still probably prefer to take their chances with India than to go to Pakistan, which they fear might suppress them altogether. Their great dream has always been reunion with Tibet, but this dream, like the inaccessibility of Ladakh, seems to belong to the past rather than the future. With the Communists now in Tibet, it seems just as well for the lamas and the Ladakhis that the dream is unlikely of fulfillment.

Srinagar, Kashmir ❀ *June 28*

Just as I was climbing up the ladder and into the plane for the ghastly trip to Srinagar, a jeep came tearing over the pebbly plateau. Bouncing in it, breathless and beaming, were the missionaries. They had come to say good-by and to bring me a *mani* stone, which must never be taken but only given as a present. It is a beautiful stone, marvelously carved. Like the missionaries, I have been affected by the spell of Ladakh: I half believe that the stone has the magic to ward off demons.

Yet already the spell is fading. This is the sadness of traveling —that people, whose faces, problems, and intensities are very real to you while you are with them, lose some of their reality when you are away from them. There are two hundred thousand men, women, and children breathing, sweating, working, loving, crying, and dreaming among those far-off mountains, but will I really believe this a month from now, or a year from now—back in America?

Srinagar, Kashmir ✿ June 29

This evening, after a splendid wild-duck dinner to celebrate my return, Ahmed Sher told us a story. It is a true tale, he
insisted as we lounged in deck chairs on the houseboat roof and
Ahmed Sher squatted by our side. It is also a modern legend
of Kashmir.

Once upon a time there lived a little old lady in the City of
Pasadena in the State of California in the country of the United
States.

Now this little old lady, so the story goes, lived in the City of
Pasadena alone, except for a son who was very preoccupied with
business. So the old lady, growing lonely, did what every southern
Californian and every Kashmiri considers right and proper:
she consulted a fortune-telling palmist.

"You will never be happy," the palmist told her, "until you
travel. You must go far, very far. You must go all the way to the
other side of the world."

So the old lady packed her bags, said farewell to her son, and
set off. She traveled to many countries, but she was still lonely.
When she came to Bombay in the land of India, she decided it
was time to consult another palmist, and she found one—an
old man with a long white beard and a purple turban.

"You must travel to the North," he said, "and there you will
find a land where your heart will be at peace. And in that land
two men will approach you and ask to be your servant. The first
will be an evil man; the second will become your son."

The old lady took a train, and then a bus, and so after many
days of travel came at last to a hotel in Srinagar, in the beautiful
Vale of Kashmir. She looked about her, at the quiet waters of
Dal Lake and at the mountains rising above, and knew that her
heart was at peace. Then she walked out onto the road beside the
lake.

The first person she met was a tall and handsome Kashmiri wrapped in a gray blanket and wearing a pink-and-gold cap. He salaamed.

"I would be a very good servant for *Mem-sahib*," he said. But the old lady remembered what the palmist in Bombay had told her and refused his services. And this was a very good thing, so the legend goes, for although Gulum Mohammed was tall and strong, he was indeed a "badmash"—a very wicked young man.

A little farther down the road she met another young man, smaller, wrapped in rags, and very unhappy. There were, in fact, tears on his cheeks. This was Samdhu.

Now Samdhu was the son of Amdhu, the venerable owner of the houseboat *Pigeon*, one of the prettiest and soundest of all the carved teakwood houseboats in Srinagar. But business was not always good, Amdhu had many children to feed, and his fifth son, Samdhu, was no help. For Samdhu was a gay young man who would much rather sing Kashmiri love songs and lie on the river's edge in the sun than help his father earn an honest living.

That very morning, driven to fury by his son's laziness, old Amdhu had disowned Samdhu for life and cast him forth from the houseboat. And now here was Samdhu, with tears on his cheeks, without a pice or an anna in his pockets, trailing down the road.

Coming toward him slowly, he saw a plump old white lady, with tight gray curls and a worn black purse dangling from her arm. Samdhu, who could usually judge immediately how much the pocketbooks of white *Mem-sahibs* held, was at a loss in this case, but he was desperate.

"*Mem-sahib*, I would be a very good servant for you," he said tentatively. The old lady looked at him sharply, then smiled.

"I will try you," she said. "First of all, we will go for a row on the river. Get me a boat."

Samdhu had no boat, but he hired the cheapest one he could find, on account. It was a leaking hulk which had to be bailed between every stroke of the paddle, but the old lady seemed pleased and sat erectly on the creaking thwarts during the tour, gazing with interest at the scenery and, occasionally, at Samdhu.

"Now Samdhu," she said when they returned to her hotel, "I want you to build me a nice little houseboat and to serve me on it as my son. How much will it cost?"

Samdhu was amazed, but he managed to retain his composure. In the interests of a long-term investment he quoted her an honest price, and the old lady produced enough rupees from her pocketbook to build the boat. And so it was done, and it was christened the *Pasadena*, and a very pretty little boat it was, and still is.

For two years the little old lady lived modestly on her boat, and Samdhu served her faithfully and honestly, only begging off now and then to sing a Kashmiri love song or lie on the river's edge in the sun. He had long since decided that she was a very nice old lady indeed, who had probably spent most of her resources in building the boat, and he treated her with affectionate respect, as a son should treat a kindly if impoverished mother.

One day, when the plane trees were turning crimson around the lake, she called him to her.

"Samdhu," she said, "I am a very old lady, and I am not much longer for this earth. For two years you have served me as a good son, and now I should like to see that your future is provided for. I am willing to pay twenty thousand dollars to buy a business for you. What do you say to this?"

Samdhu, despite his astonishment, thought very hard. He did not understand business, for in Kashmir it is generally run by Hindu pundits, very august people who wear turbans instead of caps, and who do not live on houseboats. Samdhu did not think he would like business, for he had never heard a businessman singing a Kashmiri love song. So he came to a decision.

"Lady Sahib," he said, "this is very good of you. But there is only one thing I would like. As you know, I have not spoken with my father since he disowned me on the day when you and

I met. Now I would like to be friends with him again, and to help me in this, I would like you to pay off the debt on his houseboat—a matter of perhaps two thousand dollars."

"Done!" said the little old lady, and so it was, and there was much rejoicing when the *Pasadena* and the *Pigeon* were reunited. To celebrate the event further, the old lady built Samdhu a neat little house on the bank beside the grass where he liked to lie in the sun and saw to it that the house was shortly occupied by a neat little wife.

"Now Samdhu," she said, "there is only one more thing. You are a lazy boy who likes to sing Kashmiri love songs and lie in the sun, and I do not think you will earn any more money after I am gone. So I have written to my son in America telling him that I have found another son in Kashmir, and I have told him that he is to send you in regular installments one quarter of the income from my estate. It will be a big estate."

Shortly afterward, the surprising old lady died peacefully, and deep was the mourning on the two teakwood houseboats. They buried her in the English cemetery, and though other graves have fallen into neglect, the flowers on her gravestone are always fresh.

For bad times have come to Kashmir; its people have been at war; the tourists are gone; the houseboats are empty, and many of the houseboat owners are starving. But the people of the *Pigeon* live comfortably on the bounty which trickles from Samdhu's regular check from America, and there is always plenty of rice and curry for their friends.

As for Samdhu, he lives merrily in his little house by the river's edge with his two radios, his wife, and his children—all of whom like to sing Kashmiri love songs and lie on the grass in the sun.

Srinagar, Kashmir ❀ *June 30*

It was a wise move for Eric to drive our car up to Kashmir, over the Banihal Pass, for it means that in our exploration of the countryside and our talks with the villagers we are free of the secret agents of the Kashmir government who dog our steps and our interviews in the city. Not that we have anything to hide, but the secret agents are convinced that all foreign correspondents are spies or at least instigators of trouble. Their easily-recognized presence makes it impossible to obtain any wide information on how people are really feeling in Kashmir these days, for no one speaks freely in their presence. Only the houseboatmen and the merchants can talk to us without being overheard, and by now they are almost professional pro-Pakistanis.

A Kashmir village far from the politically conscious and comparatively sophisticated town of Srinagar was what we wanted. So today we gave the slip to the soft-felt-hat boys and drove for miles through the lush green valley of summer. And after a long time we came to the village of Matipura.

In the square wooden schoolhouse, ragged boys with bare feet were singing lustily: "Ours is a magic land, full of flowers and birds; great conquerors loved the beauty of this land, and so do we, its people."

Yet Matipura, like all the villages of Kashmir, is filthy, disease-ridden, and incredibly ramshackle. The houses, patchworks of mud, bricks, and old planks, are sometimes roofed with sod on which in spring grow purple-and-white iris, but they look as if the wolf wouldn't have to huff and puff very much to blow them all down.

The streets are littered with refuse, scrawny hens, and mongrel dogs. Some of the children have no clothing but an old piece of burlap sacking to wrap around their thin shoulders. Most of them are not in school, because their parents cannot afford to pay the dollar-a-year charge for textbooks. Besides, from the age of four on, they are needed in the fields.

The beautiful girls of Kashmir are old crones at thirty, squatting suspiciously in their dark doorways, pounding a few handfuls of rice in a stone bowl. The men are rickety weeds.

Here in Matipura is the whole contrast of Kashmir: the poverty-stricken peasant in his crumbling village against a background of the rich, fertile, beautiful valley bursting with the wealth of summer.

Until now, almost nothing has been done to try to improve the lot of the Kashmiri peasant. Under a succession of maharajahs, the peasant became poorer and poorer, the landlords and the feudal aristocracy richer and richer. Few peasants owned their own land, and most of them had to pay one half to two thirds of their crop to the landlords, who later sold it back to them at inflated prices in the black market.

Today, among the many reforms which the Kashmir government is trying to initiate, the most successful is a just and peaceful land reform. Already land has been taken from many of the big landlords, each of whom is allowed to keep twenty-two and a half acres and is compensated in moderation. Already, thousands of peasants have become proprietors of the land they were cultivating, and more are receiving title to land every day.

Old Khaliq, a peasant of Matipura, was the first man to receive land in Kashmir. When we arrived at the village, he was out in his fields, but eventually he appeared, puffing with haste and the importance of being summoned, his bare feet still wet with the mud of his rice paddies.

"We never dreamed in all our lives," he said, "that land could ever belong to us. We thought that only rich people could own land, and that we people of the village would always have to cultivate it and give most of what we grew to the landlords. So naturally we didn't care how little we grew on the land, just so we had enough left over to feed our families.

"And then the government came and gave us land! At first we doubted their sincerity, and we thought maybe they would come and take it away again. But now we understand that it really does belong to us, and we feel like working harder and growing more rice, because we know that we can keep or sell most of what we grow."

Like all peasants, Khaliq was reluctant to express his pleasure too exuberantly. He complained, for instance, that the amount he had been given—about an acre—was still too small to enable him to support his large family. Furthermore, he pointed out, he now had to buy his own oxen and seed, instead of having them provided by the landlord.

But Khaliq and all the others agreed that certainly they would have been better off this year than last, had not a devastating flood hit them last autumn and destroyed most of the crops and many flocks of sheep and goats. This year, if there are no more floods, the villagers hope to have more to eat and more spare cash than they have ever known.

"Then maybe I shall send my grandsons to school," said Khaliq, waving a gnarled hand at the old schoolhouse where the ragged boys were still singing of the beauties of Kashmir.

Out in the wet rice paddies, the peasants too were singing. They sang of Alexander the Great, of the mustard fields in blossom, of the cobalt kingfishers flashing above the river, of the white snow on the mountains that ring the green valley. And some of them were singing the new songs taught to them by local government workers, songs telling of the future and of the land which, after long centuries, finally belongs to them.

Later

We are nearing the end of our stay in Kashmir, and once again I have been trying to sort out a welter of impressions and emotions and contradictions. For several years this has been one of my annual sports.

Indians and Pakistanis are so violent in their separate determinations to hold Kashmir permanently that the foreign observer instinctively rejects or at least criticizes both points of view—or accepts the validity of one statement without accepting the conclusion which is drawn from it.

I, for instance, agree with my Pakistani friends that India has been dishonest in promising a plebiscite and making it more and more evident that a plebiscite will never be held. I think her trickery and quibbling in the United Nations, while simultaneously lecturing the Western world on morality, is shocking. And it seems to me that under the terms of the British departure scheme in 1947, Kashmir ought by rights to have joined Pakistan, because it is a contiguous area with an eighty per cent Moslem population. I see the vital necessity to Pakistan of the rivers flowing through Kashmir and down into the otherwise-arid plains of the West Punjab, and I have no real conviction that India will not change the direction of those waters.

On the other hand I have now come to believe—although I did not think so at the time—that the government of Pakistan had a hand in the tribal invasion. If this is true, then the invasion was not an uncontrollable and spontaneous religious uprising, but a case of stupid aggression (or aggressive stupidity).

If Kashmir could become a sort of Switzerland of Asia, with her borders guaranteed by both nations, that would be ideal. But in view of the Russian menace to the north, it would also be dangerous and impractical.

I do not really believe in the concept of the religious state, much as I sympathize with Moslem fervor. I think that Nehru is sincere in his desire to maintain India as a secular nation. And I think that India is more determined than is Pakistan to raise the standard of living of peasants, no matter what their religion. If Pakistan held the Vale of Kashmir, I do not believe she would have gone nearly as far in land reform and in other measures to help the miserable peasants as India has.

By all of these steps I have come to the speculation that perhaps, after all, self-determination is not the answer everywhere. If the peasants of Kashmir were allowed to vote, I have no doubt that with the exception of the Hindus and the Ladakhis, they would vote overwhelmingly to join Pakistan. And I think they would be wrong. They are simply too remote, too uneducated, too primitive to make an intelligent judgment of the issues. They would throw over their reforms and their stability, and vote purely on the basis of religion. And they would land right back in the laps of misery and quarreling politicians.

And that is why I continue to be irritated at India's hypocrisy, and yet not to worry too much at the prospect of Kashmir remaining with India.

July

Delhi *July 5*

 wo days after we returned from Kashmir I went
to Dr. Buckler, the president's fine Anglo-Indian doctor, for the
cholera shot we all need from time to time. After the shot we fell
into conversation about childbirth in India. Upperclass women,
he says, have a fairly easy time despite the fact that none of them
do anything physical all day beyond pujas, or prayers. As for poor
women, there's no fuss at all.

One day, he told me, an untouchable woman in swinging
skirt and tunic was sweeping his verandah. She seemed to be
working very slowly, so after awhile he spoke to her sharply and
told her to hurry up. She finished and disappeared.

Half an hour later he was called to the nearby Red Cross Hospital, where he found the sweeper woman in the last stages of
labor. He would never even have guessed that she was pregnant,
he said ruefully.

Most Indian farm women, said Dr. Buckler, just go out into a
field, have the baby, cut the cord themselves, and come home. I
asked him why more of these field-born babies didn't die of infection.

"Nature has ways of resisting infection from natural sources," he said. "It's only when we moderns introduce unnatural things like instruments and hands that infection becomes widespread. As for the mental aspects, alas, the more education a woman has, the more difficult time she is likely to have."

When I came home I found that Sesh was waiting. He looked very sporty in cocoa-colored slacks, a bright red tie, and a hounds-tooth jacket. He was chewing gum.

"Could I have a bourbon on the rocks?" he asked. "You Americans really know how to drink, as I found out this month when I had a lot of dates with American girls. Thanks."

"Oh?" I inquired, settling down on the couch and picking up the yellow baby sweater I am knitting. I still try to pretend to company that it is a sweater for me, but I won't be able to get away with that little pretense much longer.

"Yes," said Sesh happily. "I've quite a wide group of girl friends in the Embassy now. They are very happy to know an Indian and learn about the real India from me. I cannot afford to take them to restaurants, so I take them walking through the gardens of one of the old tombs, and we sit on the steps in the moonlight, talking of philosophy and love."

"And what is to come of all this?"

"Oh, I shall marry one of them," said Sesh carelessly. "I don't know which one yet, and I don't much care. They are all pretty and intelligent, although not quite as intelligent as I am, luckily.

"Also, I have applied for a journalistic exchange scholarship in America. I want to see the tall buildings and the dams and the universities and Hollywood. Really, India has nothing to offer, compared to America!"

He laughed gaily, looked at his new wristwatch (American), and downed his bourbon expertly. "Got a date with one of the American girls—a blonde," he said. "So long."

Funny, I thought, I liked him better when he was a native-bred Communist. Then I wondered what he was like on a date, and I imagined that I knew.

When I first came to India a few years ago I was unmarried—and delighted when various Indian young men began asking me for dates. Not only did they seem exotic and very glamorous, but it seemed to me that Indians might be more revealing about India on a social occasion than they would be if I were sitting with them in an office asking journalistic questions.

They were indeed revealing, and none more than young Mr. Dabari.

I met him during my first week in India when I went to one of the government press offices for information. He was, I realized after a longer and more jaundiced acquaintance with government offices, a third assistant clerk and likely to remain so. At the time he emerged from his files to help me, however, I thought him quite dazzling.

After he had produced the report I needed, I rose to go. "I am giving a party tonight," he said suddenly. "A big party with some of my friends in Davico's Restaurant on Connaught Circle. Would you care to join us?"

I was still unsure of myself, or India, but this sounded safe—all those friends, and a big restaurant. Mr. Dabari himself seemed very polite and gentle. So I said yes, I would like very much to come.

"At eight o'clock I will call for you in my car at the Imperial Hotel and escort you to the restaurant," he announced.

In high heels and evening dress, I met Mr. Dabari in the lobby of the hotel that evening. "The car is broken down," he said. "We will walk. It is not far."

We walked out of the hotel driveway, and Mr. Dabari turned right, instead of left toward Connaught Circle.

"I thought it best to hold the party at my home," he explained. "The atmosphere is so much better than in those big restaurants."

I didn't see how he could have cancelled a reservation and called all his friends in such a short time, but I walked along quietly beside him, thinking how interesting it would be to see a real Indian home.

For about a mile I limped along in my high heels and swishing skirts, while Mr. Dabari kept saying "just one more block, one more block." At last we turned from the sidewalk and headed across an open field. Ahead of us, in the middle of the field, I could see a tiny mud-and-brick building.

"Just temporary," said Mr. Dabari, ushering me inside. "The government will soon provide me with proper quarters. And by the way, the electricity line is broken, and we must use candles. Just temporary, of course."

The house consisted of a single room, with a kind of shed outside. Down the center of the room ran a row of rickety wooden chairs, side by side. Against a far wall stood a string bed. A small table and chair were placed crossways between two walls. On the mantelpiece stood a bottle of cheap Indian rum and a lighted candle in a bottle. It looked as if wax had been running down the bottle for a long time, years maybe. There was no one else in the room, but I could hear a servant, or someone, scrabbling about in the shed, and I smelt the smoke of a charcoal fire just being lighted.

"The other guests will arrive shortly," said Mr. Dabari, and indicated that I should sit down on the chair second from the door. He poured a couple of shots of Indian rum in some chipped tea cups and handed one to me. It tasted like fire brewed with gasoline, but I sipped at it—a bit nervously by this time.

From a drawer in the table, Mr. Dabari took a paper. Then he sat down beside me, very close beside me. "I will show you the marriage advertisement I have prepared for my sister," he said. "She lives with her grandmother in Lucknow, but it is my responsibility to obtain a husband for her, and she is of an age. Here is what I have written to be put in the paper. Do you approve?"

It said: "Wanted: fair-skinned bachelor for honey-colored virgin skilled in domestic arts. Must be earning Rs. 200 a month. Apply Box —." While I read, Mr. Dabari leaned on my shoulder and breathed on my neck.

"Very explicit," I said, moving over to the next chair. "And when will the other guests come?"

"Just now, just now," said Mr. Dabari. He returned the paper to the table and came back with a miniature model of the Taj Mahal carved in ivory. He handed it to me, then walked around behind my chair—the better to lean over and examine the delicate work with me.

"Charming," I said. "Really lovely." And sidled down to the next chair.

By the end of the next hour and another cup of rum, I had seen Mr. Dabari's high school diploma, the drafts of several reports on which he was working, an indecipherable copy of the astrological predictions made at the time of his birth, and a photograph of his grandfather taken just before the day the old man renounced the world and became a sadhu. I had also sidled myself all the way down the line of chairs. As there was nowhere else to go, I rose as casually as possible and retreated to the chair behind the table. It was nearly ten o'clock, and there was no sign of food or of other guests.

"Look, Mr. Dabari," I said finally. "I don't mean to be rude, but I still have some work to do tonight, and I must leave soon. Would you please tell me whether you are really expecting anyone else to come?" Poor Mr. Dabari looked miserable.

"I am afraid I must tell you the truth," he said, spreading out his palms in despair. "The women would not come."

"The *women* would not come?"

"Yes. You see, some friends really were coming here tonight. But when the women heard that there would be a white lady present, they said they would not come. None of them have ever met any white ladies, but they are very jealous of them. You Western women have so much more freedom that they have, you see. All evening I have been thinking that perhaps curiosity would lead them to change their minds, but alas, jealousy has triumphed." He looked crestfallen for a moment, and then his mood changed abruptly. He clapped his hands, and an old barefoot woman with a wrinkled, incurious face entered. Mr. Dabari ordered dinner to be served.

"We shall have our party none the less!" he exclaimed happily.

In a few moments the old woman came back, carrying a tray covered with little brass bowls filled with various kinds of curry. She placed the tray on a small table in front of the row of chairs and disappeared.

"Come!" cried Mr. Dabari gaily. I sat down beside him with a mixture of eager hunger and wariness. Mr. Dabari thrust his fingers deep into a mixture of eggplant and peppers and held out the mess toward me.

"You shall feed me, and I shall feed you," he announced. "That is what we do in India when we are *very* good friends."

I tried not to recoil. I tried to be polite. I think I mentioned something about having hoof and mouth disease. I even considered "When in Rome" and immediately decided that Rome had gone too far. Anyway, he was dashed but gracious about my strange American reluctances, and we ended up feeding ourselves from our own fingers.

After dinner we started home, Mr. Dabari wheeling his bicycle for the trip back and walking so close beside me that every time he swung his free arm he managed to swipe against me. He insisted on walking an extra mile out of the way in order to look at the moon reflected in a pool by the India Gate. On the way back to the hotel I rode Mr. Dabari's bicycle a little way, but gave it up after I almost ran into a cow in the darkness. After that I hobbled on, zig-zagging now and then to avoid that swinging arm.

"You are the first Western woman I ever met," Mr. Dabari confessed at the door of the hotel. "You are not quite what I expected."

"You are the first Indian I ever spent an evening with," I said. "You are not quite what I expected either."

We smiled at each other, not knowing whether we had given or received compliments, and went our separate ways.

After that I had several dates with Indian men ranging from an

Oxford-educated Pakistani to a very suave Bombay movie director. Basically, all of the evenings were variations on the episode with Mr. Dabari; they were not very successful, and some of them were much more difficult. I could forget that they were Indians and talk to them simply as men, for in the Western world we are trained to meet and to talk to all kinds of people and sexes. But they could never forget for a moment that I was white and talk to me simply as a woman—the words "white" and "woman" were permanently linked in their minds. The only other women they knew were Indian women, who would never never have gone anywhere unescorted with a comparative stranger. Therefore, what basis did they have for judging me except their own preconceptions? And the general Indian preconception of the white woman is, alas, that she is a creature of low morals and easy virtue. The gradual steps of courtship which we take for granted in the West are unknown to them; it is as if they lived in a looking-glass land and wished to start at the end in order to get back to the beginning.

Delhi ❀ July 7

It is really too hot for picnics, but we picnic.

One does not take peanut-butter sandwiches and hard-boiled eggs on picnics in India if one is a proper Britisher. One takes cold baked potatoes, fresh lettuce and tomatoes, cold mutton, bread and butter, oranges or apples, and beer. One also takes, if one has an American wife, a flask of martinis and an ice bucket.

Eric mixes the martinis in a glass bottle and fills the ice bucket from our refrigerator in the bathroom. A servant brings the food from the hotel kitchen, and we pack the wax-paper packets, the beer, the silverware, the tablecloth and napkins, the glasses, the extra cigarettes, and a book or two into a large, straw drum-shaped stool, which later I can up-end and sit on. With blankets, pillows, and Jimmy on his leash, the simple picnic is ready. When Bhag Singh is here we take him along too, so that he can carry our picnic from our car to the picnic spot or change a tire if we happen to have a flat. But he is on home leave now, up in the hills of Garhwal, and these days we bravely go alone.

The country outside Delhi is wonderful to explore. Little Moghul tombs (about the size of a small railway station) dot the vast plain to the horizon and beyond. History is ours for the feeling in the larger monuments and ruins. Haus Kaus, one of our favorite places, was a university some thousand years ago, and one can still wander through the rows of cells where the students slept. Tamerlane too is said to have slept there, but then Tamerlane is as ubiquitous in these parts as George Washington is in America. One can climb high among the tower rooms and, perched amid geometrically carved red pillars, gaze at the dry bed of what was once a lake, and at the little "island" where a famous hermit meditated. Between the buildings are green lawns and flowers, and always, somehow, a breeze. Indians are said not to like picnics, and the simpler people call them "*pughal khanna*" or "mad food," but often at Haus Kaus we find Indian families picnicking—the matrons of the family chattering and gay as they fuss about with dozens of strange dishes, the men lying back on pillows and blankets, smoking and talking politics, the young people clustered around a portable phonograph, listening to current hit songs from an Indian movie.

Sometimes we go instead to Tughlakabad, the great fortress spreading over a spur of rock south of Delhi in miles of harsh battlements and empty stone chambers. The city was abandoned almost as soon as it was built by Ghiyas-ud-din, the first of the Sultans of the Tughlak dynasty, and there is, even now, an atmosphere of sullen emptiness amid the powerful stonework. According to legend, Ghiyas-ud-din displaced some gypsies when he chose this site for his fortress, and one of them cursed him. "Your city will be inhabited by goats and jackals!" a gypsy snarled. And sure enough, when the city was almost completed, it was discovered that the water supply had dried up and that nothing could bring it back.

A much happier place is Kutub Minar. Here is the handsome red-sandstone-and-marble tower, which, at two hundred and thirty feet, dominates the flat plains south of Delhi. ("You certainly don't have any buildings higher than *that* in America!" one sophisticated young Indian lady once told me.) When I was younger and sprier and less pregnant I used to like to climb the three hundred steps and look down at the stone courtyards below and think of all the pretty ladies who chose this fashionable site for suicide. Now I would rather wander through the crumbles of one of Delhi's many previous cities and browse under the great carved and pointed arches of a ruined mosque to the courtyard of the iron pillar. The pillar isn't really iron—it's said to be a compound metal, resembling bronze—but whatever it is, it stands twenty-two feet and eight inches high, smooth and uncorroded, and is supposed to have been cast some sixteen-hundred years ago as a symbol of Hindu dominance. Now it has come to be a symbol of strength too, and on Sundays young students are about it like bees all day, each young man trying to stretch his arms all the way around the base of the pillar. If he can do so, he will have proved his virility, and his friends will greet the accomplishment with laughter and the kind of jokes which even Eric refuses to translate to me.

But our favorite place for a real picnic is at Okhla, about half an hour's drive south of Delhi. We park our car near the headworks of the Okhla Canal, built by the British in 1874 (the Indians had technical assistance in those days too), and start walking cross-country toward the Jumna River. On the way we pass an enormous banyan tree in which live what seem to be thousands of monkeys; Jimmy always sets up a feverish yapping and has to be sternly restrained, while the mother monkeys gather their babies in sinuous arms and scoot for the top of the tree. If Jimmy is not with us, the larger, bolder monkeys sometimes trot up to us and try to explore our pockets and our baskets.

After awhile we cross a kind of dune, covered with low scrub, and come to a sandy beach and the river. It is very peaceful here, very private. On most of our country picnics, villagers always appear, squatting at a distance to watch us and to wait for anything, particularly glass bottles, which we might discard. But here we are alone, and there is only the sunlight, the warm sand, the murmur of the river, and sometimes at sunset a man and a herd of cows crossing the river far off to the right.

Lying on the sand, thinking of these peaceful days of the new India, I remember the turbulent India of a few years ago, and I think of a talk we had with the crossing-keeper of Okhla.

A group of American and British correspondents and their wives and girls had been celebrating something—a birthday? an anniversary?—at Maiden's Hotel. The times were so ominous, with partition and rioting just over the horizon, that we were rather desperately gay. The men wore white evening jackets, the girls their prettiest long dresses and high-heeled golden slippers. We danced and laughed and drank endless bottles of champagne and tried to forget India for a while at least.

Around two thirty in the morning someone (Eric, I fear) suggested that we all drive out to Okhla for a swim. It seemed a splendid idea, so we piled into a big car, and soon the girls were sitting on the damp sands, shivering and talking about the crocodiles which are said to inhabit the river, and the men were splashing and shouting in the water, trying to forget the crocodiles.

By the time we all climbed back into the car we were wet, sleepy, and in no mood for delay. But somewhere beyond the great night-dimmed horizon a freight train was chugging; across our road a wooden gate descended.

Before us and behind us, bullock-carts, loaded with clover for the breakfasts of New Delhi horses, bumped to a stop. The men who had been sleeping on the clover went on sleeping. The drivers of the carts climbed up beside them—*they* knew that the crossing-keeper always lowered the gate a good ten or fifteen minutes before the 4:25 a.m. slow freight from Calcutta was due. But we Westerners, who didn't know it then, waited what seemed an interminable time, and then one by one climbed from the car and wandered up toward the tracks. There was nothing else to see but the carts and bullocks, the dark hut of the crossing-keeper, and the glimmering emptiness of the Indian night. In the shadows of a gatepost the crossing-keeper half hid himself.

Eric climbed onto the gate and lighted a cigarette. "What's the delay?" he asked in Hindustani.

"Please Sahib," said the shadow of the crossing-keeper, "a train will come soon, and I must keep the buffalos from crossing the tracks. It will come just now, quite soon."

The crossing-keeper moved forward curiously, his bare feet stirring up puffs of dust. Even in the light of a half-moon his face was a dark shadow in the darker shadows of the Indian night. We leaned on the gate and looked at him, and after awhile Eric spoke again.

"How are things with you, brother?" he asked.

"Please Sahib, they are not good."

"Why?"

"Because I am hungry, and my wife and children are hungry. We are always hungry. I earn thirty-eight rupees [about twelve dollars] a month from the railroad, and that is a great deal of money, compared to other people. But somehow it is not enough to feed and clothe my family."

"How many children do you have?"

"I have four, Sahib, and one more on the way. I once had two others, but they starved to death."

The crossing-keeper spoke flatly, quietly, and when he stopped, the snorting of the buffaloes on the road behind him sounded loud in the silence. The other women and I, uneasy in our long evening dresses and our ridiculous gold sandals, shifted guiltily and turned to look at the setting moon.

"Was it always like this with you?" asked Eric.

"No Sahib, not always. A few years ago, before the war and

before all these troubles which they say will give us freedom, it was better with us. I had the same job, and I earned less money, but somehow things did not seem so expensive, and I could make ends meet."

"Do you have any idea why it is this way now?"

"No Sahib, I do not know. I only know it is bad for everyone."

"Perhaps it is the fault of the British?"

The crossing-keeper shrugged his shoulders. "Perhaps so. I, myself, take no part in these politics. But working for the railway, I and my family have eaten the salt of the British for many years. I must give them my loyalty."

As the crossing-keeper moved closer to us, I noticed the long lock of hair he wore, by which, one day, the angels would haul him up to heaven. In India this is a sign of a Hindu, although in other countries I have seen Moslems wearing these locks.

"Ask him if he is afraid of the Moslems, all alone by himself all night?" I suggested. At that time, armed raids by villagers of one religion or another were commonplace. And fatal. Sometimes, close to the border of India and Pakistan, they still happen.

Yes, said the crossing-keeper, he was afraid. No one had bothered him, but still he was afraid.

"I cannot buy arms to protect myself," he explained, "and there are not many heavy sticks out here in this sand and scrub brush. I do not know what to do except to stay in the shadows whenever I can. So far there has not been much trouble in our village, although last week some Moslems attacked the untouchables. I myself am a caste Hindu, and they did not trouble us. I do not know why this was."

"Do you know why Hindus and Moslems fight?"

"No Sahib, I do not understand such things. The only thing I understand is that I have not enough money to feed my family and that my children starve."

"Perhaps it will be better soon. Perhaps India will become peaceful, and you will earn more money and be happier."

"No Sahib, I do not think it will be that way. I think it will be the way it has always been."

The crossing-keeper looked down the track toward the horizon, where a crumbling Moghul tomb was silhouetted against the pale sky. Farther south, the lights of the freight train appeared. The crossing-keeper bowed swiftly and darted across the track toward the switches by his hut.

In a moment the train rumbled by, and the gates rose. The cart drivers woke up, climbed on their platforms, and cracked their whips. The buffaloes snorted, and with a squeal the wooden wheels began rolling. We climbed in our car and drove home.

Often, when we come to Okhla, I look for the crossing-keeper. But we are older and more staid now and do not swim by moonlight at four in the morning. And the crossing-keeper I glimpse on our afternoon or evening drives seems younger and more agile than the weary shadow I remember.

But the sad thing, the bitter thing, I know, as I lie on the sands of Okhla and think about him, is the realization that after years in India I can no longer take his words at face value—as I did when I was new and believed that in general people said what they believed. *Was* his salary only thirty-eight rupees a month? *Did* in fact two children die of starvation? Or were these swiftly conceived appeals for a handout? *Did* he admire the British, or was he seeking to please the white man he was talking to?

But, no, I think as I help to bundle our picnic things back into their basket. Even if the details of his story were not true, the essence of his poor little life, that we could see for ourselves in the waning moonlight, was true enough.

Delhi ❁ July 8

My typewriter has been on the blink since the Kashmir trip. This is always a frightening thing for a correspondent in a country where repairmen are few and a new machine costs a prince's ransom. Luckily, however, there is a branch here of the company which makes my typewriter; I telephoned them last week, and this afternoon a typewriter mechanic arrived. A gaunt, solemn young man with glittering eyes.

Eric was out, and the mechanic spoke little English. However, I pointed to the machine, and he sat down silently before it and began tearing it apart. He seemed to be coughing rather a lot, so I turned off the desert cooler, thinking that living as he probably did in the perpetual heat of India's summer, the cool temperature of our study-bedroom would be bad for him. Then I went into the living-room and read the papers for an hour, only vaguely conscious of the counterpoint of coughs and test-typing from the next room.

Gradually I became aware of silence; even the coughing had stopped. I went into the bedroom and found the mechanic slumped over the machine, his face in his hands. When I came in, he made an effort and sat up straight, pointing at the typewriter.

"Okay now," he whispered, swaying a little. I put my hand on his bony forehead, and his skin seemed to scorch my palm. So then I found our thermometer and put it in his mouth; he sat there dutifully, patiently, while we waited for the seconds to tick by.

When I looked at the thermometer at last, I couldn't find the mercury. My eyes slid along the scale, unbelieving: 103, 104, 105, 106 degrees. 106!

Just then, to my relief, Eric came home. I told him about the boy and his temperature. As usual, he was imperturbable and said that Indians often had high temperatures.

"You must go straight home and go to bed," I told the mechanic. Eric indulgently translated.

"Oh no," said the boy. "I would lose my job."

After more of this, we agreed that we would telephone his office and tell his supervisor about him. If the supervisor agreed, he would go home. So we telephoned, and after much shifting around, finally found the right man. We told him that his employee had a temperature of 106 degrees and ought to go to bed. He doubted, objected, disagreed, questioned—but at last gave in.

"Very well," he said. "You may tell him to go home, but that I will expect him at work at eight o'clock tomorrow morning."

The boy had bicycled six miles to our hotel. He now intended to bicycle six miles back. So we called a tonga and put the boy and his tools and his bicycle into the back seat, paid the tonga driver in advance, and sent them off.

Delhi ❀ July 11

I found myself worrying about the typewriter mechanic, so today I called up the supervisor at the company. For a long time he couldn't remember who I was or what I was talking about. But finally he did.

"Oh, Mohan Lal?" he said. "Why yes, he's back at work. Came back the day after he was at your place. Anything wrong?"

No, nothing wrong. The typewriter works perfectly. And so does my thermometer.

"Happens all the time," says Eric, cheerfully.

Rampur ❀ July 18

Here I am, visiting a tiny "princely" state in the heart of the United Provinces and satisfying my curiosity at last. I always *did* want to know how the maharajahs and the nawabs lived, particularly since their lavish old way of life is now thoroughly doomed by the all-embracing welfare plans of the new India. And last week, when I met the Chief Minister at a party and he politely invited me to visit Rampur, I jumped at the chance. After all, Eric was out of town (or "out of station," as we say in

India) on a news trip. And nothing could be hotter than Delhi is right now!

Arranging the train reservation, I ran into one of those typical wrangles which happen so often when foreigners deal with English-speaking clerks. Unfortunately, tempers mount quickly in this climate, and very soon the clerk and the foreigner are shouting insults at each other—all because neither understands the connotation of the perfectly clear English words the other has used. "Where is my pocket book?" I once asked Bhag Singh. Later I found that the poor man had spent hours examining all of our books, trying to find one titled "Pocket."

"The mail train for the nearest town to Rampur leaves at 4:25 a.m.," said the clerk I was consulting.

"Oh, I don't want to leave that early!" I exclaimed.

"But this is the *mail* train," he said, looking puzzled. I visualized a train loaded with milk cans and sacks of mail and began to feel equally puzzled.

"When does the express go?" I asked. The clerk looked astonished.

"Why, you couldn't travel on an express!" he said. I began to feel creepy.

"Look," I said, pointing to the time table between us. "Here's one at eight in the morning. How about that?"

"But that's a passenger train!"

"Well, that's what I am—a passenger! Do you think I'm a can of milk or a bag of mail?"

"But you don't want to travel on a *passenger* train!" he screamed. At that point I didn't want to travel on any kind of train at all, but I snarled at him and made him give me a ticket for the sensible-sounding eight a.m. passenger train.

Why couldn't I have remembered? In India, the express train is the one that carries the freight; the mail train corresponds to our express trains, and the passenger train is the local train which stops at every single village along the line.

Just the same, it was a peaceful trip, with farmers climbing in and out at each stop, loaded with baskets of fruit and braces of squawking chickens. Once we stopped for awhile at a big station —and as long as I have been in this country, I was dazzled all over again by the color and confusion of a big Indian railway station.

Quite often, the variety, the strangeness, the swirling brilliance, and the overwhelming vitality of India become too much for me. Emotionally, I am exhausted by it all, particularly when I'm traveling on an Indian train. And that is why I usually read Jane Austen or Trollope on these trips. Their clarity and common sense, their very coziness, speak of a condition I know and understand. And how delicious to be immersed in the world of Elizabeth Bennett and then, suddenly, to lift one's eyes into the world of Moradabad!

Before my window a half-naked sadhu leaned on his holy staff and stared at me with a dark, unfathomable look. Beside him a group of business men or politicians looked self-important and talked noisily while they waited to board the train. A village woman in a flaring red skirt and a mustard-colored shawl walked magnificently by, carrying a baby under one arm and a sheaf of wheat under another. Along the platform scores of other Indians milled about, wearing the most amazing variety of costumes: short pants, long pants, flowing pants, tight pants. Caps, turbans, topees, old towels. Saris, pajamas and tunics, full skirts, and scarves. Reds, greens, yellows, blues.

Hawkers selling Hindu water and other hawkers selling Moslem water appeared, and young men dashed from the train to hold their cupped hands under the sanctified liquid and drink. Over by the wall was a fountain from which, a sign proclaimed, anyone could drink. Men with straw trays hung on a strap from their neck wandered among the crowds, shrilly advertising bread or fruit, tea, cigarettes, brass or earthenware cups, cheap tinsel toys, or brightly colored statuettes of the Hindu gods. The center of the platform was jumbled with food-stalls, packing-boxes, bicycles, bedding rolls, wooden beds with string mattresses, and people sleeping on the concrete until their train should turn up in a day or two.

As our train began moving, a thin old man carrying a huge green melon on his head passed by. Behind him followed a thin young man bearing a brass tray of small yellow melons. I wanted one, but it was too late.

I was slightly dashed, when I arrived in Rampur, to find that court is not in session and that the ruler is in Bombay, having his appendix removed. No one, in fact, seems to be at the palace aside from the Chief Minister and a large flock of servants, who have installed me in an elegant room with a marble floor and blue cotton curtains at the windows. Last night I ate the most delicious dinner of my entire life, alone, at the head of a mahogany table at which sixty could easily have been served.

But as it turns out, this off-season aspect of palace life has its advantages: the Chief Minister has all the time in the world to show me around, and I can see places which otherwise would be forbidden.

This morning he took me to visit the nineteenth-century gingerbread palace which was the home of his late Highness, father of the present nawab. The old man, who died in 1930, was evidently quite a rake—as so many Indian princes are, or were—and his home is an interesting reflection of princely tastes. In the palace there seem to be enough chandeliers, cut-glass bric-a-brac, life-size candelabra, and chromos of the Swiss Alps at sunset to stock several museums as well as a number of Third Avenue junk shops. And yet this is only a tiny state, a miniature of dozens of wealthier ones!

His late Highness's palace was particularly rich in nudes—statues, paintings, bas-reliefs, and trick toys. Dusty marble nymphs guarded the corridors, while their sisters, in progressive stages of deshabille, frolicked on murals in the billiard room or swung from the pendulums of solid-gold clocks. Not one of the nudes, I noticed, is an Indian woman.

His Highness's bed (preserved as a monument) is of solid

silver, with bas-reliefs of cavorting nudes. It is hung with pink lace curtains and looks something like a sarcophagus in its lower reaches and something like a bassinet above decks. His Highness had forty-one more or less legal wives, and during his reign, prudent mothers moved their daughters to another state. The present Highness, in keeping with modern times, has only one wife.

There are thrones everywhere, even in the bathrooms. In the large reception hall is a cut-glass throne, the only one of its kind in India. A few years ago part of the roof fell in and broke off an arm of the throne, but it was repaired at a cost of $7,000.

The only really functioning part of the old palace is the museum and library, which houses the best collection of Persian manuscripts and Moghul miniatures to be found in India. Of all the princely treasures I've seen here, the ones in this little museum seem to me to be the most beautiful.

The "new" palace, built by the present nawab, is comparatively simple. About as simple, let's say, as any American movie house built in the 1920's, and much larger. On our tour this afternoon most of the furniture was shrouded in dust covers, but I still found the palace's three hundred rooms impressive. Without any trouble, the secretary told me, sixty guests and their retinues could be housed simultaneously, and they frequently are during the winter season.

Among the palace's amenities are three large ballrooms, one of which functions as a night club when the ruler is in residence. The club's equipment includes a blue billiard table which cost $10,000 and was made to order in the United States to match the color scheme, and a fine set of trap drums. On invitation, I climbed in and played at them for a bit. But then I began to worry about influencing the baby too much, so I stopped. The Chief Minister, of course, *expects* all foreigners to be insane, and I imagine that he is now firmly convinced that pregnant, American, women correspondents are particularly insane.

His Highness's bedroom is not nearly as splashy as that of his father, but there is a wonderful enameled dressing-table which rises like an orchestra out of the Music Hall basement when you press a button. Even more impressive are the figurines in ten niches around the walls: solid gold statuettes of John Held, Jr. flappers in tight short skirts, hats down to their eyebrows, and high heels with ribbon ankle straps! Why is the sexual motif always Western, I wonder? Judging from temple sculpture, it would seem to me that India, too, could contribute a great deal along this line. Why, temple sculpture alone gives you the idea of what Indian saints have been up against all these centuries.

Beyond the bedroom is the bathroom, unimpressive except for the tub. Actually, this is not a tub, but a marble swimming-pool in which it would be possible to swim at least three crawl strokes. Above it is a solid-silver, life-size head of an elephant, from whose down-curved trunk His Highness enjoys his daily shower.

After all this fantasy, I found myself feeling pallid about a suggested tour of the state factories, welfare societies, agricultural stations, and cottage industries. Nevertheless, I tramped dutifully along in the wake of my hosts and was suitably impressed. The palaces were the old, disappearing India. The factories and all the rest were the new India, the important India, the vital India of the future. There will be no more $10,000 blue billiard tables while people are starving outside palace gates, thank heavens.

Just the same, as I zip back to Delhi at dawn tomorrow morning on the mail train, I know that I will be thinking of the elephant shower and the cut-glass throne, the dusty nudes and the pop-up dressing-table, grateful that I have seen them before they all disappear forever.

Delhi ❀ July 30

When Sesh applied for a journalist's exchange scholarship to America, it seemed to me a good idea. He needs no conversion to the Western point of view; if anything, he tends to be too defensive about everything American, including Mr. Dulles. But a few months in the United States would, I thought, give him a truer basis for his liking and a clearer understanding of our culture and of his own. Recently, he has been zealously convinced that everything Western is wonderful and everything Indian is terrible.

But last week he came to call, sunk in gloom. His American clothes looked bedraggled, and his hand shook as he accepted the glass of bourbon I offered him.

"They turned me down," he announced abruptly.

"Oh Sesh! Why?"

"On the application I had to say whether or not I had ever been a Communist, and I had to say yes, because I joined the party for a few months when I was a student in Madras. Do you think I should have lied?"

"No . . . no, of course not. You had to tell the truth."

"But what is truth? What truth was once is not truth now. And what is your American truth? Why do you people *do* things like this? Why do you make us love your country, and then shut the door in our faces because of some youthful folly? Would it not be better to open your doors wide, as you used to do, and let all peoples come and see for themselves?"

"It's all because of a stupid law, Sesh. Many Americans are opposed to it."

"You only want to convince those who are already convinced," said Sesh, moodily. He gave a kind of twisted, gaunt smile. "And the funny thing is that *I* am already convinced," he said.

To try to cheer him up, we took him to dinner in the Cecil dining-room. Later we sat on the verandah, drinking crème de menthe frappés and trying to forget the hot wind, or *loo*, which blows all summer from the desert of Rajasthan. After awhile Eric and I wanted to leave, but Sesh wouldn't come.

"I shall just sit here," he announced, waving us away with a lordly sweep of his hand. "I shall just sit here drowning my sorrows and thinking about closed gates." And so we left him.

The next morning we learned to our horror that Sesh had quickly become very drunk, and what was worse, had started smashing up the wicker chairs and tables on the verandah. The police had been summoned and had taken him home.

"Please don't ever invite that terrible Indian onto our verandah again!" exclaimed Miss Hotz with justified indignation. I guess we won't.

Anyway, Sesh seems to have disappeared. We hear rumors now and then of his outrageous behavior in tap rooms and cafés around town, but thank heavens, he has not been near the Cecil. Poor Sesh, poor Sesh. A casualty of the clash of cultures? Why do people so often choose to adopt the worst of another culture rather than the best?

Well, perhaps it doesn't matter that he didn't get his exchange scholarship. I believe in international exchanges of teachers, artists, students, journalists, and tourists, but I do not really believe that they promote international understanding. The longer you are in a foreign country, the more baffled you become. At last you realize that it's like a good B.A. education: you're lucky if you end up with a small grasp of the questions and the problems, let alone the answers.

The short-term visitor may emerge from India with only a new concept of poverty, and that is good. But it doesn't mean he understands the people.

For heaven's sake, who "understands the people"? It's hard enough to understand oneself. Do men understand women, or women men? Do poor people understand rich, or rich poor? Do the British understand (or even like) Americans, although they've been "exchanging" with us for years? Do Americans really understand what it is like to be British?

Many Americans I've seen have come to India, as I did, full of eager readiness to love and to worship. A few months later, they are raging at "these damned people." And I never yet met an Indian who came back after a trip to America with any real understanding of the country. They may have liked the hospitality, admired the tall buildings, respected the willingness for hard work, but somehow they almost always missed the essential "spirit." I remember one woman journalist who had spent six months working in America; she had never been out of India before. I asked her if she liked the country, and she said no. I asked why. She answered: "Because the traffic out of town on Sundays in summer is so terrible."

It makes one humble, being a foreign correspondent. Or anyway, it ought to. Many of us write about India so glibly, as if we understand everything. We don't, and maybe we never can. We see how Indians distort our own country in their dispatches—often unintentionally—and that should make us wary about ourselves.

Loving is not understanding; to love a country or a people is not necessarily to understand it, as many old China hands discovered. Many people love God, but who understands Him?

It makes me sad to think that perhaps we never really understand another human being, black, white, brown, or yellow, until we have gone through some of his vital experiences. A very simple, homely thing has led me to this thought: I used to feel rather scornful of women who "just had babies." Now, when I go through this long, seemingly-endless, and occasionally uncomfortable experience of pregnancy, when I study the baby books and see how very much there is to caring for a baby and raising a child, I am ashamed of my former scorn. I see that being a mother is a very real and very serious job, as well as a delightful one. Unless I had found this out for myself, I'm sure I would never had known it.

Only the individual knows what has brought him to his present state of being, complete with a set of prejudices and attitudes (and perhaps he doesn't know). If one had lived through exactly the same experiences, would one also reach the same state of being?

In that case, how can one condemn anyone? The murderer, the torturer, the necrophile? If we had lived his life—if we were he—we would be the same.

But how can we *understand* this? Poets and artists have a glimpse (Dostoevsky understood Raskolnikov). They bridge this tremendous chasm of separation in understanding because they have a perceptive imagination far greater than that of most people. And sometimes they are able to communicate their bridge to other people. If I were in the State Department, I would send poets and artists to Asia, and Russia too.

Now, I think, I really understand why God is called all-seeing. Only God could have the power of imaginative projection really to understand, and therefore to forgive.

But let them talk of "international understanding on the human level," and send their professors and their students back and forth. The very act of exchange creates an atmosphere of peace, and, at least, of the *will* to understand.

But sometimes I think the world was far more peaceful before Marco Polo. And would be peaceful again if everyone stayed snugly at home! Understanding is so difficult, so complicated, so *hard*. Maybe it's better not even to try.

Or maybe I'm just very hot, very tired, and very pregnant.

August

❋

August 3

MAYBE it's just the heat. The heat which seems to have lasted forever. The damp heat in which the desert cooler no longer works. The heat which clamps like an iron band around our heads; the heat which keeps us scratching stupidly at our prickly skins. This is the riot season, when Hindu and Moslem pass each other warily on the blistering streets under a scalded gray cauldron of metallic sky. This is the time of nerves, of malice, of vituperation. This is the time when Indians and Westerners look at each other with irritation, more aware of their differences than of their similarities.

I, too, am irritated. And what irritates me particularly right now is the Indian tendency to confuse "what will be" with "what is."

"Ha!" sneers an Indian engineer. "We in India have dams just as big as your vaunted T.V.A.!"

"Where?"

"Kosi."

"Kosi isn't built yet!"

"No matter. It is bigger than T.V.A."

Land reform, complete democracy in the villages, an invincible army, perfect spirituality, cyclotrons—well, maybe India doesn't quite have all of them yet, but you are just an insensitive, materialistic, non-spiritual Westerner to point out the difference between the dream and the reality. Of course, maybe after I have been here longer I will come to believe that there *isn't* any difference. But right now, my Western training makes me argue when I run into one of these "what isn't, is" statements.

Take the question of untouchability, for instance.

"Untouchability has been abolished in India," any intellectual Indian will tell you. And indeed, the Constitution of India holds it illegal to discriminate against untouchables. Almost every state has passed laws for the protection of *harijans*, or children of God, as Gandhi called them. And this is fine; certainly a beginning of which Indians should be proud. But after all, it *is* only a beginning. If I were saying all this to an Indian, he would immediately begin talking about Negroes, and I would of course agree with him that legislation is one thing and full equality another. But then, why can't he agree with *me*, when we talk about untouchables?

Actually, it is rather hard to find out what life is like for an untouchable, and how he is feeling about things. There are highly vocal untouchable "leaders," of course, but they seem to suffer from grandiosity, over-intellectualization, and a typical Indian dislike of first-hand investigation. And in our daily life it is difficult to talk to the ordinary untouchables who cross our path. I can (and may) say: "clean the bathtub," or "wash the dog." But neither my poor command of the language nor the ancient traditions, by which I am partially bound, permit me to ask "how is life with you, friend?" And if I try to get an interpreter, I always run into the arrogance of the bi-lingual, educated man: "You don't want to ask this man any questions! He knows nothing." Even Eric dismisses my curiosity with: "They are poor, beaten-down creatures and will only be frightened if you try to question them."

Perhaps the ones in the North are different from the ones in the South, where the fight against caste has been severe. In any case, my most illuminating meeting with a group of untouchables was in Madras some time ago—just after the "Temple Entry Act and Civil Disabilities Removal Act" had been passed. The newspapers were bursting with the pride of magnaminity; hereafter untouchables would be allowed to enter temples from which they had been barred. After thousands of years of discrimination, full equality achieved at one blow!

I met a gentle professor who had been active in the movement to abolish caste. "We haven't even *begun* on the untouchables," he told me. "First we have to educate the 'educated' Indians." (I remembered a Brahmin youth I had once met, who said: "The law says I can't practice untouchability. It doesn't say I can't believe in it.")

The professor took me to visit a "model" colony of untouchables. The tiny mud houses, each only about twelve feet by six, stood in the glaring sun, with a narrow alley between each one; there were only four water taps for the forty-six families who lived there; the only bathroom was a nearby field.

I sat down on a flat stone between two houses, and the men collected in a crowd before me, staring. I asked them what they thought of the Temple Entry Act.

"How can we care about going to the temples when our bellies are empty?" asked a rickshaw puller.

From dark doorways, naked children slipped into the brilliant sunshine, many of their small stomachs puffed out in the familiar symptom of malnutrition. Between the houses, women in rags moved silently, incurious. Only one of them spoke, tossing the words over her shoulders as she scoured a brass pot with sand.

"God gives the poor only children, nothing else," she said.

The men coughed, trying to cover her indiscretion, and the rickshaw puller spoke again: "Now the caste Hindus have opened their temples to us, but none of us go to them. For what use is a temple when you are hungry? What we need is not temples, but full stomachs!"

"The main thing is to have a regular job," said a young man in a white loin cloth. "Being untouchable in itself doesn't matter, but it seems to make it harder to earn money."

The rickshaw puller pointed to his hut, where he lived in two earthen-floored rooms with his wife, his uncle, and five children.

"We don't want a fine house with electricity and beds," he said. "We will be satisfied with these mud huts and their thatched roofs, if only we have employment and food. That is the important thing for us—nothing else."

Everyone seemed to want to talk at once, but the voice of the bullock-cart driver, an old man with dragging gray mustaches, rose above the others:

"It is true that caste Hindus say they have reformed and that there are no more laws against us. But it is all only skin deep! The uppercaste people come here to see us in this colony, and some of them try to help us. But if we go to their homes, they call us to 'wait outside,' and they do not let us in, because we might defile their homes. If we go to one of the temples we are now permitted to enter, the caste Hindus go somewhere else. If we get a little money and wear clean clothes, they say we are showing off, and cut our wages. And when we die our funerals are held at a different place from theirs."

From the back of the group an angry voice spoke: "We should not criticize these things. These visitors are rich people."

"What does it matter?" the bullock-cart driver shouted. "We must tell the truth, and these things are true!"

There was never enough food, they said, for untouchables could not earn more than five to ten dollars a month, and it took ten dollars to buy the minimum amount of food to keep a family alive.

"It is not so terrible to go hungry yourself," a street sweeper said as he swung a rickety baby from one arm to the other. "But it is bad to see your children go hungry too."

As we walked out to the gate, the oldest resident of the colony came to say goodbye. A shy old man, he hesitated a long time when I asked him what had changed most in the twenty years he had lived there.

"The trees are taller now," he whispered finally.

And then there was the untouchable woman I talked to a few days after Mahatma Gandhi was assassinated. The first deep amazement had passed, and all of India—or so it seemed—was in mourning. The rioting between Hindus and Moslems, which had convulsed the country for months, had stopped completely, and the silence of tragic shock lay over the land.

Gandhi had devoted much of his life to the untouchables, and I thought it would be interesting to talk to one—although I was sure I could predict the interview in advance: "Mahatmaji was our leader, and our hearts are full of sorrow." I finally found an Indian friend who agreed to find someone for me and to interpret; he went out in the street and after awhile came back with a sweeper woman—elderly, smelling of dried dung and charcoal, quite composed at the strange circumstances in which she found herself. With a swirl of dirty, swinging skirts, she squatted on the floor and talked about Gandhi.

"He was a wicked man," she said flatly.

"How could that be?"

"He tried to say that people like me are not untouchable. That is against our religion. God meant for there to be untouchables and other peoples. Anyone who tries to tell us that we are like the other people is speaking against God and is a bad man."

Before I could recover from my surprise, she burst out: "It is *clear* he was a bad man! Before he was killed, there were riots and killings, isn't that right? And now that he is dead, the riots and killings have stopped. That shows that he was the man who made all the trouble, and, therefore, that he was a wicked man!"

I thanked her, gave her a rupee, and sent her back to her sweeping. And for a long time I wondered whether she was just a stray individual who had added two and two and reached five, or whether she represented any large body of untouchable thinking. I still don't know. But I decided then that there is a lot more to the whole untouchability question than merely talking about "*Harijan* Uplift" or passing a law.

All these recollections are prompted by a trip the Lubars and I made yesterday. For months, we in Delhi have been hearing rumors of a fierce struggle between caste Hindus and untouchables which is going on in a score of villages in the East Punjab. Congress workers we know are worried, for they feel that unless the struggle is peacefully resolved and the untouchables gain social and economic equality they may become ready prey for Communists. Then too, the struggle could spread all over India. Already there has been rioting in the south between Caste Hindus and untouchables.

There has not been much news about the situation in the papers, so the Lubars and I decided to go and see for ourselves. One of our Congress Party friends agreed to come with us and suggested that we head for the more or less typical village of Bidal.

Bidal is only forty miles from Delhi, but it is twenty miles from the nearest motor road, telephone, radio, or telegraph office; like most of the villages of India, almost no one has heard of it except its own residents. The road leading to it—a rutted bullock-cart trail whose twenty miles took us four hours to drive—dipped at last by a brown pond where black water-buffalo drowsed, and disappeared into sandy alleys between the mud walls of the houses. At the far end of the village, isolated from the main section, are the houses of the untouchables. The sun beats down equally upon all the mud roofs, the well for the untouchables, and the well for the caste Hindus.

Under a neem tree we found a group of *harijans* sprawled upon string beds. Others quickly collected. They had no work to do, they said. They had had no work for six months—except when they went to other villages where there was not yet a boycott against them.

"Things have been bad for a long time," said one young man. "Until a few years ago, one of our jobs was to take away dead cattle from the fields and dispose of them. But when freedom came, we decided we would no longer do this degrading work, which makes us so despised, unless the caste Hindus helped us with it. They would not help us, so the cattle now lie in the fields where they died.

"When we heard that untouchability had been abolished by the new constitution, we were very happy. Then the village had an election for the panchayat, and a *harijan* was elected to represent us. We were very proud. But the caste Hindus on the panchayat refused to sit with him, or to let him have any voice in the proceedings."

This made the *harijans* so angry, an old man broke in, that they found the courage to call what amounted to a strike on a matter which had rankled for a long time. A large part of their work, he said, was to crush sugar cane for the caste-Hindu landlords, in return for which they were given one seer (about two pounds) of every eighty-two pounds they crushed. This tiny proportion they felt to be unfair, and they demanded two seers, or double the old rate. The landlords, already outraged by the untouchables' refusal to remove dead cattle, declined to pay the higher rate and called a boycott on the *harijans*.

"Now they will not sell to us in their shops," said the young man. "We have to walk miles over the fields every time we want to buy anything."

"They will not give us work on their lands, as they used to do," said his father. "They use refugees from Pakistan instead and pay them at the low rate which we refused. And the refugees have to take the work because they are even poorer than we are."

"We have to graze our cows here in our sandy streets," a boy broke in. "The Hindus chase them away from the fields where they used to go."

An old woman elbowed through the crowd and with a bare toe

drew a line in the sand. She pointed on one side, then the other.

"Here in my untouchable quarter I can walk," she said. "There, in the quarter of the Hindus, I dare not walk for fear of my life."

Back on the road the village schoolmaster, a caste Hindu who is also a shopkeeper and a landlord, was waiting for us. He had a sensitive, bitter face, and he looked angry.

"They have been telling you lies," he said. "All they want is more money. There is no boycott. I myself sold some food to an untouchable a few weeks ago."

A wrinkled man with great mustaches and a yellow turban spoke to the schoolmaster: "And what happened after you sold that food? The panchayat fined you twenty-five rupees!"

The wrinkled man was a landlord himself, he told us, but he had heard the words of Gandhi, and he felt sympathy for the untouchables. He had tried to help them by allowing them to work in his fields and take some of the grain in payment, but the panchayat had fined him and forbidden him to continue. Even if they went to the nearest town and complained, he said, the police and the magistrates would not listen, because they themselves were caste Hindus.

"The trouble with these untouchables," the schoolmaster said, "is that since freedom came they've all grown uppity. They think they are as good as we are now, and deserve as much money—which is obviously wrong! Everybody is superior to somebody else in India, except the untouchable, who is inferior to us all."

"We are only demanding our rights, which you have kept from us for centuries," said a stalwart young *harijan* standing near the schoolteacher.

In hundreds of remote, forgotten villages of India, other untouchables are echoing the brave and increasingly bold voice of the young *harijans*. In many villages the caste Hindus are fighting back, sometimes bloodily. And in many other villages, it is true, the two communities are working peacefully and happily side by side, with untouchability all but forgotten. There will be more and more such peaceful villages as equality becomes an economic and emotional reality. But my own feeling is that the struggle will be a long one. Everything takes a lot of time in India, and so will this.

Delhi ❀ August 5

The silly infant has managed to turn itself upside down, or *ulta pulta*, as the Indians say. So today, the doctor and Mrs. White (the matron at the hospital) spent forty-five minutes trying to turn it back again, head down. Obstinate brat—no luck. They'll try again next week, and I only hope they know what they're doing! Anyway, I'm consoled by learning that *ulta pulta* babies are considered very lucky in India.

There are other annoyances which, because of the heat, seem more intense than they probably really are. Last week our impudent Jimmy got into a fight with a big bruiser of a mongrel and came home with a piece the size of a silver dollar ripped out of one side of his neck. Usually we take him for treatment to the municipal veterinarian in New Delhi, but this seemed so urgent that we rushed him around the corner to the little S.P.C.A. office. An old attendant there wiped his hands on his filthy pants, took two stitches in Jimmy's neck, and said he would be all right.

But five days passed, and Jimmy, who is usually lively as a Mexican jumping bean, grew more and more lethargic. So yesterday we took him to the municipal vet—who found that not only had the stitching been done so carelessly that the wound was infected, but that there was another subcutaneous wound on the other side of his neck, poisoning his whole system. Now Jimmy is his old gay self again, but we have to take him into New Delhi every day for the next ten days to have his bandage changed.

Why can't people who work with their hands in India learn to be efficient? I ask myself in rage. Why are workmen, whether they be veterinarians, auto mechanics, or electricians, all dreamy idiots with no pride in their work, no skill? Why does the municipal

government have to train and employ young Anglo-Indian veterinarians in order to be sure that there will be at least one place
in the nation's capital where animals are decently cared for?

No, I'm wrong. Could a private vet make a living in Delhi or
New Delhi? Maybe a small one in New Delhi where foreigners
live and sometimes keep animals. But not in old Delhi with its
largely Indian population. Indians hate cats and aren't much
fonder of dogs; pets are rare. A private vet would starve to death.
And the S.P.C.A. probably can't afford to hire anyone better than
that myopic butcher; their budget is too small. Indians tend to
think that if an animal is sick or dying, obviously karma is in operation. Therefore any attempt to have hospitals for animals is silly.
(And may be it is, in a country where there aren't nearly enough
hospitals for *people*.) And so the S.P.C.A. ekes out a miserable
time on the contributions of a few enlightened Indians and the
tiny gifts of many impassioned but hard-up Britishers.

As for pride in workmanship: how can there be any when no
one respects manual labor? Only low-caste people work with their
hands, and for this labor they get just enough money to stay mis-
erably alive. Where is the incentive to pride, to skill?

We're back to caste and religion again!

Delhi ✤ *August 9*

Usually, what I write about India in the paper creates not
the slightest stir here—for my work is background and feature
writing, and to Indian editors only politics matter. I doubt
whether most of them have been in a village or talked to a poor
man (outside of their own employees) in thirty years.

But in my story about the untouchables in Bidal, I seem to
have brushed a raw spot. Anyway, today I am honored by the first
public attack I have ever suffered during my years in India: a col-
umn-long editorial called "A Woman's Tears" in one of the big
English-language newspapers. Apparently I was all wrong about

those untouchables I talked to the other day. Hadn't I heard that *untouchability is abolished?* And don't I know that "under the new constitution, every *harijan* can claim complete equality with the highest in the land"? To do me justice, I am no Katherine Mayo, but so on and so on. And then comes the hook, the final inevitable hook to any discussion of untouchability: "Her picturesque description . . . should, indeed, make an ironical reading in a civilized country where even playgrounds, parks, and swimming pools cannot be used by all except without breaking heads over the color problem. Margaret Parton's copious tears for *harijans* of India could have been shed, with far greater justification, for the Negroes in the U.S.A."

All right, so here we are, right back at the color problem, as usual. What it has to do with untouchability, the subject under discussion, I'm not sure. But anyway, the Indians always bring it up whenever an American mentions untouchability. I wonder whether they believe that because an American doesn't like discrimination against untouchables in India, he therefore likes discrimination against Negroes at home?

Delhi ❀ *August 10*

Last night at dinner I sat next to an American Negro writer who had recently completed a lecture tour of Indian universities. I asked him whether he thought the educated Indian was really interested in learning the facts of Negro life in America.

"No," he said. "They are only interested in the Negro as a symbol. They are color conscious to a degree I have never encountered even in the United States. And they cannot imagine a loyalty beyond that of color. To them, every Negro is a natural enemy of every member of the white race. Several times, when I denied this, I was accused of selling my racial integrity for State Department gold."

Everywhere he went, he said, he was treated as a combination of Joe Louis, Paul Robeson, and the Shah of Persia. Introducing him, university professors would assure the audiences that in America Negroes were still bought and sold, murdered without any penalty by the whites, forbidden to attend schools, and lynched if they voiced any protest. When he tried to set this picture straight, he was shouted down by angry cries of "traitor!" Not to his country, but to the colored races of the world.

Naturally, the poor man had concluded that there is a Communist under every charpoy in India. And of course there *is* a great deal of intellectually fashionable Marxism in universities here. But it's a pity that he had so little chance to meet other Indians: the engineers and architects of the great irrigation projects, the civilized and literate army officers, the devoted civil servants. A pity, too, that he failed to understand the negative quality in the Indian character, which will take the other side of almost any argument for sheer deviltry—as many Russian propaganda speakers here have discovered. And a pity that no one had told him that humor will disarm an Indian more quickly than will any heavy-handed logic.

"I am convinced that India is going Communist!" he asserted. "What else can all this anti-Americanism mean, this lack of identification with Western goals?"

With this question still on my mind, I fell into conversation after dinner with Mr. Shri. Mr. Shri is a very high government official—British-trained, Oxford-mannered, and a Brahmin. He is devoted to Shakespeare and Shelley, cricket and vegetarianism; he would be horrified if any one suggested that he wanted Communism in India.

"But do you believe that Russian Communism is expansionist?" I asked him, feeling that this was a question which should get us into some basic problems. I should have remembered that the Hindu mind works not in blacks and whites, but in grays.

"My dear lady," Mr. Shri said. "All dynamic nations are expansionist. America, with her wealth and money to throw away, is expansive. Russia is. So is China. So too, may India be in a generation or so, after we have had a chance to develop a really powerful army.

"We know that Russia would like all nations of the world to become Communist. There are two ways she could achieve this: by overthrow from within, or by direct onslaught. In India, we control our Communists very strictly, so that the method of overthrow from within is closed to them, except by political means. And they will not get far that way. As for the second method, we do not believe that Russia will ever attack us. If they do, we are prepared to defend ourselves. That goes for China, too.

"As far as we are concerned, that more or less settles the Communist problem. But it does not settle the American problem.

"The trouble with America, and the basic cause of the present differences between us, is the American conviction that the only important issue in the world is Communism and anti-Communism.

"It seems so to you because you feel yourselves menaced by Communism. But we do not feel menaced by Communism nearly as much as we do by several other things, such as poverty within our own country, the need for economic progress, and colonialism."

"Surely colonialism is a receding force in the world today?" I asked.

"It is not receding very fast in our eyes," he said. "We ourselves have been free from it for only a few years, but we still find the Portuguese stubbornly occupying pockets of our country. Algeria, South Africa, part of Indonesia—in all of these places a colonial issue remains. How can you ask people to fight an evil like Communism, which may come some day, when you are not helping them to fight an evil they already know?

"I tell you, if America would stand by the foundation on which she was built, if she would return to the defense of subject people everywhere and to the great moral principles in which she used to believe, then she would have the admiration and support of all of Asia.

"Already you are admired for the economic aid you have given, which is helping to keep our country free and democratic. Food production has been raised, and there is a new spirit of hope among our villagers which was not there before. For these things we are grateful to you.

"Why does not America talk about these human matters, instead of shouting all the time about hydrogen bombs and massive retaliation? Keep your bombs in readiness, if you must, but do you need to talk about them all the time?"

Mr. Shri stared for a moment at the night shadows beyond the open French windows. "As for myself," he said finally, "I would rather lose my freedom altogether than drop one atom bomb as you Americans did on the people of Japan."

"What about all the millions of people who have died in Soviet slave labor camps, or been liquidated in China, or massacred in Eastern Europe?" I asked. "Do you care about them too?"

Mr. Shri shrugged his shoulders, and looked bored.

"They are human," he said indifferently. "They all have to die someday, so why does it matter when or how?"

Today I have been puzzling over Mr. Shri, whose point of view I have heard so often from so many Indians. Why his curious lack of interest in Communist doctrine, his obvious indifference to anything which happens to the West, his insularity? And why— thinking also of my earlier conversation with the Negro writer— the widespread use in India of the Negro as a symbol, the disinterest in the facts of slow progress?

These questions are too vexed for any final conclusions. But I have evolved a theory which pleases me—or will until I learn more.

Indian insularity is traditional and has been so for thousands of years. Protected by the Indian Ocean and the Himalayan barrier, the Hindu has lived his life as he chose, uninfluenced by, and uninterested in, other cultures. The early accounts of India are written by travelers from China or the West who came *in*—not

Indians who came *out*. Until very recently, to voyage across "the black waters" (which meant almost anywhere away from India) was to risk a loss of caste.

Today India is a secular nation, but she remains basically influenced by Hindu thought. And the Hindu religion is an inward one: the main task of every life is the improvement of the soul in order to earn a higher existence in the next incarnation, and eventually—after many incarnations—to lose identity in the "world soul."

But as Nehru once said: "Strong winds are blowing over Asia." These winds (which really started blowing perhaps a hundred years ago) have dropped a pebble into the placid surface of Hinduism and started widening circles of social conscience and responsibility.

One circle was the growth of the Vedanta sect of Hinduism, which emphasizes the need of helping, and loving, other human beings. But this is still a minor sect, rather like the Quakers in the West. Another circle is the recognition that society has an obligation toward individuals. Gandhiism was one expression of that new recognition, which now embraces all of India. Without it, there could be no hope that the disparate elements of India could ever be welded into a nation. Today, because of it, Indians (by and large) care about the welfare of other Indians.

Recently, a third circle has rippled outwards to embrace all of Asia, all of the "colored" world. Thus, as one Indian put it to me the other day: "Toward Russia, our attitude is correct. Toward America and Britain, it is friendly. Toward Asian nations, it is warm."

And I remember an outspoken young press officer we met when we visited the Tata Steel Works—a capitalist enterprise if there ever was one.

"Why do you Americans keep talking about the 'East-West' war?" he asked. "Don't you realize that it's a great mistake to associate the word 'Russia' with 'East'?

"We Indians have never thought of Russia as Eastern the way

we are. But when you call it East, we can't help but feel a sense of added friendship and interest in Russia. We have an instinctive emotional identification with any Eastern nation; we felt it for Japan during World War II, even though we knew it was Fascist and wrong. But we couldn't help gloating over Japanese victories, as our parents gloated in 1905.

"We feel the same way about China, although intellectually we have no sympathy with Communism. But we say to ourselves 'Oh, they are fellow Asians like us, and probably they are just trying to help themselves live a better life, the way we are.' It is very simple —the East is our family, and the West is not."

The concept of brotherhood moves slowly, and for Indians it must first embrace men who share the same dark skins and a history of struggle against Western exploitation. (Even if those men have to be forced into the role, as is the Negro.) The circle has not yet widened to include white men, be they Russian or American.

We in the West have our own guilts, of course. We too feel that the white race is "family," and all others are "not family." But the difference is that more of us are beginning to care—very slowly, very spottily—about what happens to the "not family." If an earthquake wipes out an Asian city or a province is decimated by famine, I think a lot of Westerners care about it and try to do something about it. Hiroshima was as much a shock to most Americans as it was to Asians. But sometimes, talking to Indians, I get the bleak feeling that if the entire white race wiped itself out, India wouldn't care a damn.

Delhi ❀ *August 15*

The doctor said I should have showers the last six weeks instead of baths, so the nice hotel is installing one for us. Several weeks ago some workmen came and put in the pipes and the shower head, and that seemed to be the end of the matter. The shower worked all right, but water sprayed all over the bathroom because there was no shower curtain, and not even a rod to hold a curtain. I mentioned this matter to the management several times, feeling that I was right in character as "the odd American" trying to force sybaritic luxuries on India. But this morning, two workmen arrived to put up a rod.

The bathroom is about six feet wide; the rod was seven feet long. The workmen pushed and prodded for half an hour, but obviously the rod wouldn't fit, and would have to be cut. But did they cut it? No indeed! They trotted out and came back in an hour with augurs and hammers and chisels and drills. They dug a hole in the outside wall above one end of the tub and a hole completely through the inner wall at the other end of the tub. When Eric suggested that they might better have cut the rod and placed it in brackets, they looked shocked. "Oh, no, Sahib," said one of them, "that would be too much trouble. It is much better to dig out the wall, and the rod will only stick out a little into the next room." And so it does; about six inches of metallic pipe now jut out into my dressing room. But as one of the workmen pointed out, it does very well to hang things on.

Shower curtains are a problem, too. I walked all around Connaught Circus this afternoon looking for plain or fancy or ordinary shower curtains which can be bought practically anywhere in America. Not only were there none, but no one had ever heard of them—although many homes in India have showers. Finally I decided I would have to make one, so I went to Pandit Brothers, which sells all kinds of cloth. "Have you any rubberized material?" I asked. "No, Mem-sahib," answered one of the brothers. Sorrowfully, I started to leave, when it occurred to me that maybe canvas would do. Ah yes, said the brother, they had canvas. And led me to a counter piled high with bolts of rubberized material.

Not only does this solve the shower curtain problem, but it also solves the crib sheet problem.

Delhi ✻ *August 20*

Every year there is famine somewhere in India, every year a few thousand or a few million people are living on a handful each of chicken feed every three days. Every year India becomes more and more determined to solve her economic problems. Every year there is prolonged wrangling in Washington about the amount of foreign aid which would help India toward a solution of those problems. And every year the anti-American talk explodes toward the end of the hot weather, when tempers are so short they have to explode *somewhere*.

The easiest way to start a discussion among foreigners or Indians these days is to ask: "How strong is the anti-American feeling in India?" The resulting uproar can last anywhere from fifteen minutes to two hours, for no two people ever seem able to agree on the extent of the feeling, its cause, or its implications.

There is little doubt that anti-American feeling does exist. But the old hand in India is likely to point out that it exists only in certain newspaper, government, and university circles (and even there, not very profoundly), while the American newcomer is likely to be appalled, and convinced, that nothing short of Red propaganda can be responsible.

To an American, accustomed to thinking of his countrymen as a pretty nice people, friendly, democratic, freedom-loving, and blessed with the good things of life, it is undoubtedly annoying to see his country often portrayed as a nation of lynchers, witch-hunters, gadget addicts, crude barbarians, and imperialistic oppressors. And the malicious tone in which these references are made has a sharp way of penetrating thin American skins. (We will simply have to learn to develop thick British skins.)

There is never any telling when or where the anti-American discourses will appear in the papers: a paper which writes an editorial about "America, Guardian of Free Democracy" on one day is perfectly likely to appear with one entitled "America, Land of the Slave Drivers" on the following day. In contrast to much that has been appearing lately, Nehru's remark (which heated the inside collars of American officials) that Western countries "lack all subtlety, lack any approach to the mind or heart of Asia" seems but mild and courteous chiding.

The causes of the anti-Americanism which does exist are complex. One of them, I think, is that basically even the most literate Indians are ill-informed about the United States, and not even the yeoman work of the United States Information Service has been able to penetrate the depths of misinformation and ignorance. I remember, for instance, an Indian friend who returned from a visit to Washington full of admiring amazement at the monuments; he had not known that Americans, like Indians, respected or commemorated the illustrious dead.

In general, the material on which the average educated Indian bases his conclusions are speeches by American politicians as reported in the Indian press, Hollywood films, and American weekly news and picture magazines.

Not one of these three has much appeal to the intelligent Indian mind. The speeches of most American politicians seem to him intemperate and arrogant; the ordinary Hollywood films seem vulgar, while the best films exposing and deploring some aspect of American life merely seem to confirm the Indian suspicion that America is a land of graft and racial oppression; the news magazines, with their bland assumption of American infallibility, are slick irritants to proud Indians. (Where is the boundary line between pride and jealousy? Where does envy become negativism?)

The kind of evidence an Indian will use to make up his mind about the United States often seems curious to me. Last year an elderly professor at a Moslem religious institution told me that he had lost his faith in America for four reasons: the suicides of Navy Secretary Forrestal and Harvard professor Matthiessen; the fact that the American writer Agnes Smedley, who died in England, had directed in her will that her ashes be sent not to her home, but to China; a movie about Huey Long (*All the King's Men*), which the professor took to be an accurate picture of American politics in general.

Another factor influencing Indian thinking is, of course, the long years of the fight for independence during which the young Indian was conditioned emotionally against not only Britain but all of the West, which, he was taught from childhood, represented "colonial imperialism." Now, although his country is free, his emotional reactions are still the captive of his conditioning; he is unable to react with the same emotional strength to "Russian imperialism," for all of his training has been in the opposite direction. Suspicion and lack of understanding are characteristic of this attitude.

"What then is this democracy that the Western nations and their spokesmen are holding out to us as the much-to-be-desired plum?" asked a tycoon-owned newspaper the other day. "Does it mean equality under democratic law? Does it mean freedom of thought and the opportunity to develop freely? Does it mean equal distribution of wealth and produce among the rich and poor nations alike? Or is democracy and cultural freedom only a temporary bastion against the encroaching Red Sea, to be replaced when it has served this purpose?"

Which somehow reminds me of a charming Parsi I met recently. He is a poet and also a high executive with the enormous Tata enterprises. "Even poets have to have their hobbies, you know," he said. We talked of the differences between the East and West, and of his belief that religion is responsible for differences.

"The West has adopted the Christian idea that men are sinners, but that salvation is possible," he said. "As a miserable sinner you do the best you can—which may not be the ideal of perfection—but you *do*. Compromise becomes necessary. The East, on the other hand, waits for perfection. Because the Hindu believes that perfection can be achieved, it is not necessary to do anything until it is possible to do it perfectly. In the West, if you want to write a letter, for instance, you buy the best stationery you can afford even if it is not the finest, and you write the letter. The Hindu, on the other hand, says to himself: 'There is no use getting stationery until I can afford the finest.' And either he never writes the letter at all, or else he uses a torn-off scrap of wrapping paper for it."

This makes sense of a lot of difficulties. Of what use is democracy, if it is not perfect democracy? Of what use is America, if it doesn't always sound like the land of Thomas Jefferson and Abraham Lincoln? Of what help is a gift, unless it is given purely, *perfectly?*

For this is the real crux right now, the immediate reason for the current upsurge in "anti-Americanism"—the fact that the United States is giving aid to India but not (in Indian eyes, at least) in the right spirit. But, oh dear, trying to see both sides, how complicated it becomes!

The other day a normally pro-American newspaper ran a cartoon which really hurt: At one end of a long table a blowsy blonde labeled "U.S.A." leaned possessively on a pie marked "Food for India." At the other end of the table an emaciated Indian drooped before an empty wooden bowl. And the blonde was murmuring: "First tell me you love me, honey."

The Indians hate, first of all, the necessity for help. Secondly, they hate the thought that economic help—absolutely necessary if their people are to have any hope at all—should come with "strings," or should affect their proud new independence in any way. Thirdly, they loathe the American demand for gratitude.

"We are a proud people," an angry dinner partner said to me the other night. "We hate taking gifts from any one. We are forced to ask for help, but if you attach strings to this help, seeking to remind us of our poverty, we shall hate you."

And a high government official at the same party exclaimed bitterly: "I wish we could go back to the good old days, when hundreds of thousands of people starved to death, but at least India was free from foreign gifts!"

Later, another government official gave me a more objective view of the Indian attitude. "Any indication on America's part that she expects an extravagant show of thanks for her gifts would be fatal," he said, "for it would only stiffen Indian determination not to grovel in gratitude.

"Americans must not forget that not all people are demonstrative, and that Indians—or at any rate, Hindus—are among the least demonstrative people in the world. We feel deeply, but it is not the done thing to express these feelings strongly.

"Last year, for instance, when I came home from a long trip, all my wife said was: 'Hello, you all right?' And I said: 'Yes, are you?' And that was all there was to our greeting, but neither of us had slept for several nights before, thinking of the other.

"There are few terms of endearment in any Indian language, and even the phrase we use for 'thanks' doesn't mean exactly the same thing—in other words, there is no exact phrase for 'thank you,' in the English sense. That is because we rarely express our gratitude, even though we may feel it. America would do well to realize this.

"There has been much talk, on the part of Americans, of giving aid simply as a humanitarian gesture, devoid of politics. And we wonder, why all this talk. For in the last analysis, such aid must inevitably rest on humanitarian instinct. We Indians know this as well as you do, and we don't need to have it hammered at us. The more song and dance you make about the aid, the more we will dislike you, even though we are forced to take your help.

"But if you give us help, simply and quietly, without making any fuss, you may be sure that everyone in India will know about it and thank you in their own way and in their own time."

It is perhaps too much to expect that the American people can give aid by stealth and wait to let it be found out by accident, and I certainly don't think we should follow a policy of mousy humility.

But sometimes I think that American officials and politicians would do well to ponder the ancient Indian proverb: "He who, having given, then demands thanks, throws away the good of his gift."

And this old Sanskrit proverb: "The dog wags his tail, waves his feet in the air, and shows his belly for a crumb of bread. But the elephant looks straight ahead with supreme composure and can only be enticed to eat with lengthy blandishments and the most costly dainties."

Our greatest danger in America, it seems to me, is the attitude: "If you're not for us, you're agin' us." This leads a lot of people to conclude that India, critical as she often is, is agin' us in particular. And this is unjustified. India is emotionally agin' everybody except India, which accounts for "neutralism." But in the long run, I really believe she is on our side.

Take personal contacts, for instance. Do the Indians turn cold shoulders to Americans, shout "Yank, go home," jostle us off sidewalks? Quite the contrary, they invite us to their homes, ply us with friendship and curry, exhaust themselves explaining India to us, and ask for our help in getting American scholarships for their sons. Behind our backs they may make fun of us or complain to Britishers about "adolescent America," but, basically, the Indian as a person rather likes Americans and lets them know that he does.

And while many anti-American articles, editorials, and passing cracks are printed in the Indian papers, the great weight of news which daily pours into India comes from the Western news or feature services, which day after day effectively present the Western point of view.

Today, for instance, I have been looking at one of our local newspapers which carries a lead editorial attacking America for insufficient aid. But the same edition also carries: A long article deploring Ilya Ehrenburg's "syndicated vituperations against the West"; an article on Siam, which while condemning American policy in Asia also points out the dangers of Communist infiltration; an article by the British philosopher C. E. M. Joad on Soviet double-talk; a profile of Mao Tse-tung reprinted from *United Na-*

tions World; an anti-Marxist, pro-Socialist article on British Socialism; a short *Tass* story on the Soviet peace committee, and finally, a long letter informing the editor that the Indian writer had come to the conclusion that "however grand and glorious the aims and aspirations of Communism may be" and whatever the faults and vices of the Western democracies, that at least in the West the individual was permitted freedom of thought. (Heavy reading, these Indian newspapers!)

And the other day a Calcutta newspaper turned its eyes on us: "The American way may not wholly be our way of life. But no one would, we believe, fail to discover and appreciate the enterprise, drive, confidence, and inventiveness of the Yanks . . . They have the best of everything in the world.

"The virtue of Americanism as a faith is not difficult to discover and follow as a model of enterprise. It is a faith in the liberty and happiness of the ordinary man . . . But the American should show and convince the world that it values man for what he is and not merely for what he possesses."

No, we must not confuse "anti-Americanism" with "anti-freedom" or "anti-democracy." If Indians like Nehru feel more comfortable with British restraint than with American exuberance, does it mean that they are secret Reds? Absurd! And how can anyone make this accusation when India, under Nehru's guidance, has deliberately chosen to adopt democratic methods in her great competition with Communist China to raise the standard of living of the masses? But they do, they do—and in making the accusations many Americans chip off a little more of that ideal of perfection which the Indians hold up to us. They want us to be so good, so wise, so understanding, and when we sometimes fail, unrealistic disillusion is sometimes termed "anti-Americanism."

We could begin some restoration of the image, I think, by recognizing the fact that while Asia (and in particular India) believes in democracy and rejects totalitarianism, it cannot and certainly does not look at world problems with the eyes of America. Unless we recognize the fact that this different viewpoint exists, and do not automatically characterize it as inimical, our hopes for friendship are doomed to failure. It seems pointless to me to condemn Pandit Nehru outright because he says the West fails to understand the mind and heart of Asia and lacks subtlety in its approach; perhaps it would be better to consider whether his point has validity. For myself, I think that it has.

I wish too that we Americans, in our justifiable pride of well-being, could also be proud and honest enough to acknowledge publicly some of the faults with which we are charged by Asia. If we were to recognize some of the half-truths of the charges against us, if we ceased to defend evils because we feel we cannot afford to admit them—then we would have gone a long way toward achieving the understanding and friendship of Asia.

But most of all I wish for the unobtainable, the impossible dream. I wish that every American could recognize the humanity, the individuality, the *need* of every person in the world less fortunate than himself. I wish that we could act with direct simplicity —with the same simplicity with which a woman gives a glass of milk to a hungry child, not asking anything in return but rather hoping the child will mind his manners after he's been fed. But even that hope is unimportant; the important thing is hunger and, therefore, food. The act of satisfying the need is *right*, and from right action comes right results. Not that India is a child, of course. But for me, as for so many of us, one must evoke the word "child" in order to arrive at the most important word of all: love.

September

❁

Delhi   September 3

    BHAG SINGH is back, after spending the summer in his village in Tehri Garhwal on the edge of the Himalayas. He has brought with him a young "cousin" named Anand Singh to act as a chokra after the baby is born—that is, he will wheel it in the garden, watch it while it sleeps outdoors, run errands, and generally make himself useful. Bhag Singh insists that we should not pay the lad more than twenty-five rupees a month —about five dollars—and of course his food. He will sleep on the floor of Bhag Singh's room in the servants' quarters. "He is very ignorant," says Bhag Singh with condescention, "but perhaps he will learn." The boy speaks not one word of English, but his great wide eyes are eloquent of the wonder he feels in his strange new surroundings.

    It had been a quiet summer in the village, reported Bhag Singh, squatting by the empty, bedroom fireplace to polish our shoes. No, nothing special about it—nothing much had happened.

    Well, yes, he admitted several days later and after some close questioning, there had been a few little difficulties. But nothing to speak of, and certainly nothing to interest Sahib and *Memsahib*. A few minor events of no importance . . .

There had been the matter of the drought, for instance, he began cautiously. For three months when it should have rained, it did not rain. Not a drop. Everyone's fields dried up; all the little terraces scratched out of the sides of the mountains in narrow strips were brown instead of green. He lost all his rice crop, but luckily managed to save his millet, which doesn't need as much water. Still, half a year's crop and half a year's eating was gone, right there. Mostly his family ate everything they grew.

No, he didn't think they'd go hungry this winter, but they would have to buy food with the money he sent them from Delhi, instead of saving it to buy another buffalo. Oh, hadn't he told us that the old buffalo was bitten by a snake, and died?

Yes, he said, first there was the buffalo, and then the drought. And after the drought the rains finally came, only too much rain came, and there was a big flood. Many fields were washed away, and many roads, and forty-eight men in his district were swept away by the roaring river and never seen again. Some of them were old friends of his, from his village, and some of them were relatives of his wife, from the next village. Still the rain had helped what was left of the crops.

No doubt the government would come along some time and repair the roads, he said. Perhaps, when they did, they would also build a bridge across the river, so that the smaller children could go to school. Well, you see, he explained, the school is on the other side of the river, and to get there the children have to wade waist-deep through the water. Naturally, the littlest children would drown—and some of them had—trying to reach school. Why no, he said, looking at us as if we were completely mad, the villagers had never thought of trying to build a bridge themselves. Government was supposed to do things like that, not people.

What else about the summer? Well, nothing else, much. Of course, he was sick, but then everyone is sick in the hot weather, isn't that right? Looking at him as he polished the highball glasses, we saw that the bones of his sensitive, hill-born face were outlined almost transparently under the brown skin.

"I was anxious to save as much of my crops as I could," he said, "so I worked for two days in the rain, transplanting new rice seedlings. Perhaps it was not good to be wet so much, with my feet in the water all the time, because there came a very high fever, and I had to go to bed for fifteen days. There was no doctor with your Western medicines anywhere near by, but a village doctor trained in our ancient ways treated me with herbs. He said I had the typhoid."

Yes, it was a piece of bad luck, he admitted, to get sick just then, when he was needed on his farm. Also, the typhoid made some of his hair fall out. Still, he was luckier than some other people he knew. There had been cholera in the village, and many people had died, including his mother's sister, a nice old lady.

But all of this was quite ordinary, he said. He had not yet told of the rather unusual and most unfortunate event which happened in his village this summer.

"One day," he began, "about ten of us decided to go fishing in the river. Not with hooks or nets, but with a charge of dynamite which someone had obtained." He stopped for a moment and grinned with embarassment, and we realized it was best not to ask exactly how the dynamite had been obtained. Usually there is an old soldier in a village, or someone who has worked on a road-building project.

"Of course it is forbidden to fish this way," Bhag Singh admitted. "Government says the dynamite kills all the fish in the river and then they have to stock the river all over again. But it is very exciting when the dynamite goes boom! And then the dead fish float to the top of the water, and everyone just wades out and scoops out as much fish as he wants.

"Well, we went to the river at dawn. Pyar Lal, the leader, took the stick, lighted the fuse, and started to throw it. But his sleeve caught on a rock just in front of him, and the dynamite went off right there on the rock and blew off Pyar Lal's arm. It would have killed all of us, except we were on the other side of the rock and were protected.

"Of course we had to take him to the doctor. And the doctor demanded a bribe, so that he would not tell the village police about it. But somehow the police heard anyway, and then they demanded a bribe so that they would not tell the district authorities, but the district authorities did hear about it, and we had to bribe them, too. All in all, it cost us two thousand rupees to keep the big government from learning what had happened. But if they had heard, they would have fined the whole village twice that amount."

Bhag Singh finished with the glasses and began to empty ash trays and plump up pillows. He cleared his throat, as he often does when he feels he has talked too long.

"Sahib and *Mem-sahib* have traveled so far and seen so much," he said apologetically, "that these village matters can be of little importance. And after all, as I said, it was a rather ordinary summer for us, like any other."

Delhi ❈ September 5

This afternoon I had been shopping in Connaught Circle —looking in vain for diapers—when I ran into Sesh. When I came around a corner and bumped into him, he jumped, looked for a moment as if he wanted to run, and then smiled shyly and invited me into the coffee house a few doors down the street.

He looked terrible—thin and tortured and seedy. Gone were the bright "American" clothes. Or perhaps these were the same, but if so, they had seen much fevered wear.

"Coffee is best for South Indians," he brooded as we sat at one of the little green wicker tables.

"Sesh, what has happened?"

"Nothing has happened, except that I have violated what I am and should be. And now I am trying to find out what that is."

"How?"

"I am not trying to be an American any more. I have stopped drinking and breaking up furniture and having dates with American girls . . ."

"And?"

"And . . . I am an Indian. I wish to dedicate my life to something, but to what I do not know."

"How will you find out?"

"I don't know yet. Perhaps I will become a holy man, with a begging bowl."

We talked a little more, but in a desultory not very meaningful way. And then we said goodby, and I watched him disappear in the twilight, hunched over and alone.

Delhi ❀ September 6

When Bhag Singh came back he left his wife in the hills with the new baby and brought with him his two older sons, Surendra Singh and Mehran Singh, aged six and four. Surendra will go to school here, and Mehran—well, fat and happy little Mehran will just wander around, I suppose.

Today, for fun, and to make friends with them, we took them to the circus. I had hoped secretly that a few gems of Indian wisdom might fall from their childish lips, but it must be truthfully admitted that nothing emerged but laughter and an occasional sigh of surprise. All I really learned was that an Indian circus does not differ greatly from an American small-town circus, and that small Indian boys, at least *these* small Indian boys, prefer lions and clowns to tight-rope walkers and elephants. Maybe they've seen too many elephants at home—and in the land of levitation who could think a tight-rope walker miraculous?

The circus was housed in a big tent on the open ground near the Jamma Masjid Mosque. Inside the tent there was only one ring, and around it were ranged the reserved, one-dollar seats—broken-down porch furniture with wicker seats. Beyond them rose tiers of the old-style circus board seats, jammed this afternoon with Indian men and boys. Here and there a row of village women were vivid splashes of magenta and yellow drapery, and way up at the top was a "purdah gallery," where a group of Moslem women sat in pure isolation to watch the antics below. On the sunlit roof of the tent circled the shadows of hawks.

To Westerners, accustomed to showmanship and a fast pace in their circuses, an Indian circus seems a desultory affair. There is no ringmaster, no one announcing "death-defying feats." Instead of brilliantly clad attendants whisking in and out of the ring, there is a colorless crowd of young men standing around morosely, none of whom seem quite sure what their job is. There are long intervals, during which the band sometimes plays and sometimes doesn't. Hawkers wander through the crowd selling not pink candy cotton, but curried chick peas.

The six-piece Sikh band was a raggedly affair with the musicians dressed in bits and ends of old Army uniforms and dirty flowered turbans, and they played wildly off key. However, the tunes they played were spirited numbers like "Constantinople," "Daisy, Daisy," and "Dardanella," and somehow they *did* manage to sound just as a circus band should sound. Little Mehran Singh, completely fascinated, spent most of the performance standing in his rickety chair, facing backwards, and watching the musicians with adoration.

We sat for awhile, and eventually two Indian men dressed in haphazard Western clothes trailed into the ring and placed a shaky-looking table at the center. Sometime later a Siamese girl in pink tights meandered over to the table and tied herself into contortionist knots. Then she wandered away. Time passed. The stage hands woke up, and the table was removed. A man in evening clothes did a tight-rope act climaxed by an imitation of a Western drunk—a curious performance, considering the prohibition sentiment in India. Judging from the laughter, this seemed to be popular, but we really couldn't tell very well. The custom of clapping is more or less a Western custom and has not yet reached the Indian masses. Surendra and Mehran looked both frightened and amazed when they saw us slapping our hands together; obviously, they had never seen anyone clapping before.

The drunk was followed by a second man, who threw knives at his dumpy Chinese wife in what looked like alarming boredom. They seemed to be popular, but the real *pièce de résistance* followed: two clowns hitting each other with sticks. Dressed in brightly striped, red-and-blue pajamas, their faces whitened, they might have been clowns in any circus, anywhere. Using their traditional clownly prerogatives, they sent the crowd into roars of laughter in a routine poking fun at a white man—a stooge planted in the front row who finally marched out of the tent in mock outrage, while the crowd howled with amusement, as they had at the figure of the "Western" drunk.

Other signs of the times were two Indian mythological dances representing stories of the god Krishna. These were new acts, obviously included in deference to free India, and seemed a bit odd, mixed in with Chinese knife-throwers, Polish acrobats, and horses. However, they were well received—at least by Surendra and Mehran.

The horses were followed by two elephants, and the elephants by a large, middle-aged Italian matron in spangles, the mother of a family of acrobats. This lady, who looked rather like a Brooklyn housewife in fancy dress, played around for a while with an apathetic boa constrictor. Once or twice the boa constrictor seemed to sneeze when its head came close to the fumes of an atmospheric pot of incense. The lady was followed by a tiny animal trainer, who put a crowd of truly terrifying lions through some agile tricks, and by an astonishing Indian who swallowed eight live goldfish of varying sizes, and regurgitated them in the same order in which he had swallowed them.

A trapeze act completed the afternoon—as we finally realized after a long wait, when it became evident that nothing more was going to happen. Silently the crowd poured out of the tent, Surendra and Mehran padding along beside us with equal solemnity. "Poor Indians!" I thought. "They certainly don't know how to enjoy a circus the way Americans do." But suddenly Surendra roared like a lion; Mehran began beating an imaginary drum. And we all went merrily down the road, laughing, roaring like lions, and marching to Mehran's "boom! boom! boom!"

Delhi ✾ September 8

At the moment I'm engaged in a search for an ayah. Not very seriously, because there is still lots of time, and anyway I'd really rather take care of the baby myself. But the various mothers around town have convinced me that an ayah is, after all, a rather useful person. Who will stay with the baby in the evening, if you don't have an ayah? Who will wash all the diapers and baby clothes? Why exhaust yourself doing these things when you can have an Indian woman to do them for fifteen dollars a month? Think of all the women at home and how they're tied down by their babies and have to pay a fortune every time they want to go to the movies. They'd jump at a chance for even a bad servant, wouldn't they? So if you have to have a baby in India, why not benefit from the one advantage here—servants?

So I agreed reluctantly. But I will *not* have one of those nurses who takes all the care of the baby away from the mother. One English mother told me wistfully that she wished she could bathe and dress her baby once in awhile, but that the ayah was so hurt and angry whenever she suggested such a thing that she had given up the idea. Her own baby, she said, was practically a stranger to her. Of course, she was probably a fool to let it go so far, but I'm afraid it's possible to drift into a situation like that; little by little the baby becomes the ayah's, not yours. And then,

if you're lazy (as most white women are in India), you hesitate
to give up your comfort and all that service . . .

Anyway, I have let it be known that I am looking for an ayah.

I like the old Hindu Rao Hospital, where the baby will be born.
Every week I go there for a checkup—the doctor, thank God,
having decided that her shared office is really too horrible for the
delicate sensibilities of her pregnant clients. So every Saturday
morning I drive up the hill above the Cecil Hotel, walk through
the arcaded entry, and climb the worn circular stairway. Then I
wander through the deserted inner sanctum of the hospital, with
no one to say me yea or nay, and study old engravings of the
Indian Mutiny hung tipsy-tilted on the walls of the marble-
floored reception room.

This is no crisp Western hospital with reception desks and
that polite barrier of discipline and the smell of ether which seems
to surround our mysterious and starched Western hospitals. Life
flows easily in and out of the Hindu Rao. Downstairs are many
poor Indians lined up before the door of the free clinic; their
children wander over to the private entrance to stare and sometimes say "namesteh." Upstairs, four Indian nurses, very clean and
smiling, drift about casually or occasionally bustle. And none of
this business of babies all sterile behind glass walls—these nurses
often tote in a newborn for me to see, chucking it under the
chin and ruffling its hair. All of which seems enjoyable to the
baby and, for all I can see, doesn't hurt it any.

For perhaps fifteen minutes, I wait placidly in the dim reception room, leafing through five-year-old copies of *The Tatler* or
Punch. Eventually a barefooted hospital orderly happens through,
carrying a tray or a bunch of flowers or some surgical instruments,
and I know that the word will be passed along that I am waiting.
And sometime after that the doctor sends a nurse for me, and I
am examined and pronounced fine—for an *elderly* mother, that is.
(They can never get over their amazement at anyone over twenty-
five having a baby. I feel like the Biblical Sarah.)

Afterwards, I join the doctor and Laura White, the crisp and amusing British matron, for a cup of coffee in Laura's office and a good gossip. While we talk, an old bitch dachshund, the hospital pet, usually wanders in for a lump of sugar. She looks as if she's had at least eighteen litters, and is vastly reassuring to any mother-to-be. But I can't imagine her wandering around the Harkness Pavilion of Medical Center.

Today I went up to the hospital for my regular examination and *Kaffeeklatch* with the matron—and a financial discussion. The hospital fees, she told me, are one hundred and fifty rupees flat (thirty dollars) plus ten rupees a day for the room (about two dollars). The doctor charges three hundred rupees (sixty dollars) for full prenatal care, delivery, and post-delivery care. That means that the medical cost of the baby will be around one hundred dollars.

Mrs. White also presented me with a long list of things which I am expected to bring to the hospital: antiseptic, cotton rolls, sanitary napkins, safety pins, razor blade, three dozen diapers, soap, talcum powder, roll of gauze, olive oil, and one and a half dozen "toweling squares." Never having had a baby before, I don't know whether this is the normal thing in American hospitals too, but somehow it seems a bit odd!

Over coffee, the matron, the doctor, the head nurse, and I all agreed that it was impossible to predict the sex of a baby in advance, and then agreed further that I am going to have a girl.

"When it's a girl, the bulge is horizontal," said Mrs. White, pointing to my horizontal bulging.

"The heart-beats of a girl are usually faster than those of a boy," said Dr. Passricha, who had just told me that the baby's heart-beats were fast and strong.

"Older mothers usually produce girls," said the head nurse, whose maternity patients are normally around eighteen or twenty.

The only person I know who thinks it will be a boy is the night clerk at the hotel. And why is he so sure? Very simple— when I start to walk somewhere, after standing still, I step out

with my left foot. Left foot means boy, right foot means girl.
Well, right left, I don't care; boy, girl—either one will be fine
with me!

Delhi ❀ September 10

Jane Klise is leaving India and has offered to turn over
her ayah to me. Today I went over to talk to Jane in New Delhi
and to take an unofficial look at the ayah. Her name is Mary, and
she looks competent and clean and cheerful. Jane says she's
wonderful, so everything seems settled—except for talking to
Mary, of course. And naturally she'll be looking for a job, so
what difficulties could there be?

Jane told me a ghoulish story about the experience of another
American couple, whose ayah had been well recommended and
seemed to them to be very good indeed. But when their baby developed thrush—a rather nasty infection of the mouth—it was
discovered that the ayah had been letting the baby suck her
finger, and to quiet it had resorted to the old Indian custom of
putting a little opium under the nail. The first time I heard of
this practice I wouldn't believe it, but Jane has convinced me that
sometimes it really happens. So now I'm doubly thankful to be
getting well-tried-out Mary.

Later

Jane telephoned in great distress, to say that Mary absolutely refuses to leave New Delhi and come to the Cecil in Old
Delhi. Only three miles away, but evidently a continent's width
to her. Why? Because her son brings her food twice a day, and
she can't visualize life without this arrangement. In vain Jane
has pleaded and cajoled and reasoned, pointing out that all the
other ayahs living in the Cecil's servants' quarters do very well on

food they cook themselves. But no, says Mary, she wants the food cooked in her son's kitchen, and only that food. And how could her son bring her food to her twice a day, all that great distance away?

Eric, sometimes cynical about these things, but vastly experienced in India, suggested that maybe Mary is holding out for more money. But Jane says no, she tried that too, and it didn't work. Mary knows perfectly well that good jobs for ayahs are growing scarce these days, and naturally she'd like a good job. But it has to be near her son's kitchen, because she prefers his style of cooking to her own. Nobody can tell me that the mysterious East is not mysterious.

Delhi ❀ September 11

I can never get used to the fact that most of the ordinary things a foreigner uses (and at home buys from a department store without a second thought) in India are either imported, and therefore usually not available, or else have to be made. Like the shower curtains. Or like a little bureau in which to keep baby clothes and diapers.

Naively, I had thought that I could just walk into a furniture store and buy either a bureau painted in a nice light blue or an unfinished one which I could paint myself. But I soon found that the unfinished ones are unheard of, and that the only ready-made ones available are of the type so depressingly prevalent in India homes and hotels: enormous armoires, always ugly, always dark, dark brown. Strange. If one were only visiting India for a few weeks or a few months, this sort of thing wouldn't matter. But living here, it does matter. On political and philosophical and even literary levels one can meet and talk with educated Indians. But on the subject of the arts there is a blankness. That is, the arts outside of Indian art. It is in this area that one occasionally feels really remote from "what is going on." Magazines and newspapers arrive from America and England a month or two late, but they are full of a kind of newness which seems exciting. Advertisements take on a glamor they never had at home. There is talk of architecture designed for living, of chairs and tables and bureaus conceived in beauty. Evidently people at home are interested in these things. And so am I.

But not here. Obviously, the poor cannot afford anything beyond a charpoy (which is pretty good design in itself, come to think of it). But the rich and the middle classes puzzle me. Why are they so satisfied with the hideous overstuffed armchairs and the gold velour couches set in a ring around the walls of the living-room? The clumsy Grand Rapids dining-tables and cumbersome chairs? The creaking armories in which D'Artagnan might have lurked? Are these elephantine encumbrances really suited to Indian life? Why is there rarely an effort to find something beautiful and simple and adapted to this country and this climate? Is it that the educated classes have been so preoccupied with politics for fifty years that they have had no time to become interested in the graces of life? This is the obvious answer, but I am puzzled when I think of the Japanese, with their exquisite aesthetic, or of the Chinese. It is as if a dimension had been left out of the magnificent, subtle Indian mind. Why don't they plant flowers? Well, of course they do—commercially, as offerings for the Gods. But no Indian I have ever met grows a flower as an object of beauty in itself. Everything is a symbol of something else. And trying to understand this, rather than just getting angry at it, is what makes India so fascinating and so infuriating.

Anyway, I was determined that my child should have a bureau for his diapers which, if not Swedish modern, was at least gay and functional. So last month I clipped a picture from an American baby book and went around to a carpentry shop where many Embassies have furniture made. The owner of the shop is a mop-haired old pundit with glittering gray eyes and a son studying physics at the University of California. He wasn't much interested in furniture design, but deeply interested in the relationship between the soul and the study of mathematics. Would work which contributed to a more explosive bomb, for instance, mean that his son would achieve a higher or a lower incarnation? Rather casually, he eventually accepted my photograph of the bureau I wanted, and said that it would be executed.

Two weeks later he telephoned to say that the bureau was ready. We went around to the shop, and the pundit led us through the wood and shavings and hunched-over workmen to a corner where the bureau awaited us. All the drawers stuck when we pulled them out; the whole thing tilted crazily, and the cheap wood showed through the one coat of paint it had been given.

If I had been alone in India, I would have meekly accepted the job and suffered from it. But Eric, having a more straightforward relationship with this country, blew up and gave the old pundit hell—in expert Urdu. Crisply, he outlined the faults of the bureau, the undoubted sinful ancestry of the men who had perpetrated it. And much to my surprise, the old pundit agreed completely, promised to have the faults remedied, and invited us to tea. At tea it developed that his son in California was returning shortly with an American bride—and did we think she would adjust happily to India?

Today, the bureau was brought to the hotel on a wooden cart drawn by an old horse, and installed in the big dressing room which will be the baby's room. The drawers pull in and out easily. The paint is pale blue, and there are evidently two coats. The cost was one hundred and twenty rupees, or about twenty-four dollars, which I suppose is about what it would cost at home.

Delhi ❁ *September 15*

I have now talked to six prospective ayahs, all more or less plausible, all with good chits—recommendations—and none of whom seem very impressive:

Angelina. Christian. A half-blind old creature, who is desperately in need of a job. She seems a comfortable type, but Mary Hotz, who knew her when she worked at the Cecil, says she is "a dirty old trout."

Nikki. Hindu. The Cave-Brown-Cave's ayah. They swear by her, but two women I know who also live at Maiden's Hotel, and who have watched her in action in the garden, have both told me privately they think she's dirty. Her English is abysmal, and she panicked when I asked her very slowly and quietly whether she had ever worked for an American. However, she is the best-recommended.

Bashira Kahn. A Moslem, which might make difficulties. But I like her by far the best. A big, raw-boned woman from Bengal. Has worked in a hospital, and has traveled to England, Australia, and Ceylon with various English *Mem-sahibs*. Both her English and her chits are good. She is the only ayah who has described in detail how carefully she brushes her fingernails and hands before she touches a baby. Also: "I boil everything." She is a grandmother with four children of her own. Typical of Moslems, she has a pleasant way of looking you straight in the eye, with friendliness—not cringing, like the other ayahs.

Sinairu. She comes from Simla, up in the hills, and doesn't like to stay on the plains in the summertime. She is very superior, and evidently expects to find an American duplicate of the old-style British family, whose women and children traveled to the mountains for the hot weather. She is not for us, nor we for her.

Lakshmi. The Trumbull's ayah, whom they no longer need now that the girls are old enough to go to boarding school. Bedraggled.

Parvati Ayah. The Gately's ayah. A lamb, gentle and eager-eyed. I will probably hire her, as soon as I can convince myself that someone quite as sweet and tender and nourishing really exists.

. . .

Every time I think I have a working knowledge of the Indian mind, something happens. Minor, but puzzling. Today, for instance, I went for an X-ray to a nice educated doctor (who weighed down my stomach on either side with sandbags to keep the baby quiet). Later on I was writing out a check for his Indian secretary, a pleasant young man who looked like Dopey in "*Snow White and the Seven Dwarfs*," and trying to explain to him why my bank account was in my maiden name instead of in my married name. (Easy to do in Burma, where women keep their own name, but impossible in India where they often keep their own name, but where nobody has ever heard of a *white* woman doing such a thing.) I explained that I was a journalist and had kept the name under which I write. He took my professional calling card and examined it from every angle.

"Oh," he said at last, pleased and smiling with his own powers of deduction, "and you are using a typewriter, yes?"

Now *what* was going on in his mind? Are typewriters to him always associated with journalists? Unlikely, since Indian journalist rarely use them. More likely he couldn't believe that a woman could be a journalist, so he thought I was a secretary. They never really can believe it, try as hard as they can.

Which reminds me that at a journalists' tea the other day, the Indian Minister of Commerce beamed broadly and, obviously making conversation, asked me: "You are sending mostly news now?" Of course one answers yes, that's right, or something equally inane. But *what* was in his mind? That there was some other time when I was sending cables, but *not* news?

Delhi ❀ September 16

Hurrah! My first package from America, containing an aluminum sterilizer with rack and bottles, has arrived without any trouble at all. Delivered right to the hotel and surrendered without fuss when we paid the postman seventeen rupees duty.

But the big package, the mail-order layette, is still tied up in red tape at the Bombay customs. And today I received two letters: one was from the Office of the Chief Comptroller of Imports, Ministry of Commerce, informing me that no import license would be necessary for anything I had ordered: the second was from the Bombay postal authorities informing me that they could not forward my second package unless I supplied an import license.

I called up a man I know in the Import Bureau. "Oh dear," he said. "Well, you *don't* need a license, but it would be easier to give you one than to argue with those people in Bombay." Which shows how much authority the Central Government has over the provincial governments! Anyway, he's sending me a license, and in due course I suppose I'll get the layette.

The real thing that's bothering them, he tells me, is the size of the layette. Separate packages with a few little items like crib sheets and baby nightgowns come through without any trouble. But an eighty-one piece layette for a baby which any Indian mother would just wrap up in an old sari seems fantastic nonsense! Obviously, I am going to black-market all those fancy American booties and shirties and nappies; obviously, something sinister is going on. All of which may go through the mind of just one young customs clerk, but he is enough to make trouble.

Still, I *must* have the things. Today, thinking that perhaps they would never be extricated in time, I made a really serious search through the New Delhi shops for baby clothes. I found nothing, absolutely nothing, useful or simple or functional. Everything, absolutely everything, was made of scratchy organdy and embroidered with rosettes. "These are the most fashionable baby clothes for Indian ladies who wish to dress babies like American babies," said one shopkeeper. When I asked him what one should use to dress babies like Indian babies, he just shrugged his shoulders.

Delhi ❄ *September 20*

"Coo....coo....rrhhhmmmff!" say the doves. I bury my head under the pillow, refusing the daylight of the doves. But I can still hear them, for they are ruffling and calling in the high windows near the ceiling. We need the windows for ventilation; they need the windows for preening and stretching, for telling us that the soft Indian morning is here, the few cool hours of dawn before the sun begins once more to blaze. "Coo...... rrhhhmmmff!" they say, and I roll on my back to watch the flutter of their tail-feathers, the arch of the neat gray necks.

The room is still a dusky blue. Over the desk, papers stir faintly in the air of the gently-revolving overhead fan. The fan makes a soft little whirring noise, subdued, dependable. On his small charpoy in the corner, the dachshund snores loudly once and is quiet. On the wall nearby, a little lizard squeaks in miniature alarm and darts behind a curtain. Suddenly, with a whirr of wings and voices, the doves fly off into the neem trees. Once more, the room is silent.

But it is morning now, and the hotel is waking. A splash . . . what's that? Oh yes, the bheestie filling his goatskin with water from the goldfish pond, getting ready to replenish the tanks of the desert coolers or water the roses. "Drip . . . splash . . ." goes the water, as he pads by our window.

"Look out! You misbegotten idiot!" An angry shout.

"Look out yourself, you low-caste robber!" The dhobi, with his pile of clean washing, stands and berates. The bheestie with his slippery goatskin, argues back in sullen defiance. But nothing happens; suddenly they go their ways, muttering, and the morning is quiet again.

But no . . . Mrs. Cook is crying. Usually she just cries late at night, deep strangled sobs drifting out from the transom of the room across the court. But sometimes she cries in the morning, and this morning I can hear her quite clearly. Mr. Cook is a retired British official with a pink, well-cared-for face, curly gray hair, and a soldierly posture. Mrs. Cook is also pink, but plump and anxious. They sit on the verandah and read the papers from England; they walk about the gardens; they bow good morning and good evening. They are clothed in impenetrable British correctness. To go to Mrs. Cook and say "I heard you crying, and I wish I could help you" would be unthinkable. All one can do is to bow good morning and good evening, and ignore her slightly pink nose, her slightly watery blue eyes. We will never know why she cries, I think, but only that she cries.

There are rays of sunlight now, slanting between the curtains. From the tennis courts I can hear the "whang! whang!" of balls. An early set, before the heat makes tennis impossible. And from the other direction comes the creak-bounce-recoil noise of the diving board being tested, the splash of an early swimmer.

The street outside the hotel is gathering together its noises of the day. Trot trot trot trot, the feet of the tonga ponies. Jingle jingle jingle, the bells on the harnesses. Creak . . . creak . . . creak . . . the rusty wheels of a heavy-laden ox-cart. And then a chorus of voices, far off, growing nearer, passing by, fading: "Ram, Ram, Ram, Ram . . ." A prayer procession winding down to the river for a ceremonial sunrise dip in the sacred waters.

A typical morning in India! Not a morning in a village, with its cows and the smell of dung fires. Not a morning on tour, with schedules to keep and pallid airfields at dawn. Not a morning in a clangorous bazaar or in a fishing boat or under a drain pipe. Just *my* morning—my own lazy, lucky, wonderful morning at the Cecil Hotel in Old Delhi, India.

The sunlight splashes through the curtains now and bedazzles the room. Mrs. Cook has stopped crying. But Eric still sleeps; the dog thumps his tail in ecstatic dream. The geckho is snapping silently at one droning fly. From the living-room beyond the closed mahogany door, I can hear Bhag Singh's voice giving orders in a low, furious whisper to the sweeper. Soon, very soon, he will open the door and bring us morning tea and morning newspapers. I stretch, yawn, plump up the pillow, and light a delicious forbidden cigarette. Happiness wells in my heart; contentment with life, with India, with work suffuses me.

As if to remind me that I am forgetting something else, the baby kicks. Ah yes, you there! What joy, what changes will you bring?

Delhi ✱ September 25

Well, Sesh hasn't become a swami with orange robes, shaved head, sandalwood beads, and a begging bowl—but if he had showed up in this outfit, I couldn't have been more surprised.

Suddenly, there he stood on the doorstep at teatime, looking apologetic, defiant, and even a little smug.

"I have come to take you to the new Mahatma," he said solemnly.

He wore sandals, bare legs, a dhoti, and a long white tunic-shirt. He looked very, very Indian, so much so that, God forgive me, I almost laughed. But I was so accustomed to seeing him in sports jacket and flannel slacks that it took me a minute to swallow my tea and macaroon, and gather my composure.

"The . . . new Mahatma?" I finally managed.

"Yes. You must be aware that Acharya Vinoba Bhave is in Delhi for a meeting and has set up camp near Rajghat. He is a great man, and I wish you to see him and to see how India reveres him. His prayer meeting begins just now. Come."

In a daze, I went. I was interested in Bhave but even more interested right now in Sesh. He refused to ride in our car, which he said was "materialistic," and for a moment I was afraid we would have to walk the four or five miles to Rajghat. But no, a horse and cart were spiritual enough, it seemed. As we jogged along, I tried to ask Sesh what had been happening to him.

"You will see," he said. "I am thinking of dedicating myself to others. I have thought of working with untouchables, or of sacrificing myself in some way—perhaps as a subject for new malaria experiments. Or I may become a follower of Vinobaji."

In that mood, I didn't dare ask him any more, so we rattled on in what I hoped was companionable silence. But I was puzzled. Sesh, with his worldly outlook, his intellectual approach to life, a sea-green incorruptible Gandhian? No irony, no detachment, no food, no drink, no sex? How far can the pendulum swing in India?

Behind Gandhi's cremation grounds a new village had been set up—a lovely little toy town of woven bamboo and reed shelters, clean, simple, and functional. And here, in the largest of these shelters, sat the old man who was called the New Mahatma, the old man who had been marching across the map of India, pleading with wealthy landowners to share with the less fortunate, to give one-sixth of their land to the landless.

The lean old man with the grizzled beard and the steel-rimmed spectacles sat at the center of a large white cloth which had been laid on the ground at one end of the room. Right now he seemed to be busy in conferences with various Congress politicians—a matter of intent looks and whispers in ears. Cross-legged on straw mats, the white-clad followers and disciples who filled the room murmured softly or occupied themselves with their little wooden spinning wheels. Everyone seemed to be waiting for something to happen.

We took off our shoes and sat down on the floor near the entrance—Sesh very silent and respectful but somehow . . . or did I imagine it? . . . a bit uneasy. But the room was quiet, and it was a good time to look at the *acharya* (acharya means "teacher") and think about what he had come to represent in India.

A cynical Indian once told me: "In India we manufacture holy men by the thousands, and our country is always more or less under the domination of some religious leader. The Russians' dictatorship is nothing compared to that of our holy men—for after all, the Russians are not in daily communication with the Almighty."

Like many witty observations, this one is only partially true. After all, the Indian constitution was not drafted by swamis, and holy men do not occupy Cabinet offices. Foreign policy is conducted without benefit of astrology—although there are those who think it should have the benefit, and they are not all astrologers.

Nor are the Indian people, by and large, much holier in their behavior than the peoples of any other country. Black-marketeering, corruption, inhumanity of man to man—and to animals and natural resources—flourish here as sturdily as anywhere else.

And yet there is a difference from most other countries, and the difference lies in the Indian people's yearning to be quite different from what they are, and in their desire to listen to (if not necessarily to follow) any one who speaks of a more ethical way of life. They are, in truth, people who *want* to be good.

In Hinduism it is often said that there are many paths to God. The peasant in the field, worshipping a stone, shares the same religion as the Brahmin intellectual contemplating the infinite. There is, in consequence, a unity of sorts among the thousands of men and women in India, who are all engaged in one way or another in seeking salvation.

Some people turn inward toward their own salvation: the men who recite a thousand lines from the Gita before breakfast, or who sweep the path as they walk to avoid taking the life even of an insect; the men who retire to a cave in the Himalayas to sit cross-legged for twenty years, or who crawl on their knees to all the places of holy pilgrimage.

Others turn outward: they open *ashrams*, or sanctuaries, where select students may partake of their wisdom, or they run dispensaries or schools for the poor.

A third group goes still farther: it produces men who talk not only of God and the personal salvation of the soul, but also of social reform, and who attempt to mobilize not only one small area of India or a single caste, but the entire nation. It was this group that Mahatma Gandhi so effectively crystallized.

Since the death of Gandhi, the Indian people have been lonely for a symbol of what they call their "higher aspirations." While they have a deep pride in freedom and in all the bustling "nation-building activities," life for most people is as uncomfortable, as anxious, and as quarrelsome as it ever was. All over India various saints have been preaching, as they have for milleniums, of the possible and impossible paths to salvation; in New Delhi, Nehru preaches the path of realism and rationality. But it was a reformer and religious leader in the familiar Gandhian tradition whom the people wanted. Today, Acharya Vinoba Bhave seems to be filling that need.

There are two reasons, I think, for Bhave's success. One is that he fits the specifications for a "saint" almost perfectly. Although he is only in his late fifties or early sixties, he already looks the part of the wise old man. He dresses meagerly, as did Gandhi, in sandals and a wisp of hand-spun cloth. He eats only five bowls of curds a day. He carries the message of love, brotherhood, and non-violence. And he leans on the shoulders of two comely Indian maidens.

A second and most important reason for his immense following is that he has hit upon a somewhat revolutionary idea which seems to be working. Neither Gandhi nor Bhave could have aroused any mass following unless they had fitted into the symbolic pattern. But there are many wise old men in India who fit the pattern without presenting any bold new idea, and they run their little *ashrams* without making any stir in the outside world. What is needed is the bold new idea. Gandhi's was non-violent revolution; Bhave's is land redistribution through free gifts.

For several years now, he has been marching around from village to village, holding prayer meetings and asking the rich and the poor to give one sixth of their land to landless laborers, as they might donate a sixth slice to a sixth son. And his results have been amazing: thousands, hundreds of thousands of gifts of land.

There are criticisms, of course. That he works on the emotions of those who cannot afford to have their emotions worked upon —the small landholding peasant. That like Gandhi, he maintains the economic status quo, rather than changing it. That the real need is for a rational, planned land reform, and not an emotional patchwork quilt. That people only give their worst, most unworkable lands. That he is being used as a political tool by the Congress Party. That India's planning should stem from professionals in New Delhi, and not from an emanciated holy man wandering around the countryside. That . . .

But there is a roar of motor cars outside, and a stir of voices. Everyone in the room looks up, attentive, expectant. I am closest to the door, and I can see the shadows of men on the sunlit bamboo mat which curtains the door. A puff of dust, and the mat is lifted. As I am sitting on the floor, I look down, beyond the threshold, and see a pair of feet in sandals. Quickly, as if they had done it many times, the large brown feet slip out of their sandals, and every bare toe alive with confidence, step into the room, advance across the plain straw matting. My eyes rise beyond the bare legs, the homespun white dhoti, and I recognize the President of India.

Like any other disciple, he crosses the room and sits at the feet of the *acharya*. And then, understanding symbolism as well as any other man in India, he offers as much of his own land-holdings as the holy man chooses to take. And I, irreverantly (irrelevantly?) try to imagine the bare feet of any of our American Presidents, sitting in reverence before a wise man, or before a man who has renounced the material benefits of this world in order to bring love and peace and livelihood to others. I can't.

After chanted prayers, we left in deep twilight. Sesh was subdued on the way home. In fact, he didn't say anything, and neither did I. We parted with self-consciously folded hands: *namesteh.*

October

Delhi   October 1

At THIS point, only four weeks until the baby
is due, I'm quite happy to fall in with the Indian party custom
which normally I so dislike: the business of the women sitting in
chairs in a circle around the room while the men all stand in a
huddle in the middle. Especially lately, when the weather has become cooler and the overhead fans are often turned off; evidently I am the only one with a built-in hot-water-bottle.

Tonight, at the Foreign Secretary's, I drooped into a chair
beside an amiable-looking woman. She, it turned out, had been
in Washington for a year and a half when her husband was sta-
tioned at the Embassy there, and consequently was not as tongue-
tied with foreigners as many Indian women are.

She liked Washington, she said, although she had been terrified
at first when she found out she would have to do her own shopping and much of the housework, as her husband could afford
only one servant. But apparently the terrors passed off as she discovered super-markets and electric gadgets. All in all, the only
real trial was ironing six yards of sari every day. Still, I rather
gathered that she was happy to get back to India, where husbands

or head bearers do all the shopping, and every household of her class has at least six servants. She has three children, two of whom attended school in Washington; she was somewhat non-committal on the subject of American schools and, I gathered, not too approving.

I asked her about "christening" ceremonies in India, and she told me of some of the Moslem customs which are followed in introducing a baby to life. The first ceremony, a lovely one, takes place about six days after the baby is born. In the presence of a few relatives and close friends, the baby is brought out into the garden at night and ceremoniously shown the stars while a few passages from the Koran are read aloud. Afterwards, a small feast is held for the immediate members of the family.

The second ceremony takes place anywhere from a month to six weeks after the baby's birth. This seems to be a kind of good luck observance: in the presence of close relatives and a few friends, the baby's head is shaved while passages are read from the Koran. The baby's hair is then mixed with flour and weighed on a scale against small pieces of silver. The silver is then given to the nearest beggar outside the gates. As the amount never comes to more than four to eight annas (six to twelve cents), nobody is ever impoverished by the custom, but everyone feels the baby has started off well in a life of charity and good deeds.

The third ceremony is a big bang-up and is held when the baby is about two months old. All relatives to the fifth cousin six times removed—everyone who could remotely qualify as a friend of the family's—is invited. All of them bring—or are expected to bring—presents of various sorts, ranging from jewelry to toys and clothes. These are deposited at the feet of "the bride and groom," as my informant insisted on calling the mother and father. The parents sit cross-legged under a flower-decorated pavilion, the baby lying on a cloth before them. A band plays, an enormous feast is held, and everyone (except possibly the baby) is very, very gay.

I asked my talkative friend about the belief in prenatal conditioning. She said she believed in it because of what had happened to her sister: her sister had been warned not to go out into the garden on moonlight nights during her pregnancy, but she disobeyed the warning and regularly went to the bathroom in the evening in the garden. And sure enough, the baby was born blue! She herself, said my new friend, liked very much to dance and sing during the time she was carrying her second child, a girl. And now, as you might expect, the daughter too loved to dance and sing! I have never yet met an Indian woman, even of the most educated classes and background, who did not believe in such conditioning.

Delhi ❀ *October 4*

Every morning for many months I have taken Jimmy for a walk in the hotel garden: around the swimming-pool, by the roses, under the flame tree, along the lines of the sweet-pea beds, under the bougainvillea arbor. Then while Jimmy dashes through the green tunnel made by the hibiscus bushes growing against the low wall which divides the Cecil from the Delhi Commissioner's garden, I pass sedately between the potted daisies and poppies. We meet again by the patch of yellow pansies at the end of the wall.

And every morning, somewhere between the sweet peas and the daisies, I find the same two little men: Indian gardeners (or malis) in breech clouts and dirty jackets, with red turbans around their head, scratching desultorily at the earth, arranging strings for the sweet peas, or cutting back dead branches. Mostly they don't seem to be doing anything much, just fussing.

At first, since I passed within three feet of them, I used to say a bright "Good Morning!" Then I changed it to "Salaam." Then I tried *"Namasteh."* At last I simply smiled. Now I pass by as if they weren't there.

For not once in all these months have I been able to elicit a greeting, a smile, or a nod from my two little trolls. Never have they, by the slightest motion of their bodies, indicated that they heard my morning greeting. Their eyes are downcast as I pass, although I know that like all Indians, they watch the foreigner coming, and they watch her go. But they are too humble to speak, and they make it quite clear that the foreigner does wrong in trying to make them do so.

And so, as I pass by the daisies, the poppies, and the yellow pansies, while Jimmy races after the old gray cat, my mind goes back to a rose garden on Cape Cod, far away in America, and a gardener we met there.

"Sure you can come in and see my roses," he said, smiling. Towering above us in his blue denims and white shirt, he proudly led the way down grass paths between beds of scarlet, white, and golden blossoms.

"Of course they aren't really *my* roses," he said, leaning against a sun dial and lighting a cigarette. "They belong to her up in the big house." He gestured with his cigarette at a white mansion on the hill. "But she just paid for them and never looks at them. *I* grew them."

One by one he pointed out his favorite roses, and told us how he had nursed them to their present full bloom.

"Funny how she never comes to see them," he remarked as we strolled back to the gate. "But she's rich, and I guess she has too many troubles to bother about my roses."

We shook hands. "It sure was nice of you folks to drop in," he said. He waved as we drove away.

Sometimes, for fun, I like to say that the only things about America I really miss are Macy's and the martinis at Bleeck's. But really, what I miss very deeply is the spirit of friendliness and the pride of people like the Cape Cod gardener. I understand some of the economic and social reasons for its absence in India, but I still miss it.

Never mind. One adjusts. And now that October is here, the hotel garden is once again becoming a little Eden. In northern

India, October is like a looking-glass springtime, cooling down instead of warming up, but achieving the same effect, the same feeling. Once again the grass is green, the flowers bursting with colors on their succulent stems, the air so soft that one knows this latest puff of gentle wind on the cheek can only be called a zephyr. It is a fine season to pull a wicker garden chair into the gracious sunlight and sit in dreaming indolence, sorrowing perhaps for the harassed women at home who have so little time to sit quietly and feel the universe turn beneath them and know their own part in its turning.

But with the evening comes a renewal of energy. I am ordered to walk three miles a day, so after tea we drive the car up the hill above the hotel, park, and go for the prescribed constitutional along the famous "ridge." Here, during the agonizingly long hot summer of 1857, British soldiers lived and fought and died and prepared for the final assault upon Delhi, the final destruction of the Indian Mutiny. The Hindu Rao Hospital, where my baby will be born, was their headquarters; if it had not held against innumerable attacks, the Mutiny might have been won, and as a very minor consequence, we would probably not be walking the ridge every evening.

There are few relics of that war now. Only the old roundhouse and an excruciatingly ugly Victorian memorial to the soldiers who died on the ridge. Instead, there is a wilderness of scrub trees and bridle paths, and on one side a view of the Jumna River, on the other Delhi University and the plains of India. In the blue haze of evening the plains look almost like the ocean; when the weather was hotter I pretended it was the Mediterranean I saw, and felt cooler.

Soon after we begin our walk, we pass a now deserted Moslem mosque. In the clearing in front of it, students from the university are practicing weight-lifting with stones which have tumbled from the Koranic battlements. Around a bend of the bridle path, two government clerks are sitting cross-legged and immobile on flat stones, practicing withdrawal and contemplation. Leaning against a monument, a thin boy is reading a book called *Applied Chemistry*. Nearby, a Hindu sadhu in an orange sarong, with a face like Christ, wanders alone among the camel's-thorn trees. Swarms of dragonflies hover just over our heads, and just above the trees we see flights of green parrots which Eric says are called "Rosy Pastors" because of the pink ring around their necks. Last night, miraculously, a cerulean peacock broke from the under-brush as we passed by, and flourished itself under a flame tree. Not every mother-to-be, I imagine, encounters such wonders on her dutiful daily walk.

We have both become quite interested in birds, largely be-cause of these walks, and talk of "taking up bird-watching" some day. I never seem to be able to remember which bird is which, unless it is something quite unmistakable like a peacock, but Eric is getting quite good at it. Last night, as we walked along the ridge, I asked him whether when one joined a bird-watching group, one stalked birds in Red Indian style? Then, since he didn't know what I meant, I proceeded to show him what Ameri-can Indian stalking looked like—crouching low, and tiptoeing with exaggeration, hand over eyebrows. Just then, two Indian students, marching purposefully, came around a turn in the path. I straightened up, but not quite in time, and we passed with obvious amazement on their part and embarrassment on ours. Such grotesque behavior by a clearly very pregnant woman could never, never be explained in India!

Delhi ❀ October 6

The last three evenings I have walked alone on the ridge with Jimmy, as Eric has been tied to the kind of fast-breaking news story from which I am at last free. Maternity leave has its advantages.

Two days ago, as I marched down the red-powdered path among the camel's-thorn trees, with Jimmy yelping far ahead, I came on a man crouched at the side of the path, spreading white powder in the dust. He was dressed in casual-looking, blue-and-white striped pajamas and a tattered old coat. He looked dirty, unshaven, and a little mad. So intent was he upon his mysterious work that he did not look up until I was just passing him, and the expression of his strange eyes seemed to me purely evil. I walked on quickly and took another path back to the car.

Last night he was there again, rubbing powder into the ground. I skirted him widely and fearfully, wondering why on earth he was there and what he was doing. Faintly, I remembered a madman who had once tried to poison the pigeons in Bryant Park in New York, and I thought that perhaps this man too was an eccentric poisoner.

Tonight, as Eric and I began our walk, I told him about the man with the powder. "Why didn't you just ask him what he was doing?" asked my practical husband. "I was afraid," I said.

Just then we rounded the bend beyond the old mosque and saw the crouching man with his paper bag and his powder. Eric strolled up to him and said amiably *"Kya Hal, Jenab?"* which means "How are things, friend?"

The man looked up, rose to his feet, and bowed with folded palms. The face, which I had thought evil, creased into a smile.

"Why, things are very well, Sahib," he said politely.

"How so?"

"Well, you see, I am a refugee. I was driven from my home with my wife and my son and daughter during the terrible partition, and I lost everything. But I met a friend in Delhi who advanced me enough money to open a small fruit stand in the bazaar.

"The fruit stand prospered, and I was able to repay my debt. Now I am a happy man. The fruit stand is making enough money for us to live. My wife is not a shrew. My son is in the university. I have arranged to marry my daughter to a young man of her caste earning rupees two hundred a month. So I am a happy man."

"Yes, that is good. But why are you here, and what are you doing with this powder?"

"Well Sahib, it seemed to me that since I am so happy and so fortunate, I should give thanks to God in some manner. So I thought that the best way I could give thanks would be to feed some of God's creatures. But which ones? There are special homes for the cows, and they are well cared for. The sacred monkeys too are allowed to eat as they wish.

"And then I thought of the ants of the earth. Who feeds the ants? No one, I said, no one feeds the humble ants. So every day I save a little of my flour ration and bring it up here on the ridge for the little ants. And I spread it on the ground in gratitude to God."

A few years ago I would have been incredulous at this story, would have considered the man insane, or would have been angry with him because he was feeding ants instead of hungry children. But now I am learning to think in terms of symbols; what good, after all, would his meagre ration of flour have been to all the hungry children of India? How deep and essential was his feeling that he must share the fortune of life, and how unimportant whatever choice he made for his sharing! He felt himself to be part of a whole, and to have an obligation to that whole—and I don't think it would really have mattered whether he had decided to kiss all the leaves of a single *peepul* tree as a symbol of this understanding, or to feed his cherished ration of flour to an ant hill.

Tonight I feel much chastened and have made my ten thousandth resolution not to judge Indians by appearances, and to try to understand them with deeper love and deeper sensitivity.

Delhi ❊ October 10

I am growing more and more conscious of my own awareness of the bird, animal, and insect life of India. Perhaps this is because of my nightly walks on the ridge, and particularly because of the ant-man, who has been much in my mind. Perhaps it is that now that I am not working, I have more time to look at the un-newsworthy aspects of Indian life. Or perhaps because I feel an increasingly deep bond between my fulfilled body and all other creatures, human or non-human, capable of creating life.

Drifting off to sleep, I say to myself: "I will think of India." And then the first thing I think of is birds. This is curious, for surely I might be expected to think first of people. There certainly seem to be more people than birds in India.

Yet I, no bird specialist, involuntarily think of birds. The noisy crows, very black and shining on the vivid green of the hotel lawns. The doves which roost on the wide sills of the windows set for ventilation high in the walls and wake you early in the morning with their ruffling and cooing. The sparrows flying in and out of the screenless windows of homes and offices, and sometimes into the august rotunda of Parliament. No one ever seems to mind them, and there is none of the fluttering and crying of humans which happens when a bird gets into a Western room. The sparrows always find their own way out.

These are the common birds, but somehow one notices them more in India than at home. Then there are the uncommon ones, uncommon at least to Western eyes. The hoopoe, that fine speckled fellow with feathers set backward on his head—feathers he can ruffle open like a crown. Kashmiris say that he was once a king. And the blue jay, a cerulean flash above the rice paddies. The kingfishers in the Himalayas, looking top-heavy with their long beaks on their little flaming bodies. The vultures, which were so sated during the great killings of 1947 that they hung bloated in the roadside trees, unable to fly. The kites, wheeling forever, high in the sky above the cities—some people say you can tell the cleanliness or filth of a city merely by estimating the number of kites flying above it. And always the peacocks, which continually astonish me no matter how often I see them scampering over the fields of northern India. Somehow I can never believe I am looking at a wild peacock, even when I am.

And often now, I think of monkeys, those chattering, intriguing idiots. The big silvery-gray ones bouncing on the joyfully springy pine branches in Simla. The little tawny fur-balls climbing over the erotic carvings of a temple in Benares. The long-haired, long-armed mothers scooping in their squealing youngsters among the roots of a banyan tree as we pass by on our way to picnic at Okhla. And their bright eyes peeking out between the great twisted roots, like so many fey creatures in an Arthur Rackham drawing. The big fellows who leap onto the back balconies of the hotel and who, if the doors are open, steal anything they can find. Once one of them even stole a typewriter from a Finnish tourist.

They are a scourge, of course. In some states, like Uttar Pradesh, they eat one third of the food grown, and since the food grown is just sufficient to feed the populace of Uttar Pradesh, the state has a deficit of one third of what it needs. Any sane people, we Westerners would think, would immediately eliminate, or at least control, the monkeys. And indeed, the government is trying to do so and, no doubt, will one day succeed.

But monkeys are sacred, and in India that is a very serious matter. After the beautiful Queen Sita was stolen by the wicked Ravana of Ceylon—several thousand years ago—her husband sought the aid of Hanuman, king of the monkeys. Hanuman called all the monkeys together, and they made a bridge hand to tail across the waters to Ceylon, so that Rama and his armies could go and rescue Sita. Therefore—and the "therefore" involves not only custom, but a reverence which is as alive today as it was a thousand years ago—one may not kill monkeys. One may capture the plump and insolent marauders and let them free many miles away, but one must not kill monkeys. In theory, at least. Actually, thousands of Indian monkeys are shipped every year to Western scientific laboratories, and the Indians know very well, or at least suspect, what happens to them. But there are continual protests in the newspapers against the practice, and occasionally a Government member will have to defend the shipments in Parliament. These days it is possible to make the defense on logical grounds, but on the whole the attitude seems to be one of not letting the left hand see what the right is doing.

I have never quite understood about sacred animals. Take the cow, for instance, the most sacred of sacred. I have seen an Indian grow quite hysterical as he talked of "cow preservation" and "the abolition of cow slaughter." "Would you kill your mother and your sister?" he begged, tears in his eyes. "Then how can you kill cows?" The feeling is so deep, the abhorrence of beef-eating so strong and so widespread, that I too begin to share it; somehow I feel it's fine for me to enjoy a big juicy steak, but I am faintly revolted when I see a modernized Hindu ostentatiously eating beef.

All right, so the cow is your sister and your mother, and when you die you leave your money to a home for old cows. But why then is the cow treated with a callousness which would make an Elizabethan bear-baiter blush? All over India stagger scrawny, diseased oxen, their dirty flanks scarred with the marks of many whips, pulling loads which look as if they would make an elephant hesitate. And the tails of the oxen are lumped and deformed, for it is the custom of drivers to lean over and break a segment of the tail whenever they want the beasts to move faster. The wandering cows, sickly and fly-clouded, seem no better loved or cared for than the hard-working oxen. But sacred? Ah yes, very sacred. Sometimes I wonder what "sacred" *means*.

Once I was driving a jeep along a narrow dirt road in south India, traveling rather fast because my Indian interpreter—a local schoolteacher—was late for an appointment. We rounded a curve of jungle, and a few hundred feet ahead of us I saw a cow walking on one side of the road, a man on the other.

"If I have to hit one, which should it be?" I asked, half joking.

"The man, of course," said the schoolteacher, without a trace of
a smile. Luckily, we just scraped through.

Never mind. The cows are part of the animal atmosphere of
India, and one comes to take them rather for granted, stepping
carefully around their huge flanks as they lie on the pavement in
front of the cloth shop one wishes to visit, or stopping the car and
waiting patiently until some great white animal with flapping
dewlaps and blank brown eyes chooses to arise and amble out of
the way. And by now I even feel at home with, and enjoy, the
smell of burning dung cakes cooking the evening meals.

Our life, even in the city, is full of animals. Birds, monkeys,
cows. But also the gay little ponies decorated with magenta
feathers, bells, necklaces, and blue beads, which pull the two-
wheeled carts called tongas. Geckos, the little lizards, which
scamper about our walls all evening and drive Jimmy to frenzy
because he can never catch them. Jackals, which howl outside at
night, sometimes up to the gates of the hotel, but which we
only see as gray shadows streaking across the road as we drive
home late from a party. The mangy pariah dogs, outcast of
animals, who live on bazaar scraps and offal. But very few cats,
for the Indians think they are unclean. And oddly enough, I
have seen few snakes outside the snake-charmers' baskets.

This welter of animal life seems quite natural, even in the midst
of a big city. To the Indian, animals are part of the whole flow
of life, not something distinct and apart. And I, full with child,
feel a part of this flow, sharing with the animals and the birds
about me the miracle of creation. Perhaps, after all, the cow is my
sister.

Delhi ❀ October 14

Today, a Sunday, we drove out to visit some friends at a
refugee resettlement project some miles from Delhi. And much

to my surprise, the first person we bumped into at the headquarters offices was Sesh! He wore clean khaki pants and a white
shirt open at the throat, socks and sandals—the reasonable Indian's compromise with East and West, the weather, and decorum. And he seemed a completely different person from the
solemn Gandhian of a few weeks ago.

"I *am* different," he admitted, as we walked along on an inspection tour of the new brick homes which the refugees are
building for themselves with government help. We sat down on
a pile of lumber in the shade of a newly-planted tree, and he told
me about it.

"I have been trying for so long to find a path for my life," he
said. "I tried Communism, but I have a rather literal-minded con-
ception of honesty, and I found that as a Communist I couldn't
be honest with myself. Then I tried being completely Western,
but that way seemed to lead toward ruination. I did not know
how to *live* my Westernization, except by drinking and by
dating American girls, and writing tracts against Communism.
But I wanted to be for something, and I wanted to find a good
way of life to show what it was I was living for.

"So then, naturally, I tried Gandhianism, for this seems to be a
good way, a saintly way, for many people. But again—I was uncomfortable. Maybe I'm wrong, but I can't really convince myself that the problems of India can be solved by encouraging the
peasants to be clean and pure and to practice home spinning!"

Sesh picked up a pebble and began tossing it back and forth
from one thin, nervous hand to the other. He smiled cheerfully.

"Oh, I know that's simplifying the Gandhian movement terribly, but what I mean is that I think I'm really on the side of
dams and power projects and moderate industrialization and good
strong land reform laws. Certainly we need the Gandhian kind of
movement, for it is a deep expression of Indian morality. But
for myself, I wish to work where I can see things happening,
where I can help people to help themselves."

He waved his hand across the panorama of bare fields, new

buildings, new roads, new factories, concrete mixers, and people swarming everywhere—people who had never before used their bodies in manual labor, and who were now busily building homes for themselves and their families.

"Here, for instance," said Sesh. We were silent for awhile.

"There is one more thing," he said at last. "I am not of an age or a temperament to practice *brahmacharya*."

"I know, Sesh. I have always said you should be married. But since you will not accept an arranged marriage and since interesting single girls are so hard to meet, what can you do?"

"Perhaps I must accept an arranged marriage, after all," Sesh said slowly, looking down at the ground, unhappy and a little cross.

"Oh Sesh!"

"Well, it's not so bad," he said defensively. "After all, I have learnt not to expect too much of happiness to come to one from outside. And my mother is worried; she knows it is time as well as I do. She has found a suitable girl, a Brahmin of my own sub-caste, England-returned and an instructor of history in a college. My mother sent me the girl's photograph, and she looks all right."

Sesh stood up and brushed the dust from his khaki slacks. "Mind you, I still think it's a terrible system," he said. "It's outrageous that I can't meet enough girls to pick a wife for myself, and that the only choice I have is to meet this girl and decide then whether I want to marry her or not!"

We picked our way through the rubble toward the others. Sesh suddenly laughed. "But I'm still taking the train to Madras next week," he said.

Kurukshetra, East Punjab ❀ *October 19*

The time of the child is near: I am swollen with joy; I am nearly fulfilled.

And tonight I sit on the porch of a rest house, gazing over the dark and endless plain of Kurukshetra. In the far distance I can see the campfires of half a million pilgrims who tomorrow, by their prayers, will try to rescue the sun from the demon Rahu. We of the unbelieving West will call it an eclipse, but the Hindus know that tomorrow another of the endless battles between the forces of good and the forces of evil will occur.

Kurukshetra, ninety-seven miles northwest of Delhi, is one of the holiest places of Hindu pilgrimage. It was here that the world —the world of India, at least—was created; it was at this point in formless space that the great god Vishnu sat in a trance when from his stomach a lotus flower sprouted, and from the lotus came the four-faced Brahma chanting the four eternal Vedas. Thus the world began.

But that was long ago, at the dawn of time. More recently, about twenty-five centuries ago, Kurukshetra was the bleak scene of one of India's most famous battles, and of one of the world's most famous conversations—events later recorded in the Bhagavad-Gita.

On one side of the battlefield stand the forces of the wicked Kauravas, who had stolen the kingdom of the five Pandava brothers. On the other side is arrayed the smaller army of the Pandavas, who had been given the choice of a large army or the aid of the great god Krishna; they had chosen Krishna. The third Pandava brother, Arjuna, with his mighty bow Gandiva, stands ready in his chariot, with Krishna himself for his charioteer.

The conch horns blow; the sun glints on waiting metal; the soldiers clamor for the fight. But Arjuna, their leader, is motionless. His eyes sweep over the armies of the enemy, and suddenly he sees not soldiers, not enemies, but "teachers, fathers, grandfathers, uncles, sons and brothers, husbands of sisters, grandsons and cousins . . ."

His bow slips from his hand, and the great warrior sinks to the seat of the chariot. Although he knows that the Kaurava army represents evil, he tells Krishna, he cannot bring himself to take action against this evil—knowing what the result of the action will be. Krishna, who has concealed his radiant godliness in human form, turns to speak. And then, while the opposing armies wait in what must have seemed a dreamlike trance, Krishna and Arjuna hold the discourse which has influenced India for nearly three thousand years. For it was then, once and for all, that the law was laid down that man must take action which he believes to be right, regardless of consequences; that evil must be actively opposed. And it was then that the clearest expression was given to the essential beliefs of Hinduism.

"Your words are wise, Arjuna," says Krishna, "but your sorrow is for nothing. The truly wise mourn neither for the living nor for the dead.

"There was never a time when I did not exist, nor you, nor any of these kings. Nor is there any future in which we shall cease to be.

"Just as the dweller in this body passes through childhood, youth, and old age, so at death he merely passes into another kind of body. The wise are not deceived by that.

"Feelings of heat and cold, pleasure and pain, are caused by the contact of the senses with their objects. They come, and they go, never lasting long. You must accept them.

"A serene spirit accepts pleasure and pain with an even mind and is unmoved by either. He alone is worthy of immortality.

"That which is non-existent can never come into being, and that which is can never cease to be. Those who have known the inmost Reality know also the nature of *is* and *is not*.

"That Reality which pervades the universe is indestructible. No one has power to change the Changeless.

"Bodies are said to die, but That which possesses the body is eternal. It cannot be limited, or destroyed. Therefore you must fight." *

* This passage and others concerning the conversation of Krishna and Arjuna, are taken from *Bhagavad-Gita; The Song of God*, translated by Swami Prabhavananda and Christopher Isherwood (New York: Harper & Brothers, 1951).

As the talk progresses and becomes more metaphysical, Krishna says:

"No one who seeks Brahman [God] ever comes to an evil end.

"Even if a man falls away from the practice of yoga, he will still win the heaven of the doers of good deeds and dwell there many long years. After that, he will be reborn into the home of pure and prosperous parents. He may even be born into a family of illumined yogis. But such a birth in this world is more difficult to obtain.

"He will then regain that spiritual discernment which he acquired in his former body; and so he will strive harder than ever for perfection. Because of his practices in the previous life, he will be driven on toward union with Brahman, even in spite of himself. For the man who has once asked the way to Brahman goes further than any mere fulfiller of the Vedic rituals. By struggling hard and cleansing himself of all impurities, that yogi will move gradually toward perfection through many births and reach the highest goal itself."

The campfire lights have flickered out, and the great plain of Kurukshetra is as quiet now as in the moment of that hushed conversation, before Arjuna took up his bow and led his forces to victory. Above our heads, the stars flicker and burn across the night.

Many births . . . many births. Will it be an old soul who comes into my care as he travels through the eons toward perfection? Or a new little soul, who has had to move several incarnations back in order to learn a lesson imperfectly learned before? Of one thing I'm certain, though—he's not being born into a family of illumined yogis! Or for that matter, even into a home of pure and prosperous parents. But no matter: whatever our young mysterious traveler through eternity is seeking, we welcome him —body and soul.

Kurukshetra ✿ October 20

The wicked demon Rahu sprang today from the abysses of the sky to attack his ancient enemy the sun, but thanks to the prayers of the pilgrims, failed to gain more than a toothhold upon his gleaming prey and was eventually forced to retire. "Right action" once again triumphed over evil!

As everyone in India knows, anyone who bathes in the great Lake of Kurukshetra during the period of an eclipse washes away all sins and earns eternal merit, especially if prayers are uttered in defense of the besieged sun. At the time of the eclipse, Hindus also believe, waters from all the holy rivers of India pour into the lake and thus multiply its powers of purification.

For days, tens of thousands of men, women, and children have been arriving at the camping places (hygenically prepared by government workers and boy scouts) near the sacred lake. And today all of them seemed to converge all at once on the wide dirt road leading to the lake. There were hundreds of holy men, too: some with faces painted in rainbow colors, some carrying beds of thorns, some dressed in nothing but a smearing of white ash which made them look like thin little children playing ghosts. There were women in scarlet-and-yellow cloaks and men in magenta turbans. There were thousands and thousands of farmers and their wives, wrapped in the plain gray rags of the poor. And there were cows, of course, always cows.

Suddenly I found myself separated from Eric, separated from the other correspondents, separated from everyone except myself and the baby and half a million Indians. And I was swept along, pressed on one side into the soft, dirty-white flank of a cow, pressed on the other by humanity, at the center of a softly panting inexorably moving mass. The dust swirled up around us; the sun beat down upon us; we pushed; we elbowed each other. Yet we went on; there was nothing else to do.

Separately, we moved forward; separately yet together. The whole was oneness, oneness was the whole. And I, no longer was I foreign, distinct, alone in an alien culture. I was not an American, not a woman, no longer a detached observer.

For this length of time—and it seems strange only in retrospect, for it did not seem strange then—I was part of the oneness, part of the whole, part of the flow of humanity. There was no time, no birth, no death. Only the soul, forever and forever flowing through life. And suddenly I seemed to understand, oh, for a flicker of thought, for a heartbeat of illumination, that there *is* no separation, but only the illusion of separation.

> "*I am he who causes (says Krishna)*
> *No other beside me.*
> *Upon me, these worlds are held*
> *Like pearls strung on a thread.*
>
> *I am the essence of the waters,*
> *The shining of the sun and the moon:*
> *OM in all the Vedas,*
> *The word that is God,*
> *It is I who resound in the ether*
> *And am potent in man.*
>
> *I am the sacred smell of the earth,*
> *The light of the fire,*
> *Life of all lives,*
> *Austerity of Ascetics.*
>
> *Know me, eternal seed*
> *Of everything that grows . . ."*

For a time, a soft breathing time without measurement, we flowed together down the road toward holiness, toward perfection, toward Brahman.

We reached the shores of the lake, and Eric's hand reached out from a stone wall and grasped me. And then the dream (the ecstacy?) receded, and I was clambering over the wall and joking with the other correspondents and becoming my separate self again: American woman foreign correspondent. And sitting on the battlements of an old water temple, observing the festival of the eclipse.

As the hour of ill omen approached, the mass of people thickened on the banks of the lake and on the brick steps leading down into the shallow water. Then Rahu leapt for the sun, and conch shell horns blew from all the ancient temples circling the lake. Drums beat, and bells jangled. The battle was joined.

Hundreds of thousands of men and women surged forward into the cloudy waters, ducked themselves and emerged to pray with folded, dripping hands and heads upraised to the sun. Below us, a man dipped his small son into the waters and raised him high toward the skies. An old woman knelt up to her waist in water and cried aloud toward the heavens. Over the lake bobbed thousands of coconuts, watermelons, and pumpkins tossed by the ultra devout as gifts to the elements.

And so was the sun god saved, and so did half a million souls advance another step toward heaven.

Delhi ❦ *November* 1

Child, child, where are you? I am weary now and want to get on with it. Ponderously, I pace the garden walks, jealous of the blooming sweet peas, the unfolding roses. I am strong, happy, and confident. But the child, stubborn little girl (I know it's a girl!) is more than a week overdue, and I am cross with her: I did so want her to be born in October, my favorite month.

Besides, I am so very tired of the kindly Britishers who meet me on my dutiful strolls: "Bearing up, eh? Well, better start bearing down!" Or: "Oh, you still here?" Each morning, for the last few days, I have become more and more reluctant to make an appearance before what seems the whole watching hotel, for I feel they think I am shirking my duty.

In this tense state, only the Indians console me. Bhag Singh, with his tender solicitude. The sweepers, who go about their work with downcast eyes—as if nothing unusual were expected. Their wives and the swarming children in the servants' compound beyond the garages; the women watch me walk by and a tiny, oh a very tiny smile plays about their lips, as if we were all sisters together knowing that time takes its own time. And they share this knowledge, this relaxed knowledge, in their companioning smiles.

The suitcase is packed, and has been packed for a month. My dressing room beyond the bedroom has been turned into a nursery; the blue dresser is filled at last with diapers and sheets and incredibly small shirts and nightgowns; a mattress-maker has fitted a tiny flat mattress into a laundry basket. Here it is, with its clean little sheets and its soft little blankets. Above them is stretched an extra-fine-mesh mosquito netting with a fine lawn binding, made by our ayah. She too, waits.

In the bathroom, low shelves have been built and covered with yellow oilcloth. On one end of them rests a one-burner electric stove for sterilizing bottles (if I *have* to use bottles!) and whatever else has to be sterilized. Beyond the shelves is the rather battered but still usable bathinette.

As the endless hours drag by I wander among these inanimate things, waiting for the life which will give them meaning. I finger the blankets, rearrange those ridiculously small shirts. On top of the bureau is a delicately carved wooden calf nursing a mother cow, bought in a moment of extreme sentimentality. It rests on a pink and blue "horoscope handkerchief" sent to me by someone in America.

On the desk in the bedroom are all the books on child care—my props, my guides, my saviors, my substitutes for tradition. The English women laugh at me; the Indian women smile gently when they see them. But how else am I to know what to do when I am left alone with this new life to care for?

"This new life . . ." Oh no, I really can't believe it! There's something incredible, impossible, about the whole process. How could I, really so unworthy, so unready, be entrusted with a human life? A *soul?*

Delhi ❀ November 2

Nothing.

Delhi ❀ November 3

Well, I don't know what they do at home when a baby is ten days late, but this is what they do in India, or to be more exact, what my Parsi lady-doctor is doing with me: tonight I am having four injections at one-hour intervals of something called Stilbestrol, followed by two pills of something mysterious, and then bed.

Tomorrow morning, at six a.m. exactly, I am to take an ounce of castor oil. At eight a.m. a hot enema. At ten a.m. a hot bath. This, said the doctor, must be an Indian bath—two buckets of water poured over me, including my head.

I am a little frightened now, and faintly think that right this moment it might be pleasant to be in San Francisco or New York. But never mind—Grantly Dick Read I'm on my way!

Later

Went up to the hospital for my first shot at six p.m. tonight (unfortunately missing an off-the-record conference the American ambassador is holding for the American press). While the giggly little Indian nurse on duty was preparing the shot, I asked her jokingly whether she was good at them. She looked unhappy. "Well, these needles are pretty blunt," she said. And sure enough, she darn near killed me.

I yelled bloody murder, and she apologized again for the needle, saying that the government didn't give the hospital enough money to use sharp ones. So I said—sheer bravado—that I'd drive into New Delhi and buy myself a new needle for the other shots. But *she* didn't know it was bravado, and "Okay," she said cheerfully.

I am beginning to see that if you want anything special in these government-owned hospitals you have to buy it yourself. I had to supply the Stilbestrol, for instance, and Mrs. White has already told Eric to be ready to rush out to buy penicillin, if necessary. Do-it-yourself childbirth, they call it.

Luckily, I met Mrs. White on the way out, and she sniffed a bit at the idea of my going off to buy a sharp needle. "I'll give you the next shots myself," she said—and she did. Surprise: no trouble at all. So I think the giggly little nurse should go practice on something besides me.

Now there's nothing to do but wait.

Hindu Rao Hospital ❀ *November 5, Sunday*

It's a boy!
I made it, and nobody *ever* made a baby before. There was never any magic before. There was never any miracle before. But this, this, this.

How long has this incredible marvel, this something-out-of-nothing been going on? Why didn't I notice? Why didn't I realize? Why don't people understand that this is a ruddy miracle happening every day? Good heavens, we walk around, talking about babies as if they were the most ordinary things in the world—blind to the dazzle, blind to the miracle. We act like Arjuna, talking to Krishna—treating him just like an ordinary man and forgetting he was an expression of God.

But Arjuna couldn't have stood it, if he had gazed directly at the brilliance for more than a moment. Maybe we can't, either. But now, on this day of birth, I gaze at the brilliance, and I am blinded with a joy of passion and reverence.

Hindu Rao Hospital ✿ *November 6*

And it's a *boy*.

I came out of a fog of "the Queen's Ether," and heard the matron say in an astonished tone: "It's a boy!"

"I don't believe it," said I, groggily.

She rolled me over, gently, so that I could look down at the squalling red creature in a basket beside the delivery table. Then she lifted the towel covering most of the baby. She pointed. "You gotta believe that!" she said. Most un-English, but convincing.

Before that—well, it all seems dreamlike, and I'm not sure I remember very well.

Friday night, several hours after my last shot, things began happening. I woke Eric, put on a bright red Japanese kimono, just to pretend to feel gay and brave, and telephoned the hospital. After awhile, trying to be very casual about it, we dressed, took a last look at that waiting bassinet, patted Jimmy, and went out into the crisp black night. The stars were very bright above the neem trees.

At the hospital they did this and that, and put me in a little room next to the delivery room. They let Eric stay with me, and for almost two days, poor dear, he read aloud from *Peaks and Lamas* while I practiced deep breathing and scientific relaxation. I've always been interested in Central Asia, but alas, I'm afraid I shall have to re-read the book some day.

Sunday afternoon, after thirty-six hours of nothing much, the doctor and the matron decided that they and not Dr. Grantly Dick Read were in charge of the delivery, and at that point I agreed with them. The Indian anaesthetist was attending a Guy

Fawkes Day cricket match in New Delhi, but he was paged in the stands and turned up in about an hour, only moderately grumpy. The last thing I remember was apologizing for having a baby on a big British holiday, and the next thing I remember was: "It's a boy!"

And then there was Eric, delirious from tension and relief. And for me, sleep, blessed sleep.

Eric, he tells me, went back to the hotel Sunday evening and found Bhag Singh waiting anxiously on the front doorstep. "It's a boy," said Eric, in typical British restraint. But Bhag Singh, dear emotional Indian that he is, went mad with pride and for the first time in his life (I'm sure) lost all sense of decorum. He flung his arms in the air; his eyes flashed in triumph; and he raced out of the room. "Iss boy! Iss boy!" he shouted, running down the garden and across the verandah where at least fifty people were decorously sipping sherry. Our friend, Marc Purdue, of the Associated Press, was taking a bath, but that made no difference to ecstatic Bhag Singh. He burst into Marc's living-room, through the bedroom, and into the bathroom. "Iss boy! Iss boy!"

He did the same thing with at least six other friends, all in various states of pre-dinner deshabille; with the servants quarters; the taxi stand; the tonga drivers, and the Tibetan merchants squatting by the driveway. Paul Revere couldn't have done a better job. "Iss boy! Iss boy!"

And so begins another human life, another journey. And as I watch my tiny son sleeping in the bassinet beside my bed, I think of the ceremony with which many Hindus welcome a newborn son. Shortly after birth the father touches the lips of the baby with honey and ghee (clarified butter) and repeats the Vedic words: "O long-lived one, mayst thou live a hundred years in this world, protected by the gods." Then he whispers a prayer into the ears of the baby: "May Savitri, may Sarasvati, may the Asvins grant thee wisdom." Finally he touches the shoulders of the infant and blesses it, saying: "Become firm as a rock, sharp as an axe, pure as gold; thou art called a son; live thou a hundred years. May Indra bestow on thee his best treasures."

Hindu Rao Hospital ✿ November 12

Sesh came to see me today, bringing with him a horoscope for the baby (the exact moment of birth is always noted in Indian hospitals because it would be almost impossible to live your life through in India without a horoscope). According to Sesh's astrologer, our child will be "very bright and shining," will be famous, wealthy, a leader of men, and "will love young girls too much."

Sesh looked rather bright and shining himself, and I soon discovered that he was in love, really, truly in love.

"I went to Madras to see the girl my family had picked," he said, his eyes luminous. "At first it was a little awkward, but she was very pretty, even prettier than her photograph. And when she talks she is modest, but very intelligent. And she is as happy as I am that I have found my life work in town planning. She is Indian, and yet she is modern."

"Like you, Sesh," I suggested. He looked startled for a moment, then thoughtful.

"Yes," he said slowly. "That is what all my struggling was about, wasn't it? I thought I had to choose between Communism or the West, or else adopt the Gandhian way of life. But India is India, and not Russia or America. We must do things in our own way, using our own terms of time and facts and truth. Now that I understand this, I see that it is possible to be modern and to work for the future and still remain essentially Indian . . ."

"Aren't the Gandhians essentially Indian?"

"Oh yes, of course. But I am uncomfortable with their holiness; perhaps I am not good enough to be one of them. And I believe there are other ways to help our country besides trying to reform human nature: scientists and doctors and agriculturalists and engineers and town planners and dam builders are not Gandhians, but they too are building a new India. There are many paths to God; there are many ways of being Indian."

Sesh will be married as soon as the astrologers pick a suitable day and moment. He shrugged his shoulders when he told me this, and smiled. "I know it's nonsense," he said. "But they've done it that way for thousands of years and will go on doing it for another thousand. And it doesn't really matter, does it?"

As he started to say goodby, Sesh suddenly grinned, and his eyes shone with a mischievous light. "By the way," he said dryly, "my mother is particularly happy over the marriage arrangements. I think she must have been fearing that I would bring home an untouchable or an American."

Who says Indians have no sense of humor?

Hindu Rao Hospital ❀ November 14

My room is high and airy, perched atop this old bastion palace, looking down the ridge toward the west and over the roofs of the Subzi Mundi bazaar. On one side of the room is a door leading to a wide courtyard where I can watch the sweet Indian nurses flash by like white paddybirds. On two other sides are French windows leading to the verandah where, these cool and lovely afternoons, I lie in the sun and gaze at the glimmering horizon.

Tonight is Divali, the festival of the lights. And this evening Bhag Singh arrived at the hospital bearing twenty little clay bowls, twenty wicks, and a jar of oil. Carefully, he placed the bowls on the top of the flat wall which edges the verandah, filled them with oil, placed a wick in each bowl, and lighted the wicks. Suddenly the dark verandah was fairyland.

"To welcome the Chota-Sahib [little master]," said Bhag Singh. "To bring the goddess of good luck to him."

"Sheer superstition!" sniffed the matron, who was watching. But she let them stay, and I'm happy. I love Divali.

To Indians, Divali is Christmas, New Year's Eve, and the Fourth of July rolled into one. Lying in my bed by the window and gazing at the flickering lights, I remember all the other Divalis I have seen and imagine to myself how it is down there tonight in the glowing town.

Tonight, earthenware cups like mine, myriad as the stars and far brighter in the Indian dusk, were set alight in long rows on the rooftops, on window-sills and doorsteps. The lights serve two purposes: they commemorate the safe home-coming (millenniums ago) of the god Rama, after his triumphant battle with the evil King Ravana of Ceylon, and they light the steps of Lakshmi, goddess of wealth, who will visit tonight all homes where she is made welcome.

In many homes an offering of silver marked with saffron and dipped in milk was left before a gleaming image of Lakshmi. Lights will be left burning all night, and many people are planning to stay up until dawn, waiting for a glimpse of the goddess.

Chandi Chowk, the "Street of Silver," is thronged with happy family parties, everyone wearing the new clothes which are customary for Divali. Grown-ups are buying piles of soft, sweet candies and presenting them on brass trays to relatives and friends. Little girls in new red-and-gold saris are running through the crowds waving Fourth-of-July "sparklers." On rooftops, little boys are shooting off skyrockets, and the golden shower of sparks is shimmering down onto the dark leaves of the sacred *peepul* trees.

All the shops are open on Chandi Chowk tonight, for today begins a new year for the merchants of northern India; today is the day when they discard last year's account books and last year's disappointments. Balloon vendors are everywhere; so too are the stalls of the image-sellers, their shelves bright with statuettes of Lakshmi, Krishna, Vishnu—and brilliantly chromoed pictures of Gandhi.

This is Divali for the wealthier people of India, those who can afford to spend as much as three dollars on the big day. But for the poor, the really poor who cower in the holes and crevices of this ancient city, or whose homes are a patch of earth between torn blankets tied to the branches of a thorn tree, Divali is different.

A mile from bustling, blazing Chandi Chowk is Kashmiri Gate, a portion of the old city wall where dark arcades shelter dozens of homeless, destitute families. Last Divali, in one of the tomb-like recesses, we found Mehran Singh, his grandmother, his mother, his sister, and his wife—who only that morning had given birth to their first son on the earth floor of their "home." They were recent refugees from Pakistan, and Mehran Singh had not yet found a job or a place for his family to live. He was a carpenter.

"Why talk of Divali to us?" he asked bitterly. "Divali is not for the poor."

Yet even Mehran Singh had managed to find three short candles, to stick them to the iron railing which formed one wall of his house, and to light them in the hope that Lakshmi would happen to pass by during the moments of their brief life. As the flame wavered in the night wind, the eyes of the kneeling women glowed for a moment, and even the baby seemed to watch.

And I know that this year, as every year, out among the thorn trees, under the arches of railway bridges, in ragged tents and tin shanties, shine thousands of tiny flames lighted by the poor. Too poor for honeyed sweets, cups of oil, or fireworks; rich enough for candles and for hope.

A skyrocket cuts a blaze across the black sky and explodes into golden sparks. Far off, I hear the sound of jubilant drums and clangorous bells. They fade, and then the night is silent again. My little lamps burn bright against the darkness.

The soft-stepping, smiling nurse brings the baby for his feeding. Afterwards, he falls asleep in my arms, content and warm and safe. Tomorrow we will go home together and begin a new life.

But that is tomorrow. Tonight, cradling my child and gazing at the lights of Divali, I think of the past, of all the years that have gone before, of all the years in India. Tonight I think of India.

Tomorrow is for our future, tonight is for my past . . . for the years of experiences from which I should evolve a coherent whole, but which, instead, insist on fragmenting themselves in myriad memories, unrelated. Perhaps some day they will draw together, but not now, not yet.

The old decaying pink mansions of Calcutta, with the jungle growths crawling over the porches like scavengers after the party is over. The boiling masses on the streets of Chowringee, the dark Bengali full of an inner fury with life. These remain, unresolved.

But Calcutta is not India. Nowhere is India, just as everywhere is. Once I asked Unni Nayar where I could "feel the heart of India," and he talked of the Malabar Coast in south India. If one sat silently for long enough in the green peace of the jungles, he said, one could arrive at the heart of the mystery. Unni, the finest Indian I ever met, and one of the finest human beings, is dead now. But his green Malabar is still there, gentle, quiet, significant. Alas, I did not sit silently in the jungles long enough to understand the mystery, only long enough to know that it is there.

And I think of India when I first came here. The British were still in power; the government was run by the British; the civil service was staffed at the top by British officers. The British Army was everywhere, and many of the clubs were exclusive. But the Kipling days were over, and they all knew it.

And then there was the deeply moving moment at midnight one hot August, when freedom came at last to India, and the conch horns blew in the halls of Parliament. Gandhi slept that night in a bamboo hut on the outskirts of Calcutta, ignoring the moment in time for which he had worked so long. India was divided, and Pakistan came into being.

Then the riots and the migrations, hysteria and unreason. For me, there was nothing to choose between the two sides. A month-old baby with its heart gouged out has no religion; a great-grandmother leaving the home of her girlhood and her whole long life, perched on a wagon, with blind streaming eyes, is neither a Moslem nor a Hindu.

An old Sikh, one of thousands in a sixty-two mile train of refugee wagons, ran into the road and stopped Nehru's car. "Why didn't you tell us?" he cried. "Why didn't you give us time to get out?"

Tears ran down Nehru's cheeks. "I didn't know," he said. "I didn't know."

Why does one remember the irrelevant? Now, staring into the Divali lights, I remember the look of a particular lotus blossom floating upon the blue waters of Kashmir. And the look of a particular, huge, red-bearded tribesman lying dead in a ditch by the highway to Baramullah, his hill-made rifle still clutched in his hand. He too was, no doubt, irrelevant.

But to what? Everything is irrelevant to "India" if taken separately. The old ploughs crumbling the dry earth. The wheat coming up, thinner, more meager than it would be elsewhere. The monkeys eating the grain, the scampering mice, the peacocks screaming their deified defiance under the thorn bushes. The cows, those infuriating sacred cows, lying in the roads, nuzzling at the bazaar fruit stalls. The peasants, the sharp-eyed students, the sad women in the pastel saris, with neither the defiance of the peacocks nor the boldness of the monkeys. The vigorous young officials, confident that they can build a new India, and trying hard.

But in Benares a young girl knelt before a priest and with outstretched hands accepted a green leaf on which floated a little oil and a burning wick of flame. Her face mirrored the flame, and between the girl and the priest there was peace and the joy of great belief. Her face wiped out the hysterical, credulous, or stupid faces of the women worshipping at the nearby shrine of the smallpox goddess. Her face, shining with a secret I have not learned from all my years in India, rises before me now, and will always.

It seems long ago, the night Mahatma Gandhi was killed. But vividly I see the little figure lying on a wooden bed on the verandah, the head of the bed tilted up so that the silent thousands below could have their last *darshan*. And the figure of Nehru clinging to the white palings of the closed gate to address brokenly the people who wept and despaired.

There were moments when I felt, as we all did that night, that India could not go on. There were times during the riots, times later when war with Pakistan seemed very close, times when the economic problems seemed insuperable, that collapse appeared inevitable.

But countries always do go on, somehow, and almost miraculously there was no chaos, no collapse. India is in the fields, and the peasant goes his way no matter what happens in New Delhi. The peasant in southern fields, for that matter, has often never even heard of New Delhi.

What happened in the later years, the most recent? It is hard to remember, as hard perhaps as for the ordinary Indian who has also lived through them. Droughts came and went and came again. Politicians made speeches. Anti-Americanism came and went in waves. Loans were granted, projects begun. Babies, millions of them, were born. Millions of people died. The cost of living rose, the middle class was squeezed as usual, everyone complained. But the bazaars were still thronged and year after year the great festivals brought sweetmeats to the children and excitement and release from work for their parents.

And again the disjointed pictures: villagers from the inferno whirling through clouds of red and purple and green powder on the festival of Holi; the towering papier-maché statues of the wicked Ravana and his two sinister relatives exploding into fireworks and flame on Dussera, as good triumphed over evil; the lights of Divali floating upon the oil, and the knowledge that they have so floated for thousands of years and probably will continue to do so for thousands more. Or at least for as long as human beings desire success and good luck.

And the elections: the picture in my mind of a peasant kissing the dust on the feet of an electioneering maharani. But also the vision of millions upon millions of Indians who had never before voted, conscientiously and even proudly marching to the polling booths and re-electing a government which, after all, was the soundest and the best one for them.

And the voices: Nehru, making conversation at a party or addressing Parliament in what I think is the most beautiful voice I have ever heard. Gandhi's patient little whisper. The whine of beggars. The cry of the blind man as he makes his way down a lonely street: *"Raht, raht, raht, raht!"* "Night, night, night, night!" The shy, soft murmur of women. The arrogant Oxford accents of the upper classes: "But really, what have you Americans to offer compared to Shakespeare and Shelley?" The screaming slogans of rioters: "Pakistan *Zindabad!*" or "Pakistan *Murdabad!*" The chanting of priests and the laughter of children.

Yes, I have listened. I have traveled thousands of miles from northern Kashmir to Cape Comorin, from Bombay to Calcutta; in the fields, in the jungles, and in the cities talked to hundreds of ordinary and extraordinary Indians. And I have read endlessly—the Constitution, bills up before Parliament, a dozen newspapers every day, tomes on religion and untouchability, transmigration and the sacred cow. I have learned that the rope trick is non-existent, that even the Indians consider most holy men bogus, that the much-vaunted superiority of Indian spirituality over Western materialism often cloaks a sour envy.

And during the eclipse, I began to learn something which I am still learning but which the birth of this child in my arms makes surer: the endlessness of time, the continuity of the soul, the unimportance of death.

And yet there remains an unease. Where have I missed the heart of the mystery? Surely it has been explored, and been found a human heart like every other, no better, no worse, no more mysterious? But how to explain, for instance, why India and India alone, has produced men like Buddha, Ramakrishna, Gandhi—

and yes, even Nehru with his crotchets and his woolly-mindedness and his indubitable greatness of vision? India, which has produced the doctrine of right action, the belief that means are as important as ends? India, whose people are as human and fallible as any other, but who yearn more strongly for goodness?

And what did that girl in Benares know, which shone for a moment as the grave old priest handed her the green leaf and the flame?

A Note 🌳 on the Author

THE many worlds of Margaret Parton include those of foreign correspondent, editor, reporter, writer, and mother. Her work has taken her from Kashmir to Morocco, from courtrooms to palaces, and from hot wars to cold peace conferences. Throughout it all, Margaret Parton has maintained a great sense of perspective, an attitude of humility, and an abiding interest in people, whether little or great. She is currently an associate editor of the *Ladies' Home Journal* and lives with her young son, Lemuel, in Wallingford, Pennsylvania.

A NOTE ON THE TYPE

THIS *book is set in* ELECTRA, *a Linotype face designed by* W. A. Dwiggins (1880–1956), *who was responsible for so much that is good in contemporary book design. Although much of his early work was in advertising and he was the author of the standard volume* LAYOUT IN ADVERTISING, *Mr. Dwiggins later devoted his prolific talents to book typography and type design, and worked with great distinction in both fields. In addition to his designs for Electra, he created the Metro, Caledonia, and Eldorado series of type faces, as well as a number of experimental cuttings that have never been issued commercially.*

Electra cannot be classified as either modern or old-style. It is not based on any historical model, nor does it echo a particular period or style. It avoids the extreme contrast between thick and thin elements which marks most modern faces, and attempts to give a feeling of fluidity, power, and speed.

The book was composed, printed, and bound by KINGSPORT PRESS, INC., *Kingsport, Tennessee. The paper was manufactured by* P. H. GLATFELTER COMPANY, *Spring Grove, Pennsylvania. Designed by* HARRY FORD.

Date Due

PRINTED IN U. S. A.